The American Newspaper

By Will Irwin

A Series First Appearing in **COLLIERS,** January - July, 1911

With Comments by
CLIFFORD F. WEIGLE and DAVID G. CLARK

The Iowa State University Press, Ames, Iowa

The American Newspaper by Will Irwin

The American Newspaper

By Will Irwin

A Series First Appearing in **COLLIERS,** January - July, 1911

With Comments by
CLIFFORD F. WEIGLE and DAVID G. CLARK

The Iowa State University Press, Ames, Iowa

CLIFFORD F. WEIGLE, former Executive Head, Department of Communication at Stanford University, is the Paul C. Edwards Professor in Communication at Stanford, his alma mater (A.B., 1929; A.M., 1936). A native San Franciscan, Weigle has also served in the editorial department of the San Francisco *News* and as Dean of the School of Journalism at the University of Oregon. He is a member of Phi Beta Kappa, Sigma Delta Chi, the Association for Education in Journalism, and is listed in *Who's Who in America.* He is the author of several articles in the fields of journalism history, journalism education, and personnel.

DAVID G. CLARK, associate professor, School of Journalism at the University of Wisconsin, received the B.A. degree from Texas Technological College, 1955; M.A., State University of Iowa, 1956; and Ph.D., University of Wisconsin, 1965. In addition to teaching at Stanford University and the universities of Nebraska and Cincinnati, he has been news editor at KCBD-AM-TV in Lubbock, Texas, and reporter-photographer for the Lubbock *Evening Journal* and the Lincoln (Neb.) *Star.* He is coauthor of a book on law and the mass media, soon to be published, and author of several articles in professional journals.

 Composed and printed by The Iowa State University Press. First edition, 1969. Standard Book Number: 8138-0095-1. Library of Congress Catalog Number 77-78817.

CONTENTS

PREFACE

THE AMERICAN NEWSPAPER by Will Irwin belongs properly in the mainstream of writings in American journalism history, but unfortunately it has not been generally available since its original publication as a weekly magazine series. Hence it has been read only by students and scholars persevering enough to seek it out in the bound volumes of *Collier's Magazine* and trace it through fifteen successive issues beginning January 21, 1911. Although dated in some respects after sixty years, the series can still add a great deal to the student's understanding of the emergence of the twentieth-century newspaper in the United States.

The purpose of this volume, then, is to bring Irwin's perceptive study out of hiding. The original pages have been reproduced in order to preserve the flavor of the illustrations and the 1911 national advertising common to popular magazines.

Although the compilers have collaborated in revisions, Professor Clark had primary responsibility in preparing notes for the text. Professor Weigle wrote the material about Irwin's career and his article writing. The authors share responsibility for any errors or omissions. The senior author is especially grateful to Professor Clark for taking a long-dormant wish to rescue Irwin's series from oblivion and providing the prodding needed to accomplish the job. Finally we wish to express our appreciation to Merritt E. Bailey, director of the Iowa State University Press, and his colleagues for the arduous task of finding clean file copies of *Collier's* in order to reproduce the articles for publication.

CLIFFORD F. WEIGLE
Stanford University
DAVID G. CLARK
University of Wisconsin

Will Irwin, November 1905

Will Irwin, 1906, the year he left the New York Sun

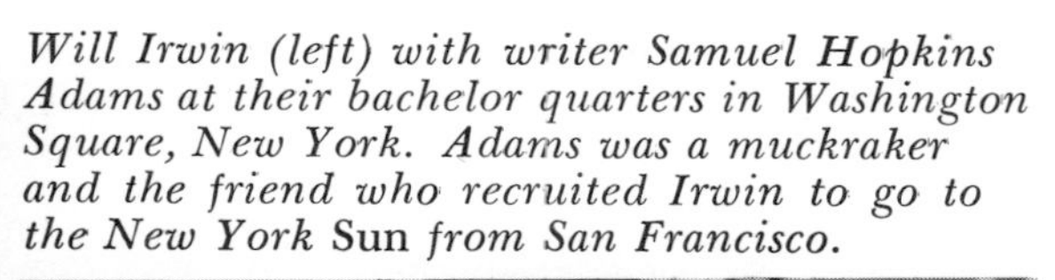

Will Irwin (left) with writer Samuel Hopkins Adams at their bachelor quarters in Washington Square, New York. Adams was a muckraker and the friend who recruited Irwin to go to the New York Sun *from San Francisco.*

Will Irwin, World War I

Will Irwin in Washington, World War I

Will Irwin in an Italian trench, October 1917

ABOUT WILL IRWIN

WILL IRWIN was among America's best young journalists and possessed at the same time the inclinations of a scholar. When he undertook his research for the series in 1910, Irwin had accumulated eleven years of intensive experience as a newspaper reporter, magazine editor, and magazine writer. He had been a reporter in two of the most exciting newspaper cities in the country—San Francisco and New York. He had written ten books, mostly fiction, and more than a dozen magazine articles.

Irwin's childhood and young manhood were like those of many thousands of other youngsters whose families were participants in the westward sweep of American population in the nineteenth century. He was born in Oneida, in the lake country of western New York, in 1873, but before he was six years old he moved with his parents and his brother Wallace to Leadville, Colorado, past its heyday but still a lively silver-mining town in the high Rocky Mountains. He moved to Denver to graduate from high school and at the age of 20 entered newly established Stanford University, on the San Francisco Peninsula. In his autobiography, *The Making of a Reporter* (1942), he recalls that he probably would have gone to Harvard had he not been threatened with tuberculosis and moved to California where the climate was believed to be more healthful. During four riotous years at Stanford, Irwin "specialized" in campus politics, undergraduate theatricals and writing, and beer drinking and inventive pranks. Expelled three weeks before he was to have received the B.A. degree in 1898, he got the degree a year later after final, solemn consideration by a somewhat reluctant faculty committee on student affairs.

Irwin's first job in journalism was at six dollars a week being what he called a "cub subeditor" (but his duties involved being both writer and assistant editor) on *The Wave,* one of five weeklies of literary miscellany, comment on contemporary affairs, and criticism then being published in San Francisco. *The Wave* died of financial starvation two years later, so in 1901 Irwin became a reporter on the *Chronicle,* one of San Francisco's three major morning papers. During his three years at the *Chronicle,* where he assumed duties of "development editor" and later of Sunday editor, he also was co-author with Gelett Burgess of two books of picaresque adventure.

As exciting as San Francisco was for young journalists, New York City was the Mecca, and the *Sun,* run by the great managing editor, Chester Lord, and Selah M.

Clarke, night editor, was the most desirable newspaper on which to work. So Irwin moved to the *Sun* as a reporter in 1904, a job obtained through Samuel Hopkins Adams, a former star reporter on the *Sun* but by 1904 an established writer who had been sent west by S. S. McClure as a talent scout.

The high point of Irwin's career as journalist came with the telegraphic flash that San Francisco had been destroyed by an earthquake. Because he knew the city so well, he was assigned to write—mostly from memory, supplemented by scant telegraphic bulletins—the story of the quake. Before the last-edition deadline on the first day, April 18, 1906, he wrote fourteen columns of copy. And he kept writing, eight columns or more a day, for the next seven days, as fire swept the ruined city. The booklet, *The City That Was,* for which Irwin is most widely known, resulted from six or seven columns of general description of pre-earthquake San Francisco that he wrote on the afternoon of the third day of the story.

After two years on the *Sun* he left newspaper work to spend the rest of his career as magazine editor and writer, war correspondent, and author of books.

McClure hired him in 1906 as managing editor of *McClure's Magazine.* But an unhappy year or so as managing editor, then editor, gave Irwin a "shuddering distaste" for executive work. Rather than return to the *Sun* he went to work for Norman Hapgood at *Collier's,* where his first muckraking assignment was a national study of fake spirit mediums. Then he dug into the story of prohibition that was creeping across the country by local option. It was after a couple of years of such assignments that *Collier's* asked him to undertake a thorough study of the American newspaper.

After the newspaper series Irwin wrote what he called "comparatively frivolous articles" until the outbreak of World War I, when he was among the first American war correspondents to sail for Europe in August, 1914. "For me," he said, "that six-month war lasted six years." In addition to becoming a well-known war correspondent, he served on the executive committee of Herbert Hoover's Commission for Relief in Belgium in 1914–15, and was chief of the foreign department of George Creel's Committee on Public Information in 1918.

During and after the war he wrote seventeen more books, including a Hoover biography and his autobiography, and two plays in addition to his magazine writing. Irwin died on February 24, 1948, at the age of 74.

ABOUT THE ARTICLES

No mass magazine had yet undertaken to "muckrake" the newspapers themselves, but indirectly papers in various cities were attacked by writers trying to follow the tangled circumstances of political corruption and business scandals. And between 1907 and 1909 at least three books about newspapers were published—*Making a Newspaper,* a highly regarded critique by John L. Given, a New York *Evening Sun* executive; *Commercialism and Journalism,* by Hamilton Holt, which discussed the evils of sensationalism and suggested endowing papers so they could resist pressures from advertisers; and *The American Newspaper,* by James Edwards Rogers. So by 1910 the American press was a rather obvious topic to assign to Irwin for a major investigative study.

Irwin had already displayed his interest in aspects of the press. In 1908 President Nicholas Murray Butler of Columbia called Irwin to his office to discuss whether or not Irwin would be available to interview newspaper editors and publishers in the United States and Europe to gather ideas for a curriculum in journalism to be established with a bequest from Joseph Pulitzer. (Although Pulitzer lived until 1911, he had arranged for the bequest with Columbia trustees in 1903.)

Before he undertook work on his series of articles, in 1909 Irwin had written articles on the New York *Sun* for the *American Magazine* and for *Collier's* on "Tainted News Methods of the Liquor Interests." Following the publication of "The American Newspaper," Irwin wrote occasional pieces on the press for the next twenty years. His articles included the "Press Agent, His Rise and Fall," in *Collier's* in 1911; "The United Press" and "What's Wrong With the Associated Press?" for *Harper's Weekly* in 1914; "Skeletons in the Newspaper Closet" in *The Literary Digest,* 1915; the "Press in Europe," on the early effects of World War I on European newspapers, for *Collier's,* 1914; "If You Are in the Papers It's ——?" 1923, and "Newspapers and Canned Thought," 1924, for *Collier's;* "Putting Copyright to Rights," *World's Work,* 1930; and the "Job of Reporting," *Scribner's,* 1931.

Thirty years later, Irwin described how he carried out his investigation for the series and soon forgot his original goal of merely muckraking in order to delve much more deeply into the origins, purposes, and principles of journalism—which is why his articles are still historically valuable after more than a half-century, while countless other "exposés" are forgotten. Here is his recollection as he recounted it in *The Making of a Reporter* (New York: G. P. Putnam's Sons, 1942, pp. 164–69):

And next, *Collier's* asked me to do a long piece of pioneering work—a series, with as thorough investigation as magazine work permits, on American daily journalism. The muckrackers had noted that in cities where gangs of machine politicians were stealing the shingles off City Hall, often the local newspapers kept silence until some magazine writer like Lincoln Steffens came from outside to unsheathe his rake. Radical reformers declared constantly that "the interests" were influencing editorial policies through control of the advertisers.

Robert Collier himself advised me to begin with a study of journalism in Britain and the Continent, in order to get a background. That, however, I had to abandon for lack of time, for when I settled down to work, the magnitude of the job appalled me. I had no precedents to go by. The only book worth looking into was Hudson's *History of American Journalism,* and valuable as it was in its sober record of men and events, it had no philosophy behind it.

Journalism was still finding itself. It had no formal code of ethics. The moral outlook of its practitioners varied from those of Oswald Garrison Villard's New York *Evening Post,* bowed down under responsibility for making this a better world, through Adolph Ochs's New York *Times* which professed merely to be manufacturing a sound and honest commodity, to a Western newspaper which was admittedly the organ of a pair of showmen, out for money and power. I scoured the country, talking intimately with publishers ranging from the esteemed Clark Howell of the old Atlanta *Constitution* and Colonel William Nelson of the Kansas City *Star* who had proved how much government by newspaper can benefit a community, to a few virtual racketeers who laughed over the tricks they were playing on the public. And not only publishers, but editors and reporters who had been balked by newspapers in conspiracy with grafters. Some of this lot talked —off the record—with astonishing frankness.

To the disappointment of Sam Adams, who favored straight muckraking, I grew rather more interested in chopping my way into this untrodden forest than in the original job of finding shame. I had been making discoveries and formulating principles. First, the real power of the American press lay not in the editorial page, as everyone supposed, but in the news columns. Nearly every publisher with whom I talked agreed with that. "The headlines are our editorials," said E. W. Scripps, whom I visited on his patriarchal ranch south of San Diego. "Give me the right-hand column front page and I won't care what they put on the editorial page," said Sam Chamberlain, Hearst's trouble shooter and doctor for sick newspapers. When I mentioned this principle to Nelson, he snorted. "We fight with all we've got—feet and teeth and toenails," he said. When I saw him again he remarked, "I've been too busy all these years to do much formulating. But I've been thinking it over. Yes, it's the news columns that do the business—mostly. But don't quote me. The boys that write our editorials wouldn't like it."

By his selection from the mass of news stories even then at command of every metropolitan newspaper, by the headlines he put on it, perhaps most importantly by the skill with which the reporter wrote it, the militant editor got his effects. It was of course a weapon which cut two ways; the insincere or purchased propagandist employed the same method with the same gratifying effect.

Getting further down toward fundamentals, the American press had a kind of franchise from the American people and the American government. We had the freest press in the world. Tacitly, it was supposed to pay for this privilege by "guarding our liberties"—in current language, by muckraking—when the process seemed necessary. Always, and especially since the rise of yellow journalism, American newspapers had been invading private lives to an extent which seemed shameful to Europeans. But if we passed laws to curb that tendency, anyone experienced in American politics and finance knew what would happen. The grafters and "interests," rather than the injured citizen in private life, would be the first to take advantage of them.

Until the "penny press" appeared in both England and the United States—and later, on the European Continent—the daily newspaper was a luxury of the rich. Something or someone had to subsidize a penny paper. In Britain, and especially in America, this angel was the advertiser. That was better than the Continental system, where some party faction, government or combination of capitalists paid the deficit. But it had always led to abuses; and in some communities, the advertisers virtually controlled all the newspapers. When reformers tried to abolish machine rule, the interests allied with the political grafters often saw the advertisers, who either withdrew their patronage or threatened to do so—and the rest was silence. This happened conspicuously in Pittsburgh.

With Pittsburgh, which I made the smirched example, I had better stop naming names; for that era is dead. But before I began to write I had a drawerful of proved instances. A bizarre scandal in the life of a department-store proprietor; and even though the press bureaus carried the story to the outside world, not a hint of it appeared in the city where he had his main store. A state chemist found that a beer which ballyhooed itself as "100% pure" was in fact adulterated. It had advertised in all the newspapers of its community except a highly intellectual organ which passed as a pillar of virtue. That day, a half-page advertisement appeared in this newspaper—which made suppression unanimous. I had three or four clear and provable instances of advertisers serving notice on a crusading newspaper that if it did not abandon its policies it would starve. In some cases, the newspaper shut up; in others, it defied the powers—and won out. A writer of signed editorials, who owned a share in the newspaper for which he wrote, had a standing arrangement with the theaters of his city. If any new show bought a full-page advertisement, he would publish a leading editorial praising the play and the performance.

Not only that; certain big corporations under fire were frankly subsidizing newspapers, Continental fashion. Which introduces a minor adventure of my own. I had the requisite proofs in one case of this sort and was writing the story in summer quarters at Scituate [Mass.] when a pleasing young newspaperman appeared in town. Somehow, he got himself invited to play on the tennis court which was the center for my group of friends, and joined me in a doubles match. As we walked away to dinner, he revealed that he had heard of my intentions concerning the corporation and the newspaper. Did I know the head of the corporation? A splendid fellow! A young Napoleon of finance! His life and rise would make a big magazine article—a much better story that the little episode of the newspaper.

"If you want to write it," he added, "you won't have to do any digging. He'll give you the dope. And if you'll take your article to him when you've finished it"— here an impressive pause—"I shouldn't wonder if he'd give you five thousand dollars!"

Was I indignant? Did I punch him in the eye? Did I even blast him with rude western language when I refused? I did not. A thrilling glow titillated my vanity. No one had ever offered me a bribe before. I felt as a debutante must feel when she gets, from a man whom she doesn't like very much, her first proposal. She's going to turn him down, of course. But oh, the compliment of it!

Let me put all this in proportion. The majority of the American newspapers were sound and honest. If occasionally they yielded to an advertiser in unimportant matters, those were only the minor compromises we all make as we go through life. But a minority of them were "out for the stuff," "edited from the business office," and they might in certain conditions endanger the whole structure of American journalism.

Then the casual remark of some veteran editor in the Pacific Northwest revealed a counter tendency. "When a woman or a newspaper goes on the street, she doesn't live long," he said. Through the records, through the memories of surviving members of their staffs, I looked into the history of a few once-famous newspapers now dead. The beginning of the end was either direct subsidy or a crawling policy toward advertisers. The graduates of those newspapers told me why. The publisher could hide the fact of control from the public for a time—but not from the staff. These hirelings lost interest and simply went through the motions. We're a gossipy people, among whom news travels almost as swiftly by word of mouth as by electric telegraph. Gossip carried the suppressed stories and the reason for their suppression. Long afterward, I had testimony from another party to such transactions when a man of great wealth said to me in a frank moment: "I bought the controlling interest in two different newspapers in those days. Something happened to them. They began to lose their pep and their interest. Within six months, they were of no use to me whatever!"

I had a feeling, which I ventured to express, that commercial common sense would prevail in the end. There, I called the turn. The American newspaper in the fourth decade of the twentieth century is not a perfect institution any more than its readers are perfect beings. But—in spite of instances to the contrary here and there—it is no longer the slave of its advertisers for the very good reason that the enslaved newspaper has nothing to offer advertisers.

In another main feature of my series, I missed the mark. In this period, the morning newspapers were the important division of journalism. They had—and have yet—a little more leisure to digest the news, to get perspective on it and to write it than the evening newspaper which appears at the time of the day when the greater part of the news is "breaking." When E. W. Scripps told me that owing to several considerations, mostly commercial, the evening newspaper was bound in the future to be the more profitable branch of the trade, frankly I did not believe him. . . . He was right, of course.

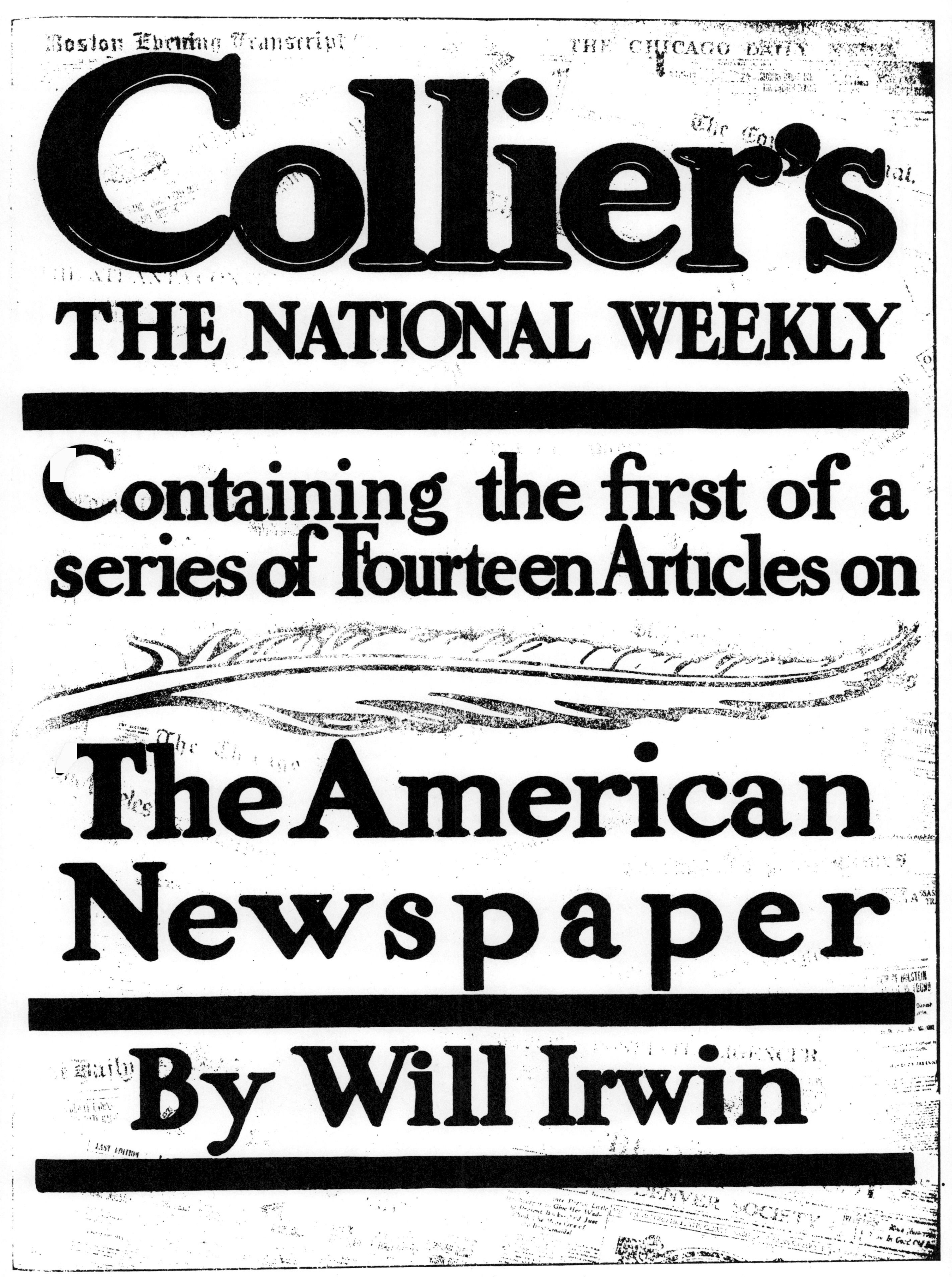

VOL XLVI NO 18 NEWS-STAND EDITION JANUARY 21 1911

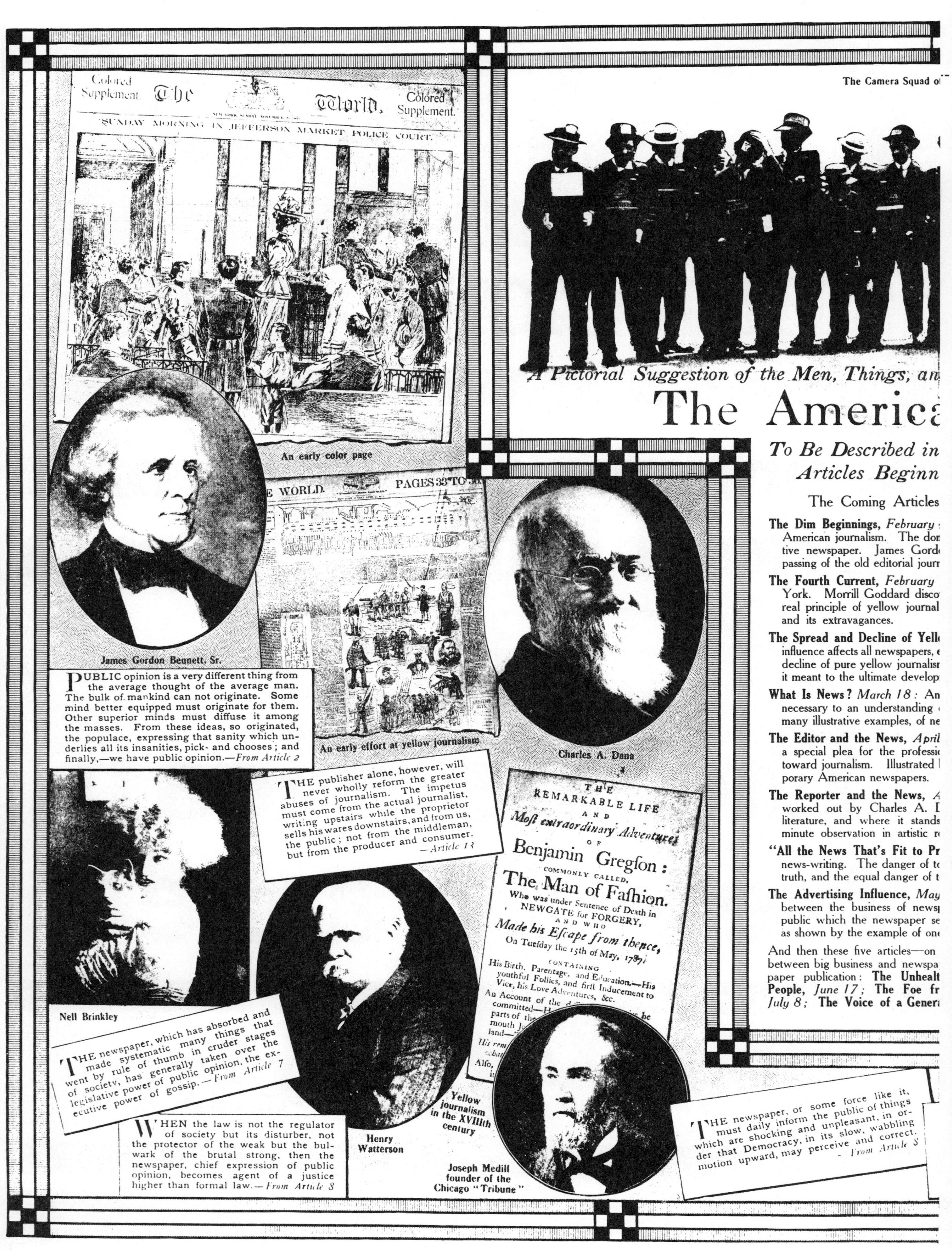

Colored Supplement. The World, Colored Supplement.

SUNDAY MORNING IN JEFFERSON MARKET POLICE COURT.

An early color page

James Gordon Bennett, Sr.

PUBLIC opinion is a very different thing from the average thought of the average man. The bulk of mankind can not originate. Some mind better equipped must originate for them. Other superior minds must diffuse it among the masses. From these ideas, so originated, the populace, expressing that sanity which underlies all its insanities, pick- and chooses; and finally,—we have public opinion.—*From Article 2*

E WORLD. PAGES 33 TO

An early effort at yellow journalism

Charles A. Dana

The Camera Squad o

A Pictorial Suggestion of the Men, Things, an

The America

To Be Described in
Articles Beginn

The Coming Articles

The Dim Beginnings, *February* American journalism. The don tive newspaper. James Gord passing of the old editorial jour

The Fourth Current, *February* York. Morrill Goddard disco real principle of yellow journal and its extravagances.

The Spread and Decline of Yell influence affects all newspapers, decline of pure yellow journalis it meant to the ultimate develop

What Is News? *March 18:* An necessary to an understanding many illustrative examples, of ne

The Editor and the News, *April* a special plea for the professi toward journalism. Illustrated porary American newspapers.

The Reporter and the News, *A* worked out by Charles A. D literature, and where it stands minute observation in artistic r

"All the News That's Fit to Pr news-writing. The danger of t truth, and the equal danger of t

The Advertising Influence, *May* between the business of news public which the newspaper se as shown by the example of on

And then these five articles—on between big business and newspa paper publication: **The Unhealt People,** *June 17;* **The Foe fr** *July 8;* **The Voice of a Gener**

THE publisher alone, however, will never wholly reform the greater abuses of journalism. The impetus must come from the actual journalist, writing upstairs while the proprietor sells his wares downstairs, and from us, the public; not from the middleman, but from the producer and consumer. —*Article 13*

THE REMARKABLE LIFE AND *Most extraordinary Adventures* OF Benjamin Gregson: COMMONLY CALLED, The Man of Fashion. Who was under Sentence of Death in NEWGATE for FORGERY, AND WHO *Made his Escape from thence,* On Tuesday the 15th of May, 1787. CONTAINING His Birth, Parentage, and Education.—His youthful Follies, and first Inducement to Vice, his Love Adventures, &c. An Account of the ... committed—H... parts of the ... mouth ... land—

Nell Brinkley

THE newspaper, which has absorbed and made systematic many things that went by rule of thumb in cruder stages of society, has generally taken over the legislative power of public opinion, the executive power of gossip.—*From Article 7*

Henry Watterson

Yellow journalism in the XVIIIth century

WHEN the law is not the regulator of society but its disturber, not the protector of the weak but the bulwark of the brutal strong, then the newspaper, chief expression of public opinion, becomes agent of a justice higher than formal law.—*From Article 8*

Joseph Medill founder of the Chicago "Tribune"

THE newspaper, or some force like it, must daily inform the public of things which are shocking and unpleasant, in order that Democracy, in its slow, wabbling motion upward, may perceive and correct. —*From Article 8*

the newspapers of to-day

d Conditions which have gone into the Making of

in Newspaper

the Series of Fourteen
ing in this Number

and Dates of Publication

1: A brief history of early English and
ninance of the editorial page in the primi-
in Bennett's discovery of news. The
alism.

'8: Pulitzer and Hearst invade New
vers, and Arthur Brisbane extends, the
sm. The yellow madness; its humors

w Journalism, *March 4:* The yellow
ven the most conservative. The sudden
. The good and bad in it; and what
nent of journalism.

understanding of the nature of news is
f journalism. This is an analysis, with
vs and news-interest in the reader.

1: The ethics of the editorial art, and
al, rather than the business, attitude
y examples from the history of contem-
The importance of the point of view.

ril 22: The art of reporting, as first
ama. Where journalism blends with
apart. The faculty of accurate and
orting. Some great news stories.

it," May 6: The ethics of news and
great delicacy in telling the scandalous
o little delicacy.

20: Beginning a study of the conflict
per-making and the interests of that
ves. Nature and causes of this system
great American city.

ommercial journalism, on the relations
er capital, and on the future of news-
y Alliance, *June 3;* **Our Kind of**
n Within, *July 1;* **The New Era,**
ion, *July 22.* : : : : :

HE HAS been several men, all extraordinary, in the course of his career,
his Pulitzer; nothing so impresses one
w regards him in the light of a historic
racter as the manner in which his able,
penetrating, highly energized mind has
s ted its point of view.—*From Article 3*

The Call=Chronicle=Examiner

SAN FRANCISCO, THURSDAY, APRIL 19, 1906.

EARTHQUAKE AND FIRE: SAN FRANCISCO IN RUINS

The combined edition of the three San Francisco newspapers, issued the morning after the earthquake

One of the first full-page cuts of yellow journalism

"WHY don't our newspapers tell the truth?" ask politicians and excellent ladies before women's clubs. Could they only know the difficulty of reaching an approximation to the hidden fact!

Horace Greeley

BY ONE of those subtle powers of mind which the science of psychology can not weigh, the world perceives sincerity; and none who ever wrote was great enough to defy his own perception of truth.—*Article 13*

Joseph Pulitzer

Julian Ralph
The greatest reporter of his period

Winifred Black or "Annie Laurie" (Mrs. C. A. Bonfils)

A chap-book illustration

WHEN Hearst began, the spirit of the old-age editor still guided newspaper publication; the majority of editors, no matter how strong their desire for circulation, served news and editorial in fashion more intellectual than the public wanted, appealed to the mind rather than the heart. Hearst's task was to cheapen the product until it sold at the coin of the gutter and the streets.—*From Article 3*

One of Brisbane's early effects in yellow headlines

Tammen of the Denver "Post"

William Randolph Hearst

I

The Power of the Press

In beginning his series with a discussion of the power of the press, Irwin made both a logical start and a justification for devoting so many articles to his topic. And, like all honest writers before or since his time, he found himself genuinely perplexed concerning the role of the press in achieving social change. Citing what seemed to be evidence of the waning power of the press, he pointed out (as many a social scientist has done since) examples of politicians elected to office in the face of solid newspaper opposition. Yet evidence that press influence was still strong was persuasive too, for he found many examples of newspapers crushing corrupt political machines. Indeed, the outstanding such case of his time was then in midcourse, the successful campaign of the Chicago *Tribune* to have the U.S. Senate declare vacant the seat of William Lorimer on account of corrupt practices in his election.

After examining the contemporary evidence, however, Irwin refused to throw up his hands on the question of press power as some later writers have done. ("Some kinds of messages, under some kinds of conditions, have some kinds of effects.") Instead he came out strongly for influence of the press as more substantial than "in any other time, in any other country." No other extrajudicial force, he said, except religion, was half so powerful. And whence came the power? Not from thundering editorial pages; they were as silent as once they had been clamorous under Greeley and Bennett. The power of the modern newspaper, Irwin realized, lay in the news columns. Perhaps this realization, which permeates the whole series, accounts for the relevance the articles have for today.

The News,—Which?

DRAWN BY ALBERT STERNER

The American Newspaper

A Study of Journalism in Its Relation to the Public

By WILL IRWIN

Beginning a series of articles on the whole subject of American journalism — the most powerful extrajudicial force in society, except religion. This article proves that the daily press, contrary to the opinion of academic critics, has more influence than ever before; and it explains the reason why

I. —"The Power of the Press"

WHEN one begins, as COLLIER'S is about to begin, a study of American journalism in its relation to the public, he finds himself perplexed by a multiplicity of squirrel tracks and a scarcity of main roads. From time to time, and especially in the past four or five years, the periodicals have burst out in condemnation or praise of the daily newspapers. The contemners say that the metropolitan newspaper has grown venal; that advertisers and great financial interests control it; that its sensationalism has vitiated the public taste; that it has lost all power of leadership in good causes. The defenders answer that it is more free and independent than ever before; that it gives its readers better mental pabulum than they want; that it leads our civilization; that it has more influence than ever the written word exercised before. When the student of journalism runs these expressions home, he finds that the criticisms are mainly by professors who, from their narrow cells, preach to an imperfect world counsels of perfection, and that the praises come exclusively from newspaper men, eager to defend their own profession, but too intimate with it for a broad and general view. Special pleaders these; truth and justice lie somewhere between their extreme views.

The Great Contradiction

THESE are the squirrel tracks, and of them is no end. Of main roads there is no beginning. When the investigator looks for some formulation of the larger principles of journalism in relation to its times, he finds nothing. Try all the books listed under "Journalism" in the Astor Library in New York or the Congressional Library in Washington. You will discover only a few treatises on the making of newspapers, a few volumes of pleasant reminiscences, one interesting but incomplete and shallow history. Dig further; the great social philosophers, who have worked out the relations of law, religion, commerce, of all the other permanent human forces, to the modern organization of society, mention journalism only in passing or not at all. Of the subtler modern philosophers, Robert Louis Stevenson presents a type. Democratic as he was in sentiment and practise, he touched journalism only to revile it as the worthless imitator of his own higher art.

Now, religion, law, science, art, infused the ancient world as well as the modern; we had recognized them, had worked out their principles and their relation to society, before the great flowering of the human spirit in the nineteenth century. Their maturity goes back always to a formative youth. But this alone of our intellectual forces is new. Two centuries ago there was no such thing. A century ago we had newspapers so-called, but they were only infant second cousins to the modern newspaper. A generation still lives which saw the birth of journalism in its present form. It has burst into the world with a flare of trumpets, but it has not even crept into the slow consciousness of the philosophers.

So, as though we began to explore law, religion, commerce, without roads or guides, we find ourselves at once bewildered by contradictions. Is the modern newspaper, with its enormous growth in size and circulation, losing that power which Greeley or Medill exercised in the older republic? Its antagonists answer yes; they cite the modern instances of Eugene E. Schmitz, elected Mayor of San Francisco with not a single newspaper favoring him; of Carter Harrison, elected Mayor of Chicago with only one newspaper favoring him; of "Honey" Fitzgerald, elected Mayor of Boston with every newspaper against him. Yet, on the other hand, we have the record of the San Francisco "Bulletin," which, unsupported, awakened San Francisco to the iniquity in the Ruef-Schmitz machine—we have even the admission from the shrewdest Californian politicians that the Heney-Calhoun battle was won and lost in the newspapers. Just now the Chicago "Tribune," in Carter Harrison's own city, has made an attack upon Senator Lorimer which may cost him his seat in the Senate and which will probably ruin his political career. The New York "World," followed by the New York "American," destroyed the cruel Ice Trust. The Atlanta "Georgian" put an end to the convict-lease system. The Mobile "Register" blocked the attempt of a railroad to gain control of the city's dock system. The newspapers of Galveston all but originated, and did make operative, the commission form of government. So there is a contradiction in the very cant phrase which we hear most commonly concerning the newspapers—"the power of the press."

Perhaps the political function of newspapers has occupied too broad a section in the limelight of commentary. For whether or not politics is boiling, the newspaper goes on day by day with its function of bringing the world to our doors. In considering this news function, commentators have been just as contradictory and shallow. What *is* "all the news that's fit to print"? One professor holds up the older standards of the New York "Evening Post." Murders, suicides, divorces, the follies of polite society—it is the duty of the good and moral newspaper, he says, to ignore these sores on the body politic. That, by the way, is a typical English view of journalism. The United Kingdom has of late been through an industrial depression, followed by an epidemic of suicides. "The fault," says one commentator, "lies with the sensational press, which has published too many accounts of misery and destitution, so that the minds of the morbid have become inflamed." On the other hand, sincere practitioners of sensational journalism declare that the publication of just such matter, through the shame which publicity brings to the criminal and the vicious, is a deterrent of crime and vice, and therefore a newspaper virtue.

Professional Ideals

AGAIN: is journalism a business or a profession? In other words, should we consider a newspaper publisher as a commercialist, aiming only to make money, bound only to pay his debts and obey the formal law of the land, or must we consider him as a professional man, seeking other rewards before money, and holding a tacit franchise from the public for which he pays by observance of an ethical code? No other perplexity of journalism is so involved as this. One would expect that the publishers of those newspapers most approved by scholars and critics would take the professional point of view. On the contrary, more than one editor of a newspaper without fear and without reproach has declared to me that it is nothing but a business. "I am responsible, just like a manufacturer of blankets, for giving people a good product—nothing more," says one. H. H. Tammen, joint publisher of the Denver "Post," a successful newspaper which has scarcely met the rich approval of the critical, expresses in different words the same point of view. "Rats!" he says. "We're out for the stuff!" Yet Colonel William R. Nelson, owner of the Kansas City "Star," a newspaper praised by its admirers for every stable virtue, holds the professional attitude and believes that in creating professional spirit lies the salvation of journalism. So does Arthur Brisbane, driving force of the New York "Journal," of whose shortcomings we have heard enough and to spare from magazine critics. So also do the authorities of the colleges which have modestly begun to teach newspaper work by the book. Those schools wander in their own maze of contradiction. By what method can one teach a thing upon whose methods no two authorities agree—whose basic principles no one has ever formulated?

Power Through the News

IN THIS series, and in later articles by other hands, COLLIER'S sets about to explore the uncharted country. That we shall say any final word upon journalism, we are not so egregious as to believe. But it is perhaps the first attempt, in the United States at least, to study the subject fully and candidly. Mainly, it will be a piece of reporting; on the lamp of civilization, itself hidden behind the brilliance of its own rays, we are about to turn our rushlight. Others, we hope, will follow with the larger philosophies of the subject, with the creation of laws, the formulation of public sentiment, which shall turn this new intellectual force, at present so wasteful and uncontrolled, into its proper relation toward progressive civilization. We are looking only for the truth, so far as our point of view permits us to perceive the truth. The work will be limited by our capacities; it will not be limited by any passion other than the passion for truth, by any desire other than the desire to know.

We shall arrive at few conclusions; but one I would better state in beginning, that we may have done with it. The "power of the press" is greater than ever before. They who deny this are looking back to the old age when all party lines were definite, when men first swallowed a formula and then bent their intellectual powers to prove it. That was the golden age of the editorial; and these panegyrists of older times assume that the editorial page still swings all the power of the press. The world runs differently now since Darwin. The power of the press has shifted; it is less tangible than it was in the days of Greeley, Dana, MacCullough, and Medill, but it is just as great. Indeed, line for line, it is greater, if for no other reason than that in the last generation not every one was a newspaper reader, while now the audience of the daily press includes all human beings with two eyes and an elementary education.

This has come to be the age of the reporter. In even its simplest form, news is the nerves of the modern world. Because of the press in its news function, San Diego, Seattle, and Boston, days apart by the swiftest trains, know as soon as New York and Washington that the insurance companies are under fire, that the Government has been swindled on glove contracts. So, and only so, is democracy possible in this immense country. Stated otherwise, the newspaper, in this simplest activity, furnishes the raw material for public opinion. If you want a concrete comparison, put our own small cities beside the Stratford of Shakespeare's time. Four or five days from London by existing means of travel, the intelligent burgher of Stratford had only the dimmest notion of events at the capital or on the far borders. His news came by inaccurate word of mouth from late visitors to London, or by an occasional royal proclamation tainted with the Government point of view. His mind was the prey of rumors and extravagant reports. From his very ignorance about the larger world, he would have been an impossible unit in a democracy. Perhaps I only state the obvious here; but I do it that we may keep fairly before us the newspaper's most important public function.

So much for colorless news; but, as we shall see when we come to consider reporting, colorless news is an impossible ideal. When Pilate asked: "What is truth?" he expressed the eternal quandary of the news editor. Truth, absolute truth, is a hypothesis. No man, from a cub reporter writing a dog-fight to a star writing a political convention, but puts into his work a point of view. Yielding to that tendency, newspapers, good and bad, honest and venal, have come more and more to put their views into their news columns, to relate events from a basis of opinion. The Chicago "Tribune," in its late exposé of Senator Lorimer, went far beyond a simple statement of the facts—that popular Representatives had taken money to vote for a United States Senator. Every paragraph in that story, as told by the "Tribune," was infused with moral indignation. When the Insurgents forced Speaker Cannon from the Committee on Rules, but did not pass the resolution calling for his resignation, the San Francisco "Bulletin," Insurgent in opinion, announced in its news headlines: "Corrupt Wealth Loses Control of the House of Representatives—Cannon is at Last Repudiated—Great Demonstration Follows the Victory." In neighboring Los Angeles is the "Times," firm for the Republican organization. "Speaker Cannon Triumphant in Defeat," announced its headlines—"Insurgents Lose Nerve in the Heat of Battle—Mercerized Republicans Dare Not Support an Attempt to Dislodge Uncle Joe." In fact, there is no colorless newspaper, though a few approximate it; every news report has some point of view, expresses some mission of God or of the Devil.

Now, these points of view, infusing the printed word, have an immeasurable long-distance effect upon the public mind. A newspaper may educate its public up or down; by the very power of constant iteration it may implant one or a number of fixed ideas. If this were not so, advertising would be of little value, whereas all the business world knows that it is of the greatest value. Advertising is the species of printed matter whereof the reader is naturally most suspicious; he knows it for the special pleading of a salesman. The most skeptical reader is more inclined to believe what he sees in the news columns. As a matter of fact, a newspaper may, by iteration, create public opinion and public taste for almost anything—provided it has not some rival contradicting all its iterations. William R. Nelson, with the Kansas City "Star" and "Times," for years had his field almost to himself. He educated his public to a taste for a calm, conservative, and well-written kind of reporting. When Tammen and Bonfils broke into Kansas City with the yellow "Post," their hardest task was to overcome the taste for Nelson's kind of journalism. Harrison Gray Otis of the Los Angeles "Times" was for years nearly as great a dictator in his community as Nelson in Kansas City. He hated labor unionism. The fact that Los Angeles is a poor union town, while its neighbors have been dominated by labor unions, is attributed to Otis; and he did it not by editorial fulminations, but by publishing all the news that tended to injure the unions and suppressing all that tended to help them. So he created in the minds of readers originally unbiased a picture of a labor union as a grotesque, unfair tyrant.

When Lincoln Steffens was city editor of the old New York "Commercial Advertiser," he decided to ram painting and the fine arts in general down the throats of his readers. A newspaper could hardly set for itself a harder task, since genuine appreciation of the fine arts is the last trimming of culture. However, by publishing the best art criticism he could get, together with educative articles on the first principles, and by reporting intelligently all the exhibitions, he created such a demand among his readers that when pressure of "live matter" crowded out art for a few days, subscribers used to write protesting. On the other extreme, the yellow journals, a few years ago, put some of their best cartoonists and cleverest writers into the sporting department. This created an artificial demand for "sporting stuff" far beyond the natural appetite of even an English-speaking people. That demand became so insistent that the other newspapers of all shades of opinion were forced to meet it; and now no newspaper is so conservative and intellectual as not to have a sporting page.

The Power of the Press is the Power of the News

"Our Constitution and State codes, formed for an eighteenth-century civilization, and warped awkwardly to fit the needs of a new era, failed in nothing as they failed in providing curbs for this new force — the power of the news. During a half century the press grew from a humble enterprise to a great business. This force surprised civilization; it was born without the law; its power kept it above the law."—*From the Second Article of the Series*

Again: Certain experts on education set about to investigate what they called the civic intelligence of school children—how much they knew about the conduct of the larger world about them, what attitude they held toward it. Springfield, Massachusetts, proved to be the banner city for civic intelligence, and the experts attributed this result mainly to the excellence of the Springfield "Republican," which has educated its young readers to a taste for matter touching on the large and vital facts in the world about them.

Concerning this "power of the press" in its news function, we have direct practical proof from the other side of the ethical fence. The gentlemen adventurers in finance who load the dice and juggle the cards on us worked formerly through bribed and influenced legislators. That became dangerous on account of the embarrassing activity of this same prying newspaper press. The fixers who elected Senator Lorimer in Illinois by direct bribery employed what Broadway slang terms "the old stuff." In the past ten years these astute gentlemen have perceived that they must get down to the influence which forms public opinion; and they have turned their brains and money upon the newspapers. True, they have done this awkwardly, the territory being far off their reservation. "What we need," said the Archbold letters, "is a permanent and healthy control of the Associated Press." After the panic of 1907 a number of them combined and raised tentatively a large fund to purchase the controlling interest in newspapers. It was their idea to have a reliable news organ in every important center. This plan failed only through one unconsidered flaw. They had expected to make money on their investment; the incidental furtherance of their financial plans was to be "velvet." And newspaper experts persuaded them that the journalism of special interests is seldom in itself profitable. Nothing but this frustrated the plan.

Directly to the point is an experience of that fighting independent journal, the Philadelphia "North American." It had declared for local option. A committee of brewers waited on the editor; they represented one of the biggest groups in their business. "This is an ultimatum," they said. "You must change your policy or lose our advertising. We'll be easy on you. We don't ask you to alter your editorial policy, *but you must stop printing news of local-option victories.*" So the deepest and shrewdest enemies of the body politic give practical testimony to the "power of the press" in its modern form.

The pedants are wrong; the American press has more influence than it ever had in any other time, in any other country. No other extrajudicial force, except religion, is half so powerful.

II

The Dim Beginnings

IRWIN IDENTIFIES four main currents in the history of American journalism. The first he calls the Anglo-American tradition of an "editorial press," meaning the press as advocate and as forum for ideas and opinions. This editorial function, he says, was the first major role of the press, and from it stem many subsequent beliefs concerning the importance of newspapers to our society. The other three currents began much later as part of what today we call the development of mass communications. Irwin lists four innovators of near-genius quality: James Gordon Bennett, whose fertile mind evolved a definition of news that was much broader than anything up to his time and that still is applied in little changed form more than 100 years later; Charles A. Dana, who brought clarity and craftsmanship to newspaper writing; and William Randolph Hearst and Joseph Pulitzer, whose great circulation war of the 1890s reinforced the sensational technique as a sure winner of mass readership.

Although Irwin was perhaps less aware than we are today that the nineteenth-century developments carried out by Bennett, Dana, Hearst, and Pulitzer were in large part stimulated by changing social conditions brought on by the Industrial Revolution, his analysis remains sound. He very clearly saw that the era of the "editorial press" was fast slipping by, and that consequently the time of the informative press, taking its power from its role as disseminator of information, had begun. This shift from advocate to carrier of information is not complete even in the midst of today's computerized information revolution, but the editorial page certainly has waned in the importance attached to it since Horace Greeley's time, and Irwin spotted this trend.

Perhaps the chief value of the article lies in the benchmark it gives the reader in assessing changes in the social role of the press since Irwin wrote. For example, he asserts that "If our American press ever renounces its ancient office of tribune of the people, it will renounce also its main excuse for its extraordinary freedom from legal restraint." Is that possibility becoming reality? Does fairly widespread agitation for press restraints reveal doubt in many minds that the press is still tribune of the people? Is today's talk of increasing restraints (codes to restrict media coverage of racial incidents, restraints on trial news coverage), and of substitutes for the press's tribune function (ombudsmen to speak for the individual to his government) an indication that the press today is serving that function less actively than once it did?

The American Newspaper

A Study of Journalism in Its Relation to the Public

By WILL IRWIN

The first article of this series, published January 21, dealt with the difficulties of studying journalism and with the influence of newspapers. It showed that the power of the press is now greater than ever before, and that the seat of that power has shifted from the editorial page to the news columns. The present article reviews the history of American journalism from the beginning, and tells what influences brought that change about

II—The Dim Beginnings

AS IT is without written philosophy, so also is journalism without adequate written history. For the United States, there is only Hudson's "History of American Journalism," inaccurate and superficial, and closing with the year 1872—or just before the profession underwent its greatest transformation. And, although readers of this present-minded age are impatient of history, we must go a little way into the past, in order that we may understand the present.

This nation inherited its journalism from England. There, before the newspaper, came the political pamphlet or broadside—nothing more than an editorial in folder form. The liberty of the press, for which Milton fought in England during the seventeenth century and Zenger in America during the eighteenth, was not so much the liberty to print the news as the liberty to express opinion in type. With the increasing complexity of modern life arose a need for some method of communication better and more general than word of mouth or palace proclamation; so was born the newspaper. In the very honeymoon of this marriage between news and editorial, the alien party began to dominate.

Immediately it took away from the pamphleteers the function of expressing and forming public opinion. Editorial smothered news, and the periodical press became rather an opinion-paper than a newspaper.

Various reasons explain this anomaly. The posing, neo-classical eighteenth century was a rather incurious age; the intellectual classes—and they were then the sole patrons of newspapers—generally held themselves above inquiry into the bald facts of life. Richardson introduced a novelty when he dared to make literature out of a servant. Obviously, the channels for communicating news were inferior, though that need not have prevented an editor from reporting his own community—which, from the modern point of view, he never did. The British libel law, proceeding on the general principle that publication of a fact injurious to an individual in private life is a crime or a wrong, no matter whether the fact be true or false, was even more strictly interpreted then than now; the simplest news item might be charged with dynamite for the editor. Finally—and to the experienced journalist most potent reason of all—an amiable weakness of human nature enters into the equation. By the editorial alone could one lead in that age, for leadership by news was as yet undiscovered; and any man with ambition enough to enter a profession would rather originate and lead than merely record. Indeed, the old-time journalist must have felt a kind of contempt for the news function of the press; must have regarded it somewhat as a painter regards his pot-boilers. Certain simple commercial and social needs he had to supply, such as information about the arrival of vessels with valuable consignments; for already he had advertisers, and both advertisers and subscribers demanded this. Otherwise, it seems, he looked upon news mainly as a feeder for his editorials. If he printed government proclamations in full and parliamentary debates up to the limit of his space, it was because these were ammunition to his heavy batteries of opinion. The startling or picturesque or humorous events of the day, which interest common-minded folk more than corn-laws or tariffs, he noticed with impatience, or ignored. A disaster, if reported at all, drew some such item as this:

"We learn of a regrettable occurrence in High Street last Thursday. During a conflagration, a linen-draper, discovering that his wife and three or four children had been abandoned to the flames, rushed into the ruins of his house and perished miserably with his unhappy family." The criminal, the horrible and the bizarre, which are the subject-matter of yellow journalism to-day, and which, considered from one point of view, are a legitimate interest of the press, the eighteenth century editor left to the chapbook. Jack Sheppard, for example, made of his career an excellent yellow story. The populace, and perhaps the intellectual readers of the daily press, had a fascinated interest in his life and death. But the newspapers hardly noticed him; he owes his pernicious immortality to the chapmen. Going to the other pole, Newton's discovery of the law of gravitation probably went unrecorded in the public press. The fact passed through the intellectual class of England by word of mouth and later by printed book. In short, news as we know it was not yet invented. The editorial, on the other hand, came to full perfection by the end of the eighteenth century.

To "mold public opinion"—that cant phrase expresses exactly the function of an editorial press as the old-time journalist worked it out. For public opinion is a very different thing from the average thought of the average man. The bulk of mankind can not originate. Some mind better equipped, better informed, must originate for them. Other superior minds must "push the idea along," diffuse it among the masses. From these ideas, so originated, so diffused, the populace, expressing that sanity underlying its insanities which mankind has displayed in all ages, picks and chooses; and finally we have public opinion.

Still another function of the newspaper press was set by the old-time journalist in the structure of British, American, and Colonial society. All fairly founded democracies have felt the need of some special pleader for the people. At the bottom are the inept and unsuccessful many; at the top the able and successful few.

From the Harvard Collection

A Chap-Book Cartoon

This Opper or Davenport of the period gave speech to his characters by means of balloons proceeding from their mouths. This method early went out of first-class newspaper cartooning, but the humorists and feature artists of yellow journalism revived it

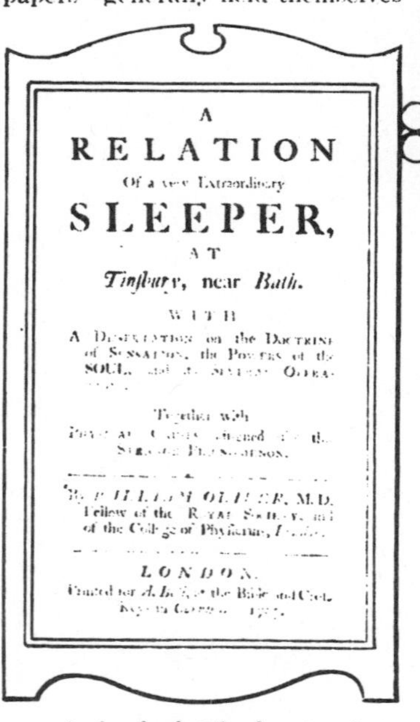

A
RELATION
Of a very Extraordinary
SLEEPER,
AT
Tinsbury, near *Bath*.
WITH
A Dissertation on the Doctrine of Sensations, the Powers of the Soul, ...
Together with
...
... M.D.
Fellow of the Royal Society, and of the College of Physicians, ...
LONDON.
...

A chap-book "Sunday story"

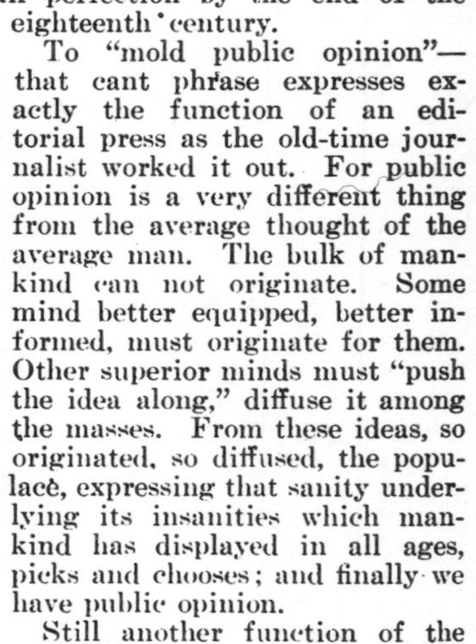

Old Bailey Trials.
LIST OF THE
Prisoners,
Convicted and Acquitted
AT THE
Old Bailey Sessions,
Held at the Sessions' House there, on Wednesday, December ..., and following Days.

A penny chap-book

Horace Greeley

"Flower of the old school. He really led; and he did it solely by the power of his editorials. Commercial necessity forced upon him daily concessions to news for news' sake, but he cursed that necessity"

James Gordon Bennett, Sr.

Who discovered news in the modern sense. "Ruthless, short in the conscience, he was yet a genius with the genius-power for creation"

Charles A. Dana

"Dana saw no good reason why journalism, the little sister of literature, should not herself dress with art. . . . As he worked it out, the art of reporting is the art of the plain, unvarnished tale"

Be your constitutions and codes never so well considered and founded, the able few will find ways to beat, ignore, and warp laws, if there be not some sentinel and advocate to guard and plead the interests of the masses. The Romans recognized this need when they incorporated the tribunes of the plebeians into the structure of their body politic. When, after the blight of the Dark Ages and the Middle Ages, democracy reappeared, the press took upon itself this function. It was an axiom of old-time journalism that the newspaper must at least assume to stand for popular causes; though less often and less clearly expressed, it is an axiom to-day. The newspapers, be they never so venial, never so inimical to popular rule, pretend to speak for the people; and the public which reads the newspapers expects this service. If our American press ever renounces its ancient office of tribune of the people, it will renounce also its main excuse for its extraordinary freedom from legal restraint.

Such was our journalistic inheritance; on such principles ran the American press when it helped create the sentiment for independence, for republican forms of government, for the Constitution; and on such principles, with minor and inconsequential differences, it continued until the thirties of the nineteenth century. Indeed, the idea has been singularly persistent. It still dominates journalism in certain regions of the United States; and when Henry Watterson, in the course of some just strictures on modern newspapers, laments the declining "power of the press," he is mourning only the decadence of the editorial as a direct political force.

Four main currents run through the history of American journalism; four elements fused to make our press what it is. Our Anglo-Saxon inheritance of an editorial press was the first current. Each of the others had for a source some man, owed its inception to some king-figure. This produced its best type just when it ceased to dominate; for Horace Greeley, whose career reached its climax in the period of our Civil War, was the flower of the old school. He really led; and he did it solely through the power of his editorials. By virtue of his honesty, his mental vigor, and his journalistic style, he really "molded public opinion." Commercial necessity forced upon him daily concessions to news for news' sake, but he cursed that necessity. He, like all his kind, was a publicist, not a newspaper man.

James Gordon Bennett invented news as we know it. Yet even before he came, we needed and consumed more news of a sort than our European contemporaries. In the first place, this was a republic; and a large republic can not proceed without some accurate means of communication, by which the remotest settler may know what his fellows on the other border are doing, what the Government is planning for him. Then, too, we had no artificial barriers against free publication. The founders of our States, understanding how greatly journalism had assisted our struggle to free and to find ourselves, gave the fullest liberty to the press. In English common law, a derogatory fact is an unpublishable fact. Anything which comes out in court or in public records, anything which concerns the relations of an official to the body politic, is privileged; it may be published. Otherwise, to print a damaging fact is actionable or criminal, and "the greater the truth the greater the libel." Our States, on the other hand, generally established the principle that truth is always justification if the writer or publisher be not actuated by malice. So we opened the way to the editor; and if he did not discover the news function at once, it was because he held the old-time idea of the journalistic mission and cherished the delusion of editorial grandeur. Indeed, these early American newspapers did, roughly and briefly, record some local events other than those which touched politics; they did try, for example, to inform the Atlantic Coast about that western advance to which every American family had contributed a member or a friend. They discovered even the germs of modern journalistic enterprise. By 1820 Harry Blake, first in the line of American star reporters, had a system for meeting the European packets in Boston Harbor and getting the news into the "Palladium" ahead of his contemporaries. At about the same period the more stable New York newspapers began to collect and to print accurate market reports—the A B C of modern news journalism. In 1829 Hale and Hallock of the old New York "Journal of Commerce" were employing fast news schooners to meet vessels outside the port of New York for the swifter transmission of European and Mexican news letters.

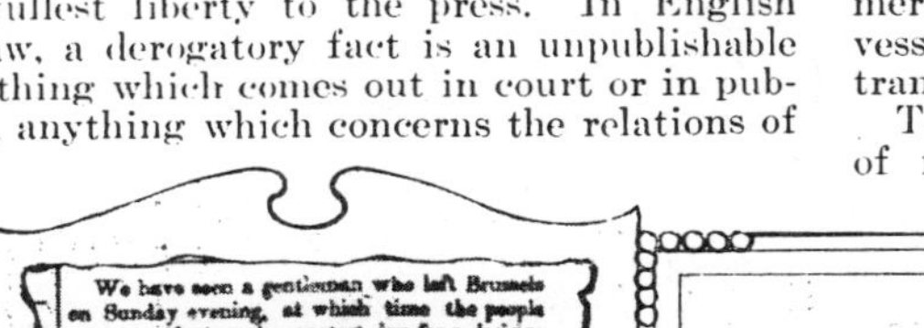

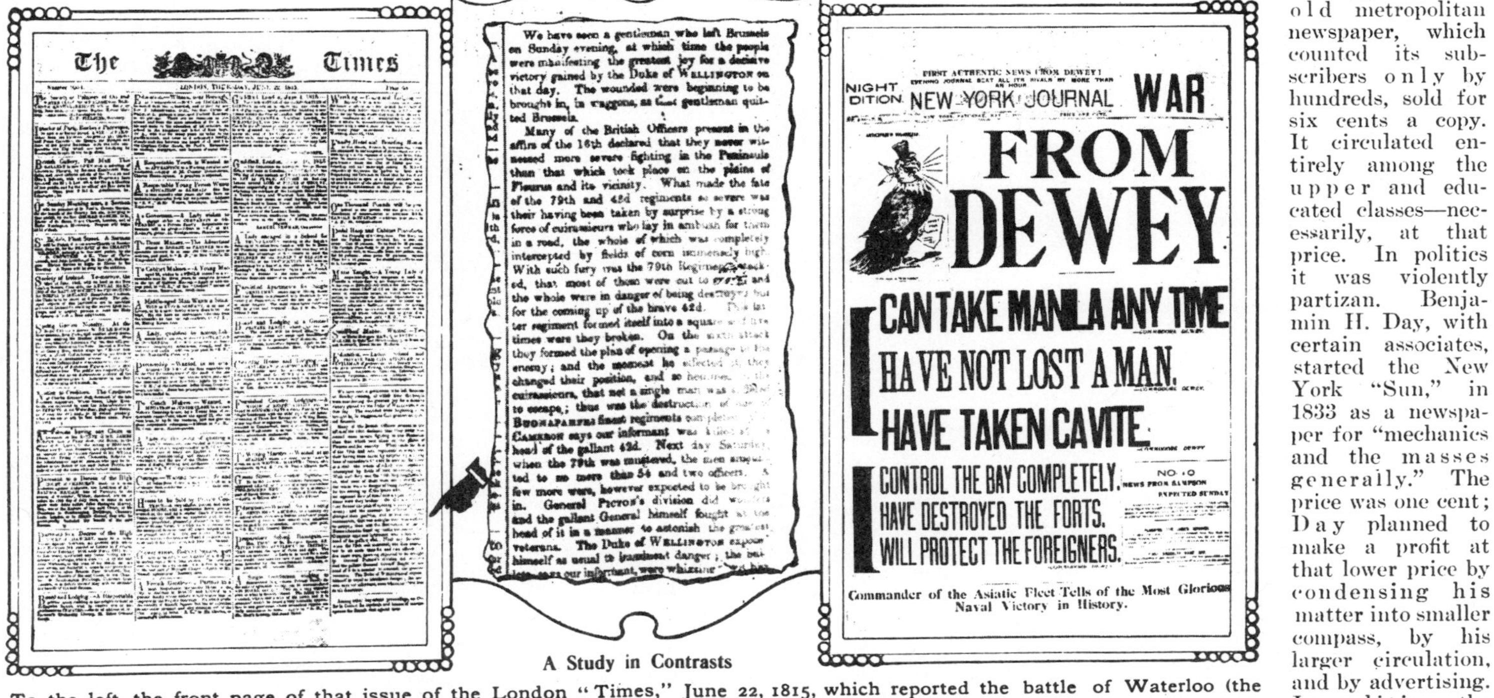

The Times

We have seen a gentleman who left Brussels on Sunday evening, at which time the people were manifesting the greatest joy for a decisive victory gained by the Duke of WELLINGTON on that day. The wounded were beginning to be brought in, in waggons, as that gentleman quitted Brussels.

Many of the British Officers present in the affirs of the 16th declared that they never witnessed more severe fighting in the Peninsula than that which took place on the plains of Fleurus and its vicinity. What made the fate of the 79th and 42d regiments so severe was their having been taken by surprise by a strong force of cuirassieurs who lay in ambush for them in a road, the whole of which was completely intercepted by fields of corn immensely high. With such fury was the 79th Regiment attacked, that most of them were cut to [illegible] and the whole were in danger of being destroyed but for the coming up of the brave 42d. This latter regiment formed itself into a square [illegible] times were they broken. On the sixth attack they formed the plan of opening a passage [illegible] enemy; and the moment he effected [illegible] they changed their position, and so hemmed [illegible] cuirassieurs, that not a single man was [illegible] to escape; thus was the destruction of [illegible] BUONAPARTE's finest regiments completed. [illegible] CAMERON says our informant was killed at [illegible] head of the gallant 42d. Next day Saturday, when the 79th was mustered, the men amounted to no more than 54 and two officers. A few more were, however expected to be brought in. General PICTON's division did wonders and the gallant General himself fought at the head of it in a manner to astonish the greatest veterans. The Duke of WELLINGTON exposed himself as usual to imminent danger; the bullets, says our informant, were whizzing [illegible]

NIGHT EDITION
NEW YORK JOURNAL
WAR
FROM DEWEY
I CAN TAKE MANILA ANY TIME
HAVE NOT LOST A MAN.
HAVE TAKEN CAVITE.
I CONTROL THE BAY COMPLETELY.
HAVE DESTROYED THE FORTS.
WILL PROTECT THE FOREIGNERS.
Commander of the Asiatic Fleet Tells of the Most Glorious Naval Victory in History.

A Study in Contrasts

To the left, the front page of that issue of the London "Times," June 22, 1815, which reported the battle of Waterloo (the finger points at the brief article). To the right, the front page of that issue of the New York "Journal" of May 7, 1898, which reported the battle of Manila Bay. In the center is an enlargement of the paragraph as it appeared in the "Times"

Though James Gordon Bennett was the evangel of news, one came before him to announce the dawning era. The old metropolitan newspaper, which counted its subscribers only by hundreds, sold for six cents a copy. It circulated entirely among the upper and educated classes—necessarily, at that price. In politics it was violently partizan. Benjamin H. Day, with certain associates, started the New York "Sun," in 1833 as a newspaper for "mechanics and the masses generally." The price was one cent; Day planned to make a profit at that lower price by condensing his matter into smaller compass, by his larger circulation, and by advertising. In politics, the "Sun" was to be absolutely, firmly independent. These two innovations made more stir in Day's time then the greatest departure of all, as the future worked it out. The "Sun's" primary object was "to cultivate public intelligence by publishing all obtainable advices of the day." In short, here was a *news*paper, the first on our soil.

Within a year the "Sun" threatened the old sixpenny papers, which began looking to their circulation fences. Then James Gordon Bennett started the penny "Herald"; and from that time forth the "Sun" was never first in the field which it discovered, though it came afterward to hold supremacy in quite another field. For Bennett, ruthless, short in the conscience, expressing in his own person all the atrocious bad taste of his age, was yet a genius with the genius power of creation. And he, through two stormy, dirty decades, set an idea of news upon which we have proceeded ever since. "I renounce all so-called principles," he said in his salutatory. He set out to find the news, and to print it first. The "Herald's" commercial success—within three years it had taken the lead from all the New York newspapers—forced the others to follow him; newspaper work became a struggle then for beats and for earliest publication. When Bennett began, two short railroads comprised all the means of rapid communication in the United States. Working with the tools he had, Bennett performed prodigies. His marine couriers transmitted European news hours ahead of his rivals; he kept in touch with our borders by private lines of pony messengers. In the Mexican War, his despatches so far beat the Government advices and the United States mails that it became a matter for official complaint at Washington. Before the telegraph he had experimented with schemes for quicker transmission by semaphore, pneumatic tube and even balloon; the poles on the first telegraph lines were still green when Bennett had made the invention a part of his own system.

These enterprises dealt with mere transmission of news. In getting news, however, he was equally keen and eager. He, first of all Americans—except some outcast journalists who lived on the fringe of society and died sometimes on the fringe of a rope—violated the sanctity of the home; he made private scandals, personal troubles, the business of a newspaper. The financiers of Bennett's generation held a counting-room as sacred as a home; they resented newspaper inquiries about their business. Bennett invaded Wall Street. Day by day he revealed the financial situation exactly as it appeared to him—for he was long his own Wall Street reporter. Criminal news, so important nowadays, attracted little attention in the thirties. Bennett found a method of watching systematically the police stations, of giving all the police news all the time.

The Triumph of Bennett

THE period in America was one of a commercialism worse than vulgar, of a spread-eagle flamboyance in private manners and of unlimited abuse in public affairs. The other newspapers of New York, Philadelphia, and Boston turned all their vulgarity, all their flamboyance, all their abuse upon Bennett; he responded by going them one better. They combined, in what he called "The Wall Street Holy Alliance," to ruin him by cutting off his news sources and bullying away his advertisers. Bennett simply tightened his belt, sharpened his weapons, and drove two or three of the weakest allies into bankruptcy. Then, failing to ruin him, they obeyed the law of necessity—and imitated.

The penny newspaper had created a great new body of readers. News, not editorial opinion, was what they wanted; for news, be it understood by this age, was then a novelty. Though such men as Greeley and Godkin in the East and Medill and McCullough in the West had afterward great personal influence through their writings, though Watterson and Hemphill in the South maintain such an influence even now, the editorial never regained its old supremacy in American journalism.

So entered the second current. And before the Civil War we find our press transformed. The preacher has become a gossip, the evangel a bellman. Now from printer's case and press sprang the old type of American reporter—prying, overcurious, unclean of person, dissolute, reckless, counting life and honor no whit against the latest news. Up sprang, too, certain false professional ideals about news which we have found it hard to live down even to this day. The excessive respect for a scoop or a beat—trade slang meaning an exclusive item of news—arose in this period; he was the best reporter who scored the most beats, though his point of view were that of the gutter and his English made a fog seem crystal-clear. So, too, the criminal department began to sprout and to grow lusty at the expense of the other higher departments; and to this day we get and consume an amount of criminal news which shocks the English. For this also the reason is plain.

Under our libel laws, the newspapers may publish any and every detail of crime, provided only they publish the truth. We do not have to wait for a coroner to accuse John Smith or a policeman to arrest him before stating that Smith probably murdered Jones. This kind of news is attractive to all classes of readers; even the truly cultivated usually get only so far as to delude themselves into believing that they dislike it. And, under our system, it is easiest of all news to get. Simply keep reporters on a basis of friendship at the police stations. The police will do the real work; the reporters need only send in the results.

Day in and day out, this news is always present and coming, while the news which demands more initiative and originality from the reporter comes irregularly. Increase of public appetite for any form of printed matter grows with what it feeds upon; that is true to the experience of publishing journalists and to the principle of book psychology. And our taste for criminal news has been educated through two generations by our metropolitan newspapers.

Success is partly an accident, and genius partly a product of the soil on which it grows. Bennett struck exactly in the nick of time. The railroad, the telegraph, the transatlantic cable were building or planned just when he began; his development ran parallel with improvement in these mechanical assistants. Not only that; the printing trades, which had stood still since the great days of Aldus and Elzevir, took a spurt forward in the first decade of his editorship. The "Sun" began with the old hand press, the mechanical tool of the "Spectator" and of Ben Franklin, its extreme capacity three hundred sheets an hour. Day had scarcely installed his plant before he replaced his Washington hand presses with a flat-bed steam press, capable of printing its thousands of copies an hour. Then, in the late forties, and when Bennett was ready to conquer new worlds, Richard

THE SUN.

NUMBER 1.] NEW YORK, TUESDAY, SEPTEMBER 3, 1833. [PRICE ONE PENNY.

PUBLISHED DAILY,

FOR ALBANY—PASSAGE ONLY $1.

FOR NEWPORT AND PROVIDENCE.

FOR HARTFORD—PASSAGE 1 DOLLAR.

AN IRISH CAPTAIN.

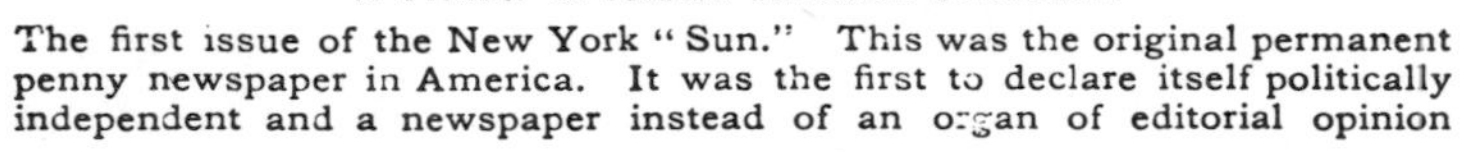
A Pioneer of Modern American Journalism

The first issue of the New York "Sun." This was the original permanent penny newspaper in America. It was the first to declare itself politically independent and a newspaper instead of an organ of editorial opinion

Hoe discovered that the way to get speed out of a press was to put the type on the cylinder, not on the bed. Eight thousand copies an hour on one four-feeder press became an immediate possibility, and circulation could proceed without limitation from the mechanical plant. The times worked with him; the first quarter-century of his long career led up toward the Civil War. Before that crisis the ordinary American had not been characteristically a newspaper reader. But that great people's war, whose levies entered the struggle by choice, not compulsion, vitally interested every literate person—which means, practically, every American. Each family had a son, or its neighbor had many sons, fighting along the Mississippi or the Rappahannock; everywhere farmers and mechanics waited for train or stage to bring lists of the dead from the latest battle. When we began the Civil War, news and the newspapers were partly a luxury. When we left it behind, news had become a necessity. From that time forth no American family was so remote or so incurious as not to want its daily or weekly newspaper.

Last of all, in 1859, Darwin crowned his century by publishing his "Origin of Species." From now on men were to accept ready-made theories less and less, and require more and more the data by which they might form their own conclusions.

So was our press established in its present form. Blindly, as progress goes, our editors had stumbled upon a private want, a public need, hitherto unsatisfied; a new factor in democracy. They held the triggers of a force whose full power they failed to understand. Our Constitution and State codes, formed for an eighteenth century civilization and warped awkwardly sometimes to fit the needs of a new industrial era, failed in nothing as it failed in providing curbs for this new force—the power of the news. During a half-century in which the press grew from a humble professional enterprise to a great business, turning out its millions in profits every year, there was nothing to restrain the baser members of the craft except public disgust as expressed by the withdrawal of public patronage, or the opposition and exposure of better contemporaries. This force surprised civilization; it was born without the law; its power kept it above the law.

Dana and the "Sun"

CHARLES A. DANA with his New York "Sun" made the next step forward, brought in the next current. As art is less than life, so his was a lesser influence than that of Greeley or Bennett; and it has always been better understood within the profession of journalism than without.

Though news had become the approved product of journalism, workmanship lingered behind. He was the best reporter, as I have said, who found the greatest amount of exclusive news, rushed it most rapidly into print. Editors, in the craze for news, did not consider that a slight story well told may attract more attention than a great one mumbled. Writers of force and vigor we had always here and there; but they were mainly accidents. Later, daring editors and reporters tried to get some writing into the press. The star reporters who did this work imitated the novelists, and produced a form of writing as grotesquely unsuited to its needs as a dress-suit to a hunting expedition. The best newspapers of the seventies include a mass of affected, stilted writing with which we have no patience to-day. There lingers in my memory a report of the Crittenden murder in San Francisco, written in the seventies by one of the high-priced American stars. This was a crime as sensational in its community and time as the late Thaw murder in New York. Mr. Crittenden, leader of the California bar, was embracing his wife, just returned from Europe, when a woman shot him from behind. The report begins:

"The old adage, 'Hell hath no fury like a woman scorned,' was amply exemplified yesterday on the Oakland ferry when an attorney, type of the profession sworn to support the Commonwealth," etc.—halfway down the column through this mass of verbiage before the reader learned that some one had been murdered, three-quarters of the way before he learned who had been murdered, next column before it dawned who committed the murder!

The plain, ordinary news mechanic went to the other extreme. The news was the thing; tell it in stereotyped phrases if you would, but tell it absolutely baldly; and look to nothing for effect and interest but a plain statement of the facts themselves. From this arose the rule, still hammered into cub reporters: "Tell your story in the head; tell it again in the first sentence, again in the first paragraph, and again in the body of the story." This plain perversion of the manner in which the human mind has been accustomed to tell and grasp stories since the race began, presupposes that the one big fact of the news—that some one has been killed, has eloped, been enriched or married—is the only thing which can possibly interest a reader.

What Dana Taught

DANA saw no reason why journalism, the little sister of literature, should not herself dress with art. Perceiving that the news reports in the daily papers must henceforth be the chief intellectual food for three-quarters of our people, he came to believe that the clever, subtle, and sound narration of these reports was a task worthy of all the taste, the culture, and the soul-force that there is in any man. He perceived that this art must be limited, that any striving for extraordinary combinations of words was beyond the scope of the reporter. As he worked it out, the art of reporting is the art of the plain tale, beginning at the beginning and proceeding to the end, and decked mainly with those details which the trained eye of the good reporter comes to perceive. So appeared the "Sun" style—easy, often witty, full of detail and incident, but always clear. The public will never know all the influence which Dana had upon newspaper men. "Sun" writing became the standard and criterion; the old, stilted, highfalutin style retreated to the country and the frontiers; and every good writing reporter became debtor to Dana. He put a premium upon that same writing reporter; the pure news-getter was never supreme again after Dana entered the field.

So stood our journalism in the late seventies and early eighties, a decade before Pulitzer and Hearst came out of the West on the fourth current which changed the whole stream so curiously. For before the yellows appeared, our press was settled into a certain form. Though circulation, properties, receipts, and profits had become enormous, enough of the old editorial ideal lingered to keep our newspaper publishers editors instead of business men. They still took pride in their papers as intellectual organs. The power was not yet gone from their editorial pages; by this halter they still led their public. News, however, was already the main consideration; but it was passive rather than active news, static rather than aggressive. They did not yet go out to throw the light upon dark places; else that system of corporative ownership in public affairs which grew up after the Civil War might have been discovered before the palmy days of Mark Hanna. Certain perversions of editorial power which we consider evils to-day proceeded without ruffle of conscience. The newspaper being usually a party organ, the publisher saw no good reason against sharing the spoils of party. He took subsidies brazenly from one side or the other, he backed candidates on their pledge of city or county advertising. Though our press published much criminal news—as American papers always have since the time of Bennett—his journal was moderate and conservative compared to the average newspaper of 1911. It clung still to the theory that news about public affairs interests readers more than mere personal items. Congressional debates on important measures brought forth column after column of full, literal reports, where such debates draw half-columns of condensation to-day. Already newspapers were expanding greatly in size; for the presses could now meet almost any demand of circulation. White paper was the only handicap; still we must depend on the Italian output of linen rags for our paper stock. Near the end of this era, however, our chemists capped ten years of experiment by discovering a practical process for making web paper from wood-pulp; and the last barrier to size disappeared. The field lay cleared when the first yellows came into their own.

The Panama Canal's Defense

Shore Batteries Equipped with Gruson Turrets Are More Effective Than a Fleet Patrol

By Captain GODFREY L. CARDEN, U. S. R. C. S.

IT IS asserted that the Panama Canal can best be defended by fleets. This is known as the mobile form of defense, in contradistinction to the fixed, as exemplified by permanent fortifications. In the proposed safeguarding by fleets, we have a form of defense offered which may or may not be counted upon to be always on hand. The very fact that it possesses mobility may offer at some time the opening which a resourceful enemy will embrace to gain a shore footing.

To defend the canal by ships is greatly to favor an opposing fleet, for, generally speaking, naval men ask for nothing better than to be given ships to fight. An opposing fleet offers something tangible to engage—something, in other words, that can be reached by gun-fire and destroyed—the very opposite to what holds good in the case of fortifications provided with well-protected guns and with a practically unlimited supply of ammunition and guns' crews. It is an old axiom that one gun on shore is the equal of five guns on shipboard.

Lord Charles Beresford, recently in command of the British Home Fleet, was once questioned in Parliament as to the chances naval ships had to-day against shore guns mounted in Gruson turrets. The British admiral's reply was in effect that no naval commander would be so rash as to engage ships in a contest with Gruson turrets. When we speak of Gruson turrets, we are not speaking of the ordinary type of turret as mounted to-day on ships of war, where weight considerations limit the thickness to twelve inches. The Gruson turret, as now found in many modern coast batteries, is made of chilled cast-iron, having thicknesses varying from four to five feet. These turrets are impregnable in the face of ship artillery.

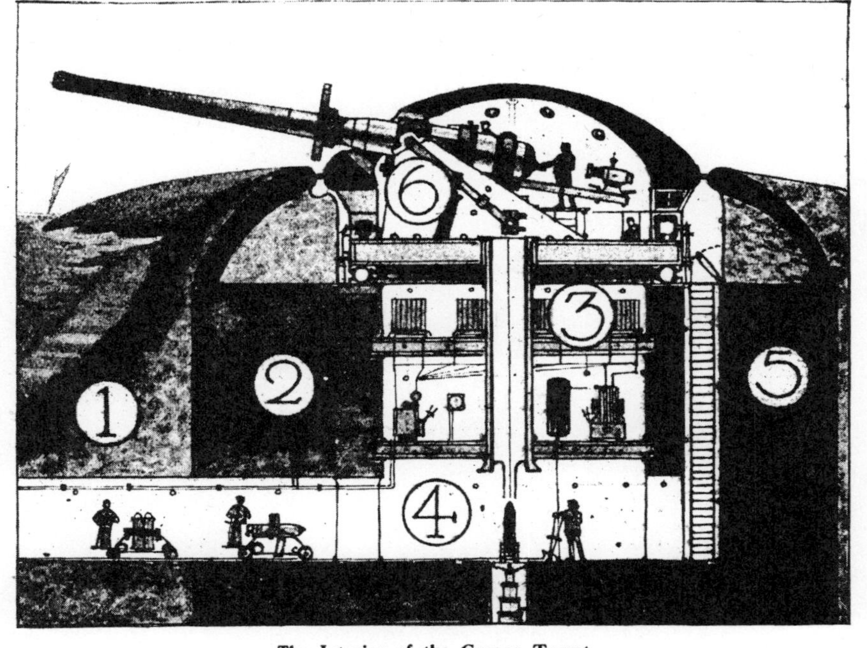

The Interior of the Gruson Turret

1, Portland cement; 2, storage batteries; 3, refrigerating room; 4, handling room; 5, iron-cement; 6, interior of turret proper. The dark turtle back and the two dark side pieces represent the armor and constitute the Gruson idea

Let us assume that the two canal entrances are covered by fleets cruising in the near vicinity. How long would those fleets remain off the canal approaches if a strong force of the enemy were threatening a section of the New England or Pacific Coast? It is to be supposed the enemy will demonstrate at a number of points, with the avowed object of concealing his intentions as to where he proposes to attack. How long does the reader imagine that we could afford to permit a number of our best ships to lie idle in the canal zone, doing guard duty, as it were. United States vessels, for the most part, are powerfully engined and powerfully gunned. They are designed to follow up, search out, and destroy the enemy—not to lie supinely by awaiting the approach of a fleet, which will never attack *unless it be stronger*. The enemy's demonstrations may be for the sole purpose of withdrawing the force on guard off the canal.

No one can dare assert that the strategy will not succeed. What has happened in land warfare is equally true of operations at sea. One has only to regard the facility with which Stonewall Jackson maneuvered the Union forces opposed to him in the Shenandoah Valley. There was seldom a time when Jackson was not weaker than the combined Federal forces, yet, through strategy, he was generally enabled to so draw out the Union forces that when he attacked he was invariably stronger in numbers.

So long as the defense of the canal is left to a mobile force, it is possible to draw off that force, and no matter what the cause may be which occasions the temporary relinquishment of the defense, even if it be dictated by the best military reasons, there is at once presented an opening for a naval commander with three or four ships to jump in, beach his guns, sink his ships for all they are now worth, and the canal is his. If he can afford protection for his gunners, he can defy any fleet to clear him out before a strong supporting force has reenforced him with men and guns. Essentially the ship is a means of attack and not a means of defense. If any one has any doubt of the ability of shore works to stand off a fleet, let him consider the attack of the British fleet on Alexandria, or the operations of our monitor fleet during the Civil War against the defenses of Charleston. Fleets may sometimes run by a battery, as in the case of the taking of New Orleans, but no such opportunity is offered at the canal entrance.

To go further, we have the comparatively recent experiments of the French Government against specially erected fortifications on the Ile de Levant. These experiments were carried on through arrangements between the war and naval authorities of the French Government. The shore batteries were built after the most approved manner, and consisted of

(Concluded on page 22)

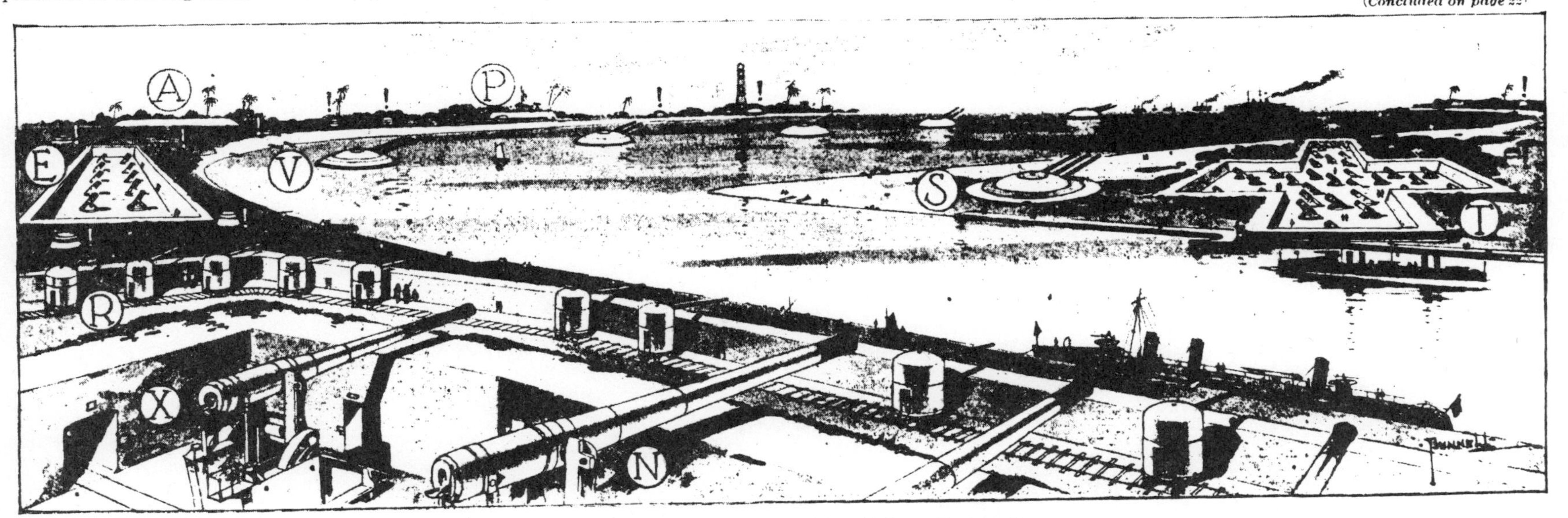

A General Idea of the Modern Coast Defense Equipment

A, battery of 13-inch rifles; E, 10-inch turn-table mortar battery; N, 13-inch D rifles; P, plane table or torpedo control; R, the Gruson movable rapid-fire gun, which makes any railroad a line of defense and any gully a fort; S, Gruson land turret mounting three 16-inch rifles; T, battery of 12-inch rifled mortars; T-T mounts; V, five submerged Gruson turrets carrying 13-inch rifles; X, 10-inch disappearing rifle. The points (!) indicate the positions of the small Gruson turrets in which the officers are stationed during action, and from which the batteries are aimed and fired. The trees and entire landscape are artificial productions, prearranged to make the view from the sea misleading

III

The Fourth Current

"YELLOW JOURNALISM," a term of opprobrium today both inside and outside the journalism profession, in reality was a phenomenon that explored a different dimension of the audience-newspaper relationship. As newspapers began to have primary importance to their owners as business enterprises even as early as the eighteenth century, proprietors sought ways to increase circulation. And gradually newspapers began to take on more of the characteristics they have today. Hence Bennett, with his expanded definition of news that embraced much more than the traditional newspaper fare. Hence Dana, and others, who stressed clarity and simplicity in newswriting. Hence, too, Hearst and Pulitzer.

The times were ripe for the rapid development of sensationalism and for pursuit of it virtually to its outermost limits. The country's population was increasing rapidly, but the immigrants were in the main neither educated nor concerned with the significant issues of the day. Lives of the masses, particularly in the big cities, particularly during the daily drudgery of the Industrial Revolution, were drab and dreary. The escapism provided by the sensationlism of the cheap papers was welcome and, a Marxist might argue, probably essential to the continued functioning of the system. Only the belated onset of Pulitzer's conscience, causing him to forswear the yellow method in his circulation battle with Hearst, halted for a time exploration of this new dimension. The so-called "jazz journalism" of the 1920s renewed the quest for bad taste and found new boundaries that undoubtedly would have shocked Pulitzer, had he lived, but which seemed not to astound Hearst, who did.

The American Newspaper

A Study of Journalism in Its Relation to the Public

By WILL IRWIN

The first article of this series showed that the modern power of the press is the power of the news. The second article described the three currents which united to make the American press what it was before the yellows came. The first of these was our Anglo-Saxon inheritance of an editorial press. The second had its source in James Gordon Bennett, Sr.; it was the discovery of news. The third, which Charles A. Dana typified, was the idea of art in news-writing. Enter, now, the fourth current—yellow journalism

III.—The Fourth Current

Joseph Pulitzer
At the time of his entry into New York journalism

THE seeds of yellow journalism, so called for want of a better name, sprouted at St. Louis and San Francisco during the eighties; they came to fruition in New York, thrashing-floor for changes in journalism, during the early nineties. In the decade which preceded the full flowering of Hearst and Pulitzer, however, a change in the spirit of newspaper publication had crept in by way of the business office—a change which prepared the ground for this new seed. From a rather humble professional enterprise, the newspaper had become a great "business proposition," holding infinite possibilities of profit.

Dana, Medill, Greeley, Godkin, even Bennett, adopted their vocation from that mixture of motive and chance which leads a man into any profession; they certainly reckoned the chance of getting rich very slightly among possibilities. But the field for newspaper circulation grew, as I have shown; and with it grew the perfection of swift mechanical processes. By 1891 a quadruple Hoe press would print, fold, cut, paste, and count 72,000 eight-page papers an hour. The linotype, or mechanical typesetting machine, climax of delicate mechanism, was not yet perfected; that was to come just after the yellows made their start. Our publishers had facilities, therefore, to handle any imaginable increase in circulation. It was necessary only to enlarge basement spaces and increase the number of presses. And now big retail business discovered the newspaper as a salesman. Yankee advertising had been a jest of Europe for a half-century long, before experience proved that for most commodities advertisement in a regular and respectable periodical pays better, dollar for dollar, than advertisement by circular or sign-board.

The New Salesmanship

IN THE same period the retail dry goods business, consistently an advertiser since the first newspapers, began to concentrate in department stores and to drag into these great emporiums other forms of retail business, such as hardware, jewelry, and groceries. With their bargain days, their special offerings, designed to attract customers to the store, their advertising became a matter of news. They did not now announce, as in 1810: "We offer prints and calicoes at lowest prices," but: "Special to-day: A hundred dozen pairs of ladies' lisle hose, worth 75 cents, at 49 cents." For this form of publicity the newspaper was the only possible medium except privately distributed circulars; and a circular, as experience has shown, is usually thrown into the ash-can, while a newspaper notice, surrounded by matter which commands some respect, is kept and read. Newspaper and periodical advertising grew from tiny beginnings to a great force of distribution. Where the senior Bennett's old "Herald" got its advertising revenue by hundreds of dollars, the junior Bennett's "Herald" of the eighties got it by tens of thousands. There came, then, a gradual shift of power from the editorial rooms to the business office.

The stalwart old-time newspaper proprietor, who had entered the editorial game for love of it, still held his paper to editorial ideals, though he grew rich incidentally. McCullagh of the St. Louis "Globe-Democrat," it is remembered now in these changed days, would not let a business office man come on to the editorial floor, lest his staff become commercialized. There remained, however, a multitude of lesser souls who yielded to the temptation of the flesh-pots and trained their eyes solely on commercial possibilities. Their advertising solicitors raked the city for copy; the less scrupulous coerced advertisers by a species of blackmail—"You advertise with us and we'll leave you alone." Above all—and this is where the commercial movement ties up with "yellow" journalism—they were ripe and ready for any method which would serve to extend circulation and therefore make their advertising space more valuable.

During the seventies, a young German-American, a pest to his fellows with his truculence, a blessing to his employers with his news sense and his vigorous writing, shuttled back and forth between the German and English newspapers of St. Louis. Joseph Pulitzer had been a soldier of bad fortune for some years before he entered journalism; he had served as coachman, as waiter, as common laborer, as private in the burial squad which laid away the dead after the St. Louis cholera epidemic; and he had learned the common man's attitude toward life and the news. His fellows of the police stations in his early journalistic days remember him as a restless, inquiring youth, ready to try almost any experiment with life, if he might learn thereby what was inside the sealed envelope: above all, as a man with his own opinions, ready to back them with fist and tongue. He rose; he did his turn at Washington, where his writing attracted the attention of Dana; and he might have taken service with the New York "Sun." He preferred the power of the game to its art, however; and in 1878 he raised money to acquire the old St. Louis "Post-Dispatch," an obscure paper, dying of inanition.

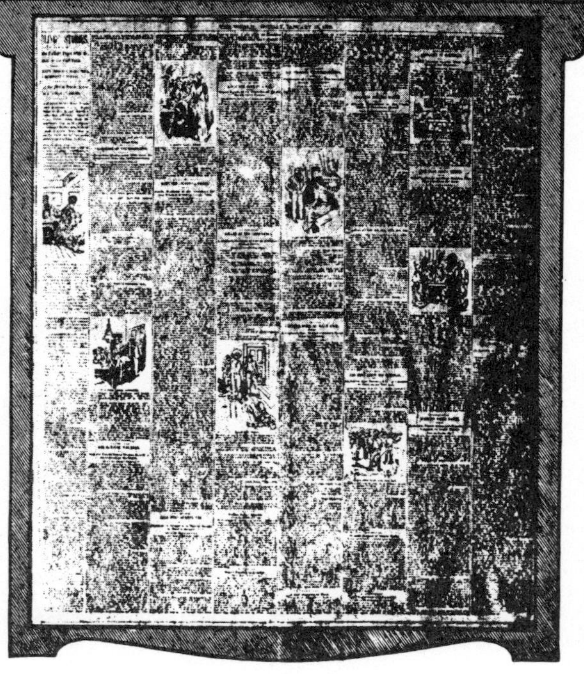

The Old Sunday "World"
Just before Morrill Goddard started yellow journalism

What Pulitzer Found

IT IS not true, as some assume, that Pulitzer founded yellow journalism then and there. What he did discover—and that is only one element in yellow journalism—was the means of fighting popular causes by the news. The process was not wholly original with him; the New York "Times" had smashed the Tweed Ring by publishing plain accounts of their corrupt transactions. Perhaps, however, Pulitzer was first to go out systematically and find evil before evil obtruded itself on public notice. He had a conservative community to serve. In such an atmosphere certain set and old injustices always flourish for lack of popular opposition. Pulitzer scratched this surface and showed what lay beneath. He made himself the bugaboo of the big cinch; he made his organ such a champion of popular rights that to this day the humble citizen of St. Louis who has a grievance tends to write to the "P.-D." before he employs a lawyer. That was the kind of journalism which Pulitzer brought to the hospitable-minded metropolis when, in the middle eighties, he bought the New York "World."

William Randolph Hearst
Shortly after he took charge of the San Francisco "Examiner"

The Beginnings of Hearst

THE yellow streak was working from quite another beginning at the other end of the continent. William Randolph Hearst, only son of rich and able parents, had come out of Harvard. His father, Senator George Hearst, a rough, hustling mining millionaire and politician, had bought the San Francisco "Examiner" as a kind of flyer in connection with his political and commercial schemes. The son had taken a fancy to journalism, and had his eye already on the "Examiner." Even in college he made a daily study and comparison of the current newspapers. The "Examiner," as he found it, was an old, conservative paper, weak in the spine through many changes of political ownership.

Unbiased and unblinded, as though this were the first and only publication in the world, Hearst set out to find how he could make it the greatest, the controlling newspaper of the Pacific Coast region. His father's old employees, and especially one "Petey" Bigelow, a wild genius of a reporter who flourished in San Francisco at that period, took him in hand and taught him all they knew. He listened to their advice—and rejected it, mainly. Not until he discovered that S. S. Chamberlain was willing to take a position on the far coast of the United States did Hearst find the man to show him the way.

Chamberlain had seen service with both Bennett and Pulitzer; for the former, he had edited the Paris "Herald"; and he had started "Le Matin." He came to the "Examiner," therefore, schooled in the most sensational journalism which had appeared up to that time. He was—and is—a master of popular psychology, a seer at perceiving the subtle values in public taste. Through all the subsequent years of the yellow craze he remained a rock of real news-journalism in the Hearst organization. To Hearst, experimenting blindly with what the public wanted, this exponent of sensationalism was a godsend. Under his tutelage the young millionaire began to make a noise. He attacked the Southern Pacific, the eternal corporation bugaboo of California—did it with such success that, during his first long absence from California, Collis P. Huntington compounded with his resident manager and bought the paper off for a thousand dollars a month. A schooner went ashore on Brandt Rock, a dangerous reef outside the harbor mouth. Hearst equipped a tug under command of "Petey" Bigelow and rescued the survivors—on behalf of the "Examiner." He sent up balloons to distribute prizes to the populace—on behalf of the "Examiner." Whenever, in all his radius of interest, occurred a disaster or a startling crime, he despatched to the scene a special train loaded to the window with "Examiner" writers and illustrators. The public park of San Francisco wanted a specimen of the fast-dying Californian grizzly. Hearst set hunters to work; they trapped the biggest bear to be had; "Monarch, the 'Examiner's' Grizzly," made space for weeks. This caught the fickle and unaccountable public fancy, and Hearst pushed the movement along by adopting the bear as the "Examiner" trademark. James Swinnerton, in the first flush of his powers as a rough-and-ready cartoonist, drew bears for a year, until people tired of the feature.

Whenever the other newspapers produced a man suited to his purposes, Hearst bought him over at his own figures. So he got E. H. Hamilton, one of the great American reporters; Homer Davenport, destined as a cartoonist to play his part in political history; Arthur McEwen, second only to Brisbane as a writer of editorials in the Hearst manner. Chamberlain conceived the idea that the city hospital was badly managed. He picked a little slip of a girl from among his cub reporters, and assigned her to the investigation. She invented her own method—she "fainted" on the street, and was carried to the hospital for treatment. She turned out a story[1] "with a sob for the unfortunate in every line." That was the professional beginning of "Annie Laurie" or Winifred Black, and of a departure in newspaper writing. For she came to have many imitators; but none other could ever so well stir up the primitive emotions of sympathy and pity; she was a "sob squad" all by herself. Indeed, in the discovery of this sympathetic "woman writing," Hearst broke through the crust into the thing he was after. His greatest single hit, before he left San Francisco for wider fields, was the "Little Jim Ward"—simply a movement to establish a ward for incurables in the local children's hospital. "Little Jim" was a helpless cripple whom Annie Laurie discovered and whom she used as an example. Every day for weeks the women of San Francisco exchanged tears across the back fences over "Little Jim."

Hearst was experimenting every week, every day; trying a hundred expensive departures, only to abandon ninety-nine for the sake of the one which "panned out." This week, he arranged the heads in certain symmetrical patterns — for "make-up" or the physical appearance of the paper, was always a hobby with him. Next week, he tried the effect of veiled salaciousness. Another, he got such sensation as he could out of Sunday's sermons to see if his readers "really cared for religion in the news." And he experimented always with one object in view—to find what the public wanted, how he might sell the greatest number of copies.

Consciously or unconsciously, Hearst and Chamberlain were working on a principle whose formulation was as original to our Occidental journalism as Bennett's discovery of news. He who serves the intellectual and artistic demands of the populace must give them in some measure what they want. If he proceed from the very highest ethical and artistic ideals, he must make concessions, or they will not listen. But having established a common ground with his public, he may give them a little better than they want, so leading them up by the slow process of education to his own better ideals; or he may give them a great deal worse. The gentlemen who conduct our theatrical affairs, for example, have of late given the public worse than it wants, so that when some sound, sincere, and artistic piece of work like "The Three of Us," "The Great Divide," or "Paid in Full" slips past them to success, they stand amazed. When Hearst began, the spirit of the old-age editor still guided newspaper publication; the great majority of editors, no matter how strong their desire for circulation, still served news and editorial in fashion much more intellectual than the public wanted, still appealed to the mind rather than the heart. Hearst's task was to cheapen the product until it sold at the coin of the gutter and the streets.

So he came generally to reject all news stories which did not contain that thrill of sensation loved by the man on the street and the woman in the kitchen; no paper ever published fewer news items to the issue. He trained his men to look for the one sensational, picturesque fact in every occurrence which came to the desk, and to twist that fact to the fore.

The First Full-Sized Colored Supplement

The coloring of the original is faithfully reproduced here. Notice how dim and uncertain it appears. For months the newspaper mechanics had great trouble with inks and register. This was considered, at the time, a doubtful and expensive experiment, and for nearly a year it was a flat failure as a circulation winner

"What we're after," said Arthur McEwen, "is the 'gee-whiz' emotion." Pressed for further explanation, he said: "We run our paper so that when the reader opens it he says: 'Gee-whiz!' An issue is a failure which doesn't make him say that." The basic human passions—"Love for the woman, power for the man"—Hearst was after them. A story to be available for his purposes must have romance, sympathy, hate, gain, in the first sentence, the first line, the first paragraph.

Necessarily, since he was reaching out to grip and to hold the populace, his editorial policy leaned to the people's side. He began as a Democrat, that being then the party of the under dog. At once he ran clear beyond Democracy until he impinged on Socialism. He adopted the union labor cause, even at the cost of an expensive mechanical department in his own newspaper. For years, or until rows and bickerings over the political support of union labor broke the alliance, this was a foundation-stone of Hearst editorial policy. Here convenience wed sincerity, doubtless; those who knew Hearst best in this early era declare that under his cold exterior he kept a real sympathy for the submerged man and woman, a real feeling of his own mission to plead their cause.

When he took the "Examiner" it was dying. In 1888, when Chamberlain came, he had brought it to 30,000 circulation. By 1893 he had 72,000; and he held a secure lead over the other San Francisco newspapers. That lead he never lost; year in and year out, except for the set-back of the great disaster in 1906, the "Examiner" has returned its $30,000 to $40,000 a month to keep the other Hearst papers floating.

This journalism he brought to New York when he bought the "Journal" in 1895. It was not yet quite what we call yellow, though it approximated that happy condition. For real yellow journalism had beaten him by a few months. Joseph Pulitzer had been fighting his way on the New York "World" with the sensational, militant style which he perfected in St. Louis. He took personal charge of the "World" in 1884. Within two years he had attacked so many things which the other newspapers had not perceived as copy, or had not dared to touch, that he was disputing circulation with Bennett the Younger and Dana. By the end of the decade the "World" was altogether the most reckless, the most sensational, and the most widely discussed newspaper in New York. He has been several men, all extraordinary, in the course of his career, this Pulitzer; nothing so impresses one who regards him in the light of a historic character as the manner in which his able, penetrating, highly energized mind has shifted its point of view. In that stage he was a creature of infinite recklessness and incredible suspicion. By mental habit he scratched every fair surface to find the inner corrupt motive. Journalism, it appears, bounded his ambition; that was one secret of his extraordinary freedom from control. Had he cared for political position, for pure financial power, the history of American journalism in the past twenty years might have been very different. Within that narrow limit he, like the silent, cold, light-eyed young man experimenting out on the Pacific Coast, had the passion for leadership. "If you should put Hearst in a monastery," said one of his early associates, "he would become abbot or die." The gods cut Pulitzer off the same stripe.

The Sunday supplement was by this time an integral part of metropolitan journalism. As early as the Civil War period, the newspapers had been giving space on Sunday mornings to entertaining matter bearing

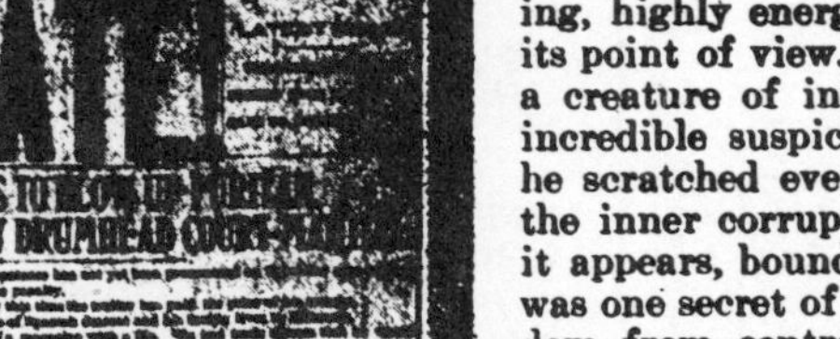

Brisbane's effect on the "Evening Journal"—A front page published in July, 1897, before Brisbane became editor of the "Journal," and a war-time number issued nine months later

[1] I find that I must ask the reader to accept one piece of professional argot. A "story," in the newspaper sense, is any contribution, from a market report to a leading editorial. What the English purist calls a "story" the newspaper man calls a "fiction story."

TWENTY-THIRD STREET AND FIFTH AVENUE ON SATURDAY AFTERNOON

THE MISSING LINK FOUND AT LAST.

French Scientist and Explorer Discovers a Race of Savages with Well-Developed Tails.

REMARKABLE REPORT TO THE FRENCH GEOGRAPHICAL SOCIETY.

The Missing Link

THE HUMAN MAN-MONKEY WITH A TAIL, DISCOVERED BY A FRENCH EXPLORER.

FRANCE'S TAX ON THE RICH

An effect of Goddard's, issued October 29, 1893. This looks mild now; then it was a sensation

Two years later—December 15, 1895—Goddard had achieved real yellow journalism

The evolution of Yellow Journalism as Morrill Goddard and Arthur Brisbane

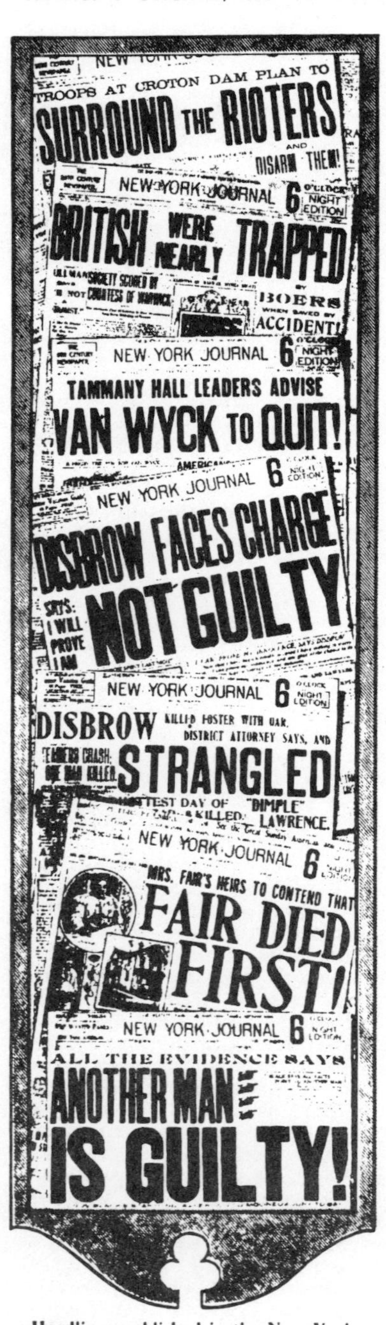
TROOPS AT CROTON DAM PLAN TO SURROUND THE RIOTERS AND DISARM THEM!

NEW YORK JOURNAL 6 O'CLOCK NIGHT EDITION

BRITISH WERE NEARLY TRAPPED

BOERS

ACCIDENT

NEW YORK JOURNAL 6 O'CLOCK NIGHT EDITION

TAMMANY HALL LEADERS ADVISE VAN WYCK TO QUIT!

NEW YORK JOURNAL 6

DISBROW FACES CHARGE

SAYS: I WILL PROVE I AM NOT GUILTY

NEW YORK JOURNAL 6

DISBROW KILLED FOSTER WITH OAR, DISTRICT ATTORNEY SAYS, AND STRANGLED

"DIMPLE" LAWRENCE

NEW YORK JOURNAL 6

MRS. FAIR'S HEIRS TO CONTEND THAT FAIR DIED FIRST!

NEW YORK JOURNAL 6

ALL THE EVIDENCE SAYS ANOTHER MAN IS GUILTY!

Headlines published in the New York "Journal" between 1899 and 1903

only indirect relation to the news. When, with the development of the rotary press, they were able to print large issues by eight-page sections, the most advanced journals began to add one of these sections on Sunday mornings as a kind of catch-all for routine semi-news matter, like notes of the fraternal orders and women's clubs, and mild write-ups of picturesque features of city life, together with such embellishment of fiction and beauty hints as they could afford. S. S. McClure, breaking into the world of print at about that time, made a fortune from his idea of selling the best current literature to newspapers for simultaneous publication on Sunday mornings—the famous McClure Syndicate.

Pulitzer Finds the Man

PULITZER, like the rest, published a supplement. Although by 1891 he had brought his Sunday circulation up to 300,000 copies, the "World" did not show so great a proportionate increase over daily circulation as the "Herald" or the "Sun"; and Pulitzer worried and tinkered over it. In 1891, H. H. Kohlsaat, then part owner of the Chicago "Inter-Ocean," saw in Paris the rotary color presses of the "Petit Journal." Printing in colors, be it known to the layman, had hitherto been done almost exclusively on slow, flat-bed presses, fed by hand, not from a roll or web. It had been thought impossible to the swift rotary press. When Kohlsaat returned to Chicago, he had Scott build him a color rotary on the European model. This would not handle whole sections, but only small inserts; Kohlsaat used it mainly for premium World's Fair views and the like. Pulitzer, alert to anything new, sent a man to see this press. The report was favorable. He consulted the Hoes, who informed him that they were already manufacturing color rotaries for small sheets. As a costly experiment, he ordered a rotary, turning out full-size pages in three colors and black. With this the "World" printed colored cartoons and beauty pictures on the outside pages of one Sunday section.

The process was costly and infinitely troublesome; and the dash of color had no visible effect upon the Sunday circulation. At the end of the year the heads of departments sent a round-robin to Pulitzer, who was fighting blindness in Europe, begging him to drop it. "The very building groaned," says an old executive of the "World," "when the boss cabled back ordering us to put a new man in charge of that section, and use the color pages for funny pictures, like 'Puck' and 'Judge.' "

Already, Pulitzer had found his editor for the Sunday supplement. Morrill Goddard, a young city editor "with a dynamo inside," had developed a faculty for getting "features" out of the news. Against his earnest protests, Pulitzer sent him over to the Sunday supplement. Once established at his new desk, Goddard, like Hearst, set out, naked-eyed, to find what the common mind wanted. An instinct quite extraordinary, considering that Goddard is a ripe scholar, led him to it; within the year he was running in that supplement what we now call "yellow journalism" as distinguished from "sensational journalism."

Pictures first—for ten grasp with the eye to one with the mind. He brought the size of pictures up from one column to two, to five; and, finally, the first "seven-column cut" made its appearance in his Sunday "World." Then reading matter so easy, with the startling points so often emphasized, that the weariest mechanic, sitting in his socks on Sunday morning, could not fail to get a thrill of interest. "Economy of attention"—that, unconsciously to him probably, made up his whole formula. Nothing which called for any close attention; something which first caught the eye and then startled, tickled, and interested without wear on brain tissue. For subject-matter he clung close to the news, choosing and expanding the bizarre, the startling, the emotional, though the item occupied only a line in the daily paper. When such subject matter failed, he was capable of making history yellow. Did a treatise on "The Man in the Iron Mask" appear, Goddard, taking the publication of this book as an excuse, would rush into print a page of the "Iron Mask," with nightmare pictures, three inches of "snappy" introduction "playing up" the mystery, and two or three "box freaks" distributed among the pictures, giving learned opinions by great historians. So he played on still another popular weakness; he made his readers believe that they were on the royal road to learning.

One of Goddard's old associates has given his formula for a page in a yellow Sunday supplement. "Suppose it's Halley's comet," he says. "Well, first you have a half-page of decoration showing the comet, with historical pictures of previous appearances thrown in. If you can work a pretty girl into the decoration, so much the better. If not, get some good nightmare idea like the inhabitants of Mars watching it pass. Then you want a quarter of a page of big-type heads—snappy. Then four inches of story, written right off the bat. Then a picture of Professor Halley down here and another of Professor Lowell up there, and a two-column boxed freak containing a scientific opinion, which nobody will understand, just to give it class."

The "Sectional View"

FROM the smallest opening, Goddard would develop a road to popular interest. He and Andrew E. Murphy, his assistant, used to walk home to their lodgings in Washington Square, talking newspaper as they went. "Have you noticed," said Murphy one night, "how the crowd stops to watch the picture in that drug-store window? It's nothing but a cheap chromo. What's the reason?" This was indeed the crudest kind of chromo—it represented "sponge fishing on the Florida coast." Goddard studied it a long time. "I have it," he said that night. "It's a sectional view. You can watch the ships above and the shark eating the diver below at the same time. Let's try it." And the Sunday magazine of the New York "World" had a "sectional view," first of its kind, in the next issue. This bit of prospecting opened a paying streak. A hundred others ended in blind pockets, and Goddard abandoned them at once.

And just when the comic section and the Sunday magazine of the "World" were beginning to bear fruit in increased circulation, Hearst bought the New York "Journal" and broke

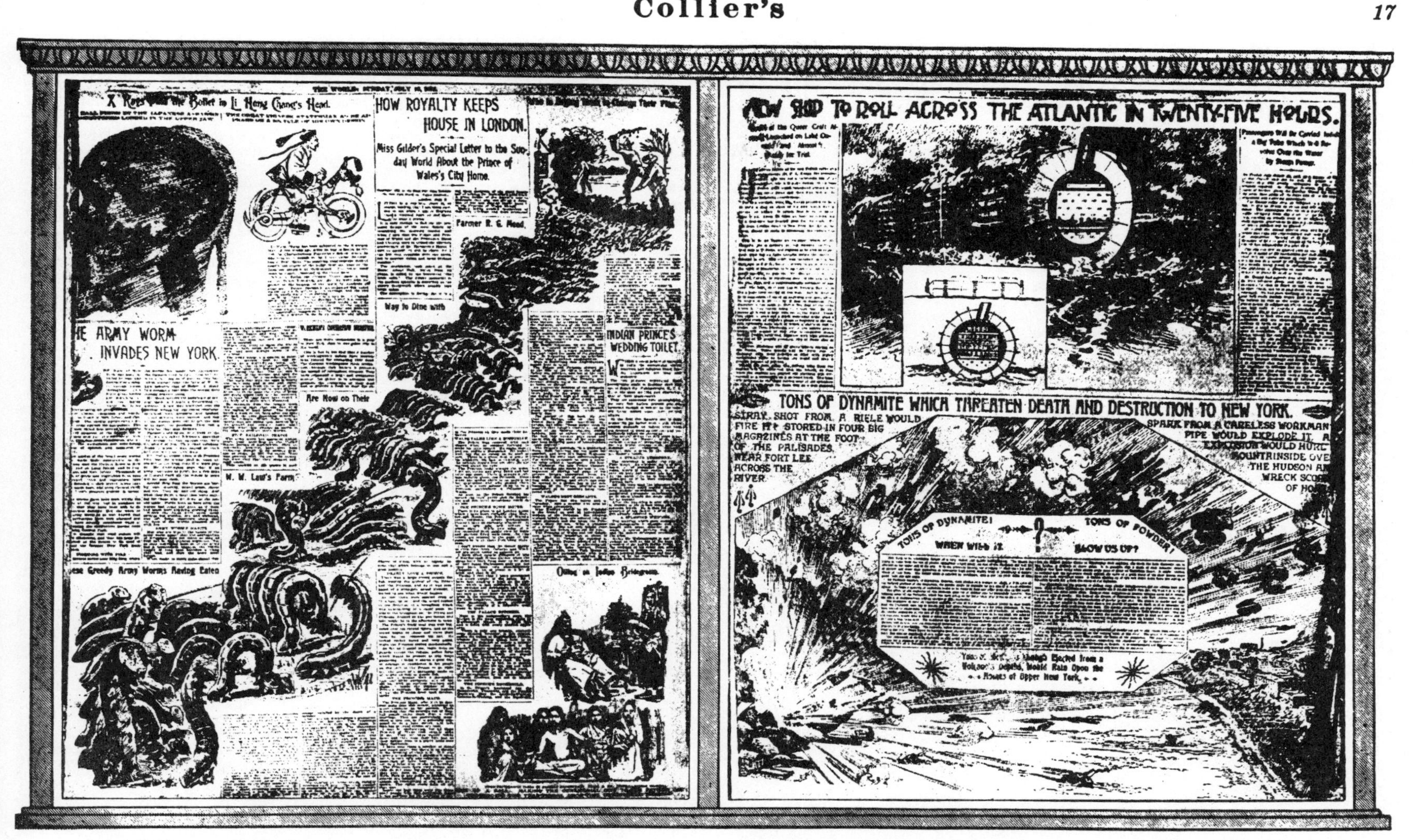
HOW ROYALTY KEEPS HOUSE IN LONDON.
Miss Gilder's Special Letter to the Sunday World About the Prince of Wales's City Home.
HE ARMY WORM INVADES NEW YORK.
INDIAN PRINCE'S WEDDING TOILET.
SHIP TO ROLL ACROSS THE ATLANTIC IN TWENTY-FIVE HOURS.
TONS OF DYNAMITE WHICH THREATEN DEATH AND DESTRUCTION TO NEW YORK.
TONS OF DYNAMITE! TONS OF POWDER!

Arthur Brisbane, as Goddard's successor, produced this page on July 19, 1896 — By September 19, 1897, just before he left the "World," Brisbane turned out the above

worked out the principle in the Sunday Supplement of the New York "World"

into the metropolis—"with all the discreet secrecy," some one has said, "of a wooden-legged burglar having a fit on a tin roof." He brought his Chamberlains and McEwens, his Hamiltons and Winifred Blacks; brought his own sensational, ruthless style of journalism; brought also the Hearst millions and the steady profits of the "Examiner." He began to win over the Pulitzer men by offers of increased salary; Goddard was one of the first whom he lured away. Forthwith, the yellow supplement burst out on the "Journal." A carnival of bids and counter-bids for men followed. Newspaper salaries, in the sensational division, went up never to fall back to their old level; newspaper desks became tenancies of a day.

Some one met "Cosey" Noble, Hearst man, in a restaurant. "What are you doing now, Noble?" he asked. "When I left the office," Noble replied, "I was city editor."

Brisbane Goes to the "Journal"

ARTHUR BRISBANE, a graduate of the New York "Sun," was then a kind of factotum on the "World." He admired the Goddard discoveries in journalism, and had maintained, against Pulitzer's own pride of invention, that the supplement, and not the colored comics, was responsible for the steady rise of Sunday circulation. When Goddard went over to Hearst, Pulitzer made Brisbane his Sunday editor. At once this section went still further in audacity, so that Goddard, to maintain the pace, had to outdo even himself. The Sunday "World" had 450,000 circulation when Hearst appeared. By 1897 Brisbane had raised it to 600,000. And now the yellow flood flowed over from the Sunday magazine to the daily paper. "What are you fellows doing?" asked Pulitzer and Hearst, in effect, of the managing editors and city editors. "The Sunday is going ahead; you are standing still." Having no great discovery of their own to stimulate circulation, the editors of the daily paper imitated the Sunday supplement. Into their own product they brought this fake, shallow, supersensational method, this predigested information, this striving for hitting effect at any cost.

Sensational newspapers tremble always with office politics. In 1897, after the club boycott on yellow journalism, Brisbane found his position on the "World" fading away from him. Hearst, meantime, had established a circulation for his morning "Journal" (now the "American"), and was making inroads on the "World" with his Sunday paper; but the evening paper lagged at little more than 100,000 a day. Brisbane, who had already received bids from across the street, approached Hearst with a proposition. "I'll take charge of your evening paper at a hundred dollars a week," he said, in effect. "But I'll expect a dollar a week raise for every thousand I add to the circulation." Hearst accepted. Brisbane, with a free hand, started to make an evening newspaper on the plan of a yellow supplement. He invented the job-type head—half the front page devoted to two or three smashing words, blaring forth sensation. He went further and devised that trick headline wherein the first and third lines, in immense type, proclaim a sensation, while the interlarded second line, in small type, reduces the whole head to a commonplace meaning ("WAR Will Probably be DECLARED," for example). Then fortune filled his sails. He took the "Evening Journal" late in 1897. On February 14, 1898, the *Maine* was blown up in Havana Harbor. There followed six months of rumors of war, preparation for war, and, finally, war. Never had sensational editor such an opportunity. In heads which occupied sometimes three-quarters of the page, the "Journal" blazoned forth the latest rumors. In smashing, one-sentence-to-the-paragraph Brisbane editorials, it bellowed at the Government the mob demand for vengeance on Spain. In one year the "Journal" touched the million mark; and Brisbane was earning, by his agreement, $50,000 per annum. It is said that the agreement was in form of a short note, and that Hearst might have broken it had he gone to law. But he paid gladly, personal liberality being one of his virtues. And liberality was wisdom, for Brisbane has been a gold-mine to his employer.

There followed the climax of the yellow craze, an episode in social history which we may yet come to regard with as much amazement as the tulip craze in Holland or the Mississippi Bubble. Now did the "World" and "Journal" go insane with violent scareheads, worded to get the last drop of sensation from the "story" and throw it to the fore; now did they make fact out of hint, history out of rumor; now did they create, for their believing readers, a picture of a world all flash and sensation; now did they change their bill day by day like a vaudeville house, striving always for some new and startling method of attracting a crowd. Now they hunted down the criminal with blaring horns, so playing on the mob weakness for the thief chase; now, with the criminal caught and condemned and sentenced, they howled for his reprieve, glorified him in hysterics, so availing themselves of the old mob sympathy for the victim of the law, mob hatred for the executioner. Now they dressed out the most silly and frivolous discussion of the day with symposiums of solemn opinion from prominent citizens; now they went a step further in audacity and headed an interview from Bishop Potter or Chauncey M. Depew "By Bishop Potter" or "By Chauncey M. Depew," as though these eminent citizens were real contributors. Now they discovered the snob in all humanity and turned reporters, artists, and—after the half-tones became possible—photographers loose on "Society." The Four Hundred of New York, largely a newspaper myth, was the target for this army. Their doings, with the follies emphasized, bedecked column after column, daily and Sunday, of hysterical slush. Life, as it percolated through the "World" and "Journal," became melodrama, the song of the spheres a screech.

Pulitzer Shifts Ground

SUDDENLY the "World" dropped the whole game; changed almost in a week from yellow to merely sensational. This came almost coincidentally with those three months in a dark room from which Pulitzer emerged totally blind. There are those who believe that Pulitzer, had he retained his sight, would have drawn a string of yellow newspapers across the country as Hearst has done. I prefer to think, as do his best old counselors, that Pulitzer perceived the end of this mad-

(Continued on page 24)

CRANK SENDS THREATS OF DEATH BY SLOW POISON TO RICH MEN!
JOURNAL HAUGHEY LOSES!
ODELL SAYS HE WILL VETO TUNNEL GRAB BILL
NEW YORK JOURNAL
POWDER THAT LOOKS LIKE THE POISON FOUND
MOLINEUX LAYS BARE DEATH CELL SECRETS
NEW YORK JOURNAL
ENGLAND AND GERMANY UNITED IN WAR!
DECLARE
NEW YORK JOURNAL
SHIPS CLEAR FOR BATTLE
NEW YORK JOURNAL
JEROME BEGINS HIS HEARING HOPING IT WILL INDICT CANFIELD!

Headlines published in the New York "Journal" between 1899 and 1902

The American Newspaper

(Continued from page 17)

ness; that he came to one of his sudden transformations in point of view. This blind man sees further into his times than any other American journalist; he must have known that it could not last. Change he did in the spring of 1901, so that now the worst one can say of his evening "World" is to call it a little sensational and rather silly, while his morning "World" is possibly the freest and most truthful popular newspaper in New York.

Hearst went on; as he grew great in influence and money he spread out to Chicago, to Boston, to Los Angeles, carrying his journalism in a form modified for the environment. Only his New York "Journal" and his Chicago papers were ever supremely yellow; but in these, for a few years after Pulitzer dropped out, his office staffs, and especially the lesser reporters, went on to the very madness of journalism. At its best the form stretched truth to the bursting point; for it consisted in warping facts to suit a distorted, melodramatic point of view. From this to outright falsehood was but a step, taken without perception by men no longer capable of seeing truth. The fact became but a peg whereon to hang the lie. Did the police find a poor, tired, sodden servant girl dead by her own hand near the park lake?—"Mystery of the Park—Pretty Girl Richly Dressed—Believed to be Member of Prominent Family." Did the reporters need an interview to dress out any large general story? If the "prominent citizen" refused the interview, the reporter wrote it just the same. Often he did not even attempt to see the "prominent citizen." The method for avoiding the trouble which naturally followed was, one of the Hearst arts.

"Riot at Morgue!"

AFTER the *Slocum* disaster I, as reporter for a conservative New York newspaper, had the mournful assignment of watching that temporary morgue where the police and divers were laying out the bodies. A new consignment had just arrived when I started back for the office. The crowd outside, mainly relatives of the dead, had grown impatient with delay, and one little German shook his fist at the police. For a minute the crowd pushed and jostled; then the doors flew open and they filed soberly in. When I reached the newspaper offices, an extra was pouring out from the "Journal" basement—"Riot at Morgue—Frantic Mob Charges Police!" This all over the front page in red letters three inches high. Later, in that summer, the hypothetical Black Hand kidnaped one Tony Manino, six years old. Since this was an Italian case, the reporters could do no work of their own on it; we merely loitered about the police station or the house, getting our news second-hand. Of course, with its appeal to emotion and mystery, this was a great yellow feature; the "Journal" went daft with it. And day by day the cubs and younglings of the "Journal" seized at every absurd rumor and shot it over the telephone as fact. "I heard a kid kind of yelling in one of the tenements and I followed it up. Nothing doing," a detective would remark. A rush to the telephone by the "Journal" delegation; in an hour we would have it in an extra, something like this: "Hears Tony Manino Weeping for His Mother." I mention these instances as typical, not exceptional, in the height of the yellow insanity.

The "Pretty Girl" Picture

AS FOR photographs—what offenses were committed in their name! For people who will yield up the news gladly are conservative about giving up pictures; and pictures the yellows must have, especially for "pretty girl stories." There was a time when they used the various poses of photographic models for the "pretty girl" whose picture was unobtainable. This growing monotonous, they placed orders with photographic agencies for photographs of foreign women in private life—people who would never know that their pictures were serving in America for the "Pretty Girl Who Whipped Burglar" or the "Prominent Society Leader of Evanston."

So much for its vices, of which its falsity was chief and its rowdy denial of the right of privacy in news-getting only second. Let me not omit its virtues, which loom larger now that the madness is over. Publishers, in relation to the public, may be divided roughly into two classes. On one side are the instinctive worshipers of wealth and money, the men hypnotized by success and its rewards. The other and smaller class—which includes, it happens, most of our greatest editors—go just as far to the other extreme in suspecting the rich and great. To this class belonged both Pulitzer and Hearst in their most active days. Question not too far the motives of great, strenuous spirits like these two. Such must find outlet for their energies without conscious direction toward an end; "the job" itself is their objective. Yet each—Hearst probably the more definitely—had somewhere down among his tangled motives a genuine sympathy for the under dog in the industrial fight. This sympathy, and the convenience which traveled parallel with it, made and kept them advocates of the common man at a period when he needed an advocate. Nothing made Pulitzer so indignant as "corporate iniquity"; and, as for Hearst, this may suffice to illustrate: the common schools have always been his hobby, and his editorial associates have seen him walking the floor with indignation at some injury to the system.

Some Yellow Virtues

I HAVE shown how Pulitzer brought to New York, as the nucleus of yellow journalism, the method of finding and fighting public evils through the news. This method the yellow newspapers perfected with their growth in general efficiency. They learned how to fight; they taught the method to other newspapers. Their period of greatest power was also the period of unchecked corporation abuses, of alliance between bad ward politics and bad high finance. The ten-cent magazine, with its healthful "muck-raking," had not yet arrived. These blatant voices, husky with much bawling, were almost the only voices raised, for a decade long, against such principles as Mark Hanna typified.

Again, like the French philosopher, they "brought philosophy from the library and the cloister to dwell in the kitchen and the workshop." A parade of learning, of scientific and philosophical knowledge, was always among their little tricks. They gave it to their readers predigested, the sensational detail to the fore, with an eye always on "economy of attention"; but they did hammer the big principles home, I believe, to people who could have accepted them in no other form. Their "stories" were an edge of interest for the wedge of knowledge. So always philosophies first reach the bottom of popular intelligence. Had we an accurate and critical record of early Christianity, we should find, probably, that after its first pure flow the people in general accepted its picturesque superstitions before they grasped its spirit; and the Darwinian theories had been mentor to the laboratories for a quarter century before the mob believed that Darwin taught anything except the bizarre idea—which he never did teach—of man's descent from the monkey.

"This Man Brisbane"

IN THIS last activity of yellow journalism, Brisbane stands supreme. The country has forgotten, if it ever knew, his influence in making sensational journalism yellow journalism. We think of him as the writer of those "heart-to-heart" editorials which even the judicious sometimes admire. With the hindsight so much better than foresight, the men who built with Hearst in his building days at San Francisco see what a chance they missed when they walked on the edge of Brisbane's methods. For Hearst said again and again: "I wish I could get the same 'snap' into my editorials that you fellows get into the news columns." Arthur McEwen tried the hardest and came nearest to grasping what Hearst wanted. The truth is, McEwen had too much of what the prize-ring calls "class." His talents as journalist and writer were basically too high and sound.

Now arrived Brisbane; he became the genius of the "Evening Journal," deepest yellow of all newspapers. He was a man after Hearst's own kidney. He, too, had a sympathy with popular causes underneath an amazing ruthlessness of method and a talent for insincere sincerities. He found how to get "snap" into the editorial page, how to talk politics and philosophy in the language of truckmen and lumbermen. Day by day for ten years he has shouted at the populace the moral philosophies of Kant and Hegel, the social and scientific philosophies of Spencer and Huxley, in lurid words of one syllable. On alternate days he has shouted, just as powerfully, the inconsistencies which suited Hearst's convenience of the day, the fallacies which would boost circulation, pull in advertising, kill rivals. No man can be so sincere or so plausibly insincere as Brisbane. To analyze his best flights, to show how artfully he conceals the one necessary flaw in an otherwise perfect chain of logic, is an exercise which I recommend to our university classes in forensics.

His violence of language and expression, which has led to so many assaults on the Hearst newspapers, is, in fact, a trick of method. At the risk of mental snobbery, it must be said that the comparatively uneducated class to which he appeals is weak in fine intellectual dis-

(Concluded on page 27)

The American Newspaper

(Concluded from page 24)

tinctions. Not only is black black and white white to them, but gray and cream and pearl are white, and brown and purple are black. "I've done hard work in the ditches," says one of the great, sane editorial writers of his time, "and let me tell you when a ditch-digger calls a man an unlimited whelp he doesn't mean what you and I mean. He may mean a slightly disagreeable person or a real scoundrel. In short, he has no language to express disapproval except the most violent. So, when Brisbane called McKinley 'the most hated creature on the American continent,' he shocked the educated, but he conveyed to his readers, in the only kind of language which they understood, merely general disapproval of McKinley." As a writer, with these editorials, as an editor, with thorough grasp of what his kind of reader wanted, he came to typify yellow journalism in its last period of real power. The profession of journalism rightly calls him the one widely influential editorial writer in these declining days of the daily editorial page. Such Hearst newspapers as use his work publish a million and a half copies for at least five million readers. In the nature of Hearst circulation, he reaches that class least infused with the modern intellectual spirit of inquiry, least apt to study their facts before forming their theories—the class most ready to accept the powerfully expressed opinions of another and superior being. We can not view American civilization without reckoning in this young exponent of means which justify ends, any more than we can view it without reckoning in his employer and discoverer—Hearst.

The $50,000 Verdict

Public Opinion About Fake Medical Advertising

COLLIER'S has done a wonderful work for humanity in the past few years in exposing the fakes and frauds in foodstuffs and patent medicines, but it never did anything better than in the exposé of the fake that has sucked so many innocent people into the Post vortex of plain, every-day graft.—Hibbing (Minn.) *The Mesaba Ore.*

✚

That notorious labor-union baiter, Charles W. Post, of Battle Creek, Michigan, has come to grief in a libel suit with COLLIER'S.
—Union (N. Y.) *News.*

✚

If COLLIER'S doesn't let up in its crusade against Post, the manufacturer of Postum and Grape-Nuts, against whom it recently secured a judgment of $50,000 in a damage suit, it is going to hurt business. And not alone Post's business. What about those 8,000,000 pounds of bran and innumerable barrels of molasses?
Tulare (Cal.) *Register.*

✚

Here we have it, the kernel of the whole matter. To sell his food products, to make his million a year in profits, his million a year in advertising, C. W. Post bargains and compounds with death exactly as do the patent-medicine fakers. If any one, feeling the first pains of acute appendicitis, ever took the advice of C. W. Post and "ate only Grape-Nuts," he doubtless added his epitaph to the "unsolicited testimonials" which Post would not produce in court.—Kokomo (Ind.) *Dispatch.*

✚

The evidence in the trial brought out many interesting facts to the detriment of the cereal company. . . . It proved in fact, as Collier says, "C. W. Post is a faker," pure and simple.
—Cogswell (N. Dak.) *Enterprise.*

✚

It may seem peculiar to you that the only newspaper in Sioux City which printed the news of this trial was the "News."

Now read the accompanying editorial from COLLIER'S again very carefully.

Just to add to the gaiety of the Christmas season, the "News" hereby challenges the Sioux City "Journal" and the Sioux City "Tribune" to print the result of this great legal battle.

We assume that their readers would be greatly interested in knowing how it resulted.—Sioux City (Iowa) *News.*

✚

There may be many "reasons" why people buy freely of such as Grape-Nuts and Toasties. But there was also a verdict which was not in Post's favor. We speak of this matter that "Sentinel" readers may understand the truth and not be groping in the dark under a misconception of the facts.—Waterville (Me.) *Sentinel.*

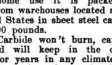

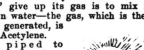

IV

The Spread and Decline of Yellow Journalism

IN THIS SECOND ARTICLE on yellow journalism Irwin again underlines the pervading influence of Hearst on the form and content of the modern newspaper. And yet Irwin wisely refrains from making Hearst the whipping boy, as other critics have done. The techniques Hearst employed were not original with him. They came from the men whom he gathered around him; some methods had been employed for generations. Irwin realized that while William Randolph Hearst was not inevitable, a "Hearst" was.

All this is very close to saying that the press, or any social institution, may have a natural history of its own. While this may be too much to assert, the reader will doubtless be struck by the similarities between the circulation wars of the yellow period and the viewership battles of today's television networks. In the second paragraph of this article, Irwin describes a young Sunday editor caught up in the struggle: "And here sat a young man whose success was measured, in the eyes of his employer, solely by the circulation of his department." Sad times, for the young man, for the respectable newspaper which had fallen into the mire of half-truth, falsehood, and shrill ballyhoo that comprised yellow journalism, but most of all, sad times for the society the paper thought to serve.

Yet, dismayed though he was at the evils of sensationalism, Irwin felt that the technique had accomplished certain things of positive value. And he saw reasons to hope. "Generally," he concluded, "the good that it did lived after it; the evil is becoming interred with its bones." His error seems to have been his failure to see that the appeal inherent in sensationalism would permit subsequent resurrections, of the evil as well as the good.

The American Newspaper

A Study of Journalism in Its Relation to the Public

By WILL IRWIN

IV

The Spread and Decline of *Yellow Journalism*

¶ This article completes the short history of journalism; the rest of this series will deal with present conditions. Herein the author shows the process by which the yellow principle tinged nearly every American newspaper

F. B. Opper: One of the most effective and witty cartoonists of the day

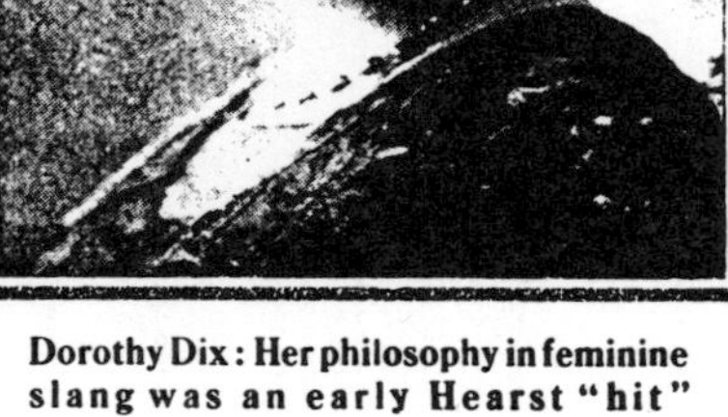

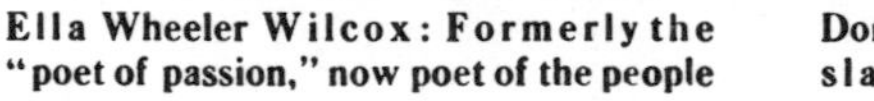

Ella Wheeler Wilcox: Formerly the "poet of passion," now poet of the people

Dorothy Dix: Her philosophy in feminine slang was an early Hearst "hit"

R. F. Outcault: His "Yellow Kid" was the beginning of the comic supplement

THE consideration of Brisbane and Brisbaneism as a social phenomenon rushed this story ahead of its purpose; it goes back now to the nineties, when Pulitzer and Hearst were adding circulation by thousands each week, when the linotype and monotype machines, last mechanical aid to speed of production, were crowding out the hand process, when the clever mechanics of those most clever mechanisms by which the newspaper gets on the street had made possible color printing and direct reproduction of photographs. Now was the spirit of journalism become mostly commercial, and the typical publisher was a business man, running a million-dollar property for money—not an editor. Here came two men out of the West to get the metropolitan seal and stamp on a kind of journalism which went like a prairie fire. A hundred publishers would have done the same thing years before had they possessed that priceless jewel of originality which Pulitzer, Hearst, Chamberlain, Goddard, received from the fairies at their birth. Now that the yellows had shown the way, other publishers fell in and imitated them either wholly or in part. Tammen and Bonfils arose in Denver with the super-yellow "Post," and bludgeoned their way to circulation and great profits; Blethen swept Seattle with the "Times." But the whole-hearted imitators were few compared to those who copied a feature or a twist of method here and there. Other men there were, more editor than publisher still, who, in face of yellow competition, had to modify their methods or go to the wall.

How the Process Worked

IN NEARLY every metropolitan newspaper office one saw the process at work. The Sunday editor had been going on his own ideas of a supplement—a publication interesting and breezy, but sound and informative, full of the best popular writing which he could buy from local writers or the syndicates; something which a man or woman would like to read in Sunday's loafing. To him would come the publisher: "We dropped four hundred circulation last Sunday, Kid. What's the matter? And the 'Blazer' is piling them up! Why don't you get some *snap* into your paper?" Next week, another four hundred or five hundred gone. And there sat a young man whose success was measured, in the eyes of his employer, solely by the circulation of his department. In despair, he would begin to imitate—to increase the size of pictures and heads, to revamp the sensations of the week's news in short, nervous, bawling paragraphs. Back would flow the circulation. After which his newspaper must have a color press, and then colored comic pictures in imitation, from some syndicate or other, of the Hearst comics. Next the daily paper must "ginger up" all along the line to meet yellow competition. Headlines must grow in size, melodrama in importance. Certain old, conservative newspapers managed to go their way unscathed, by virtue of an educated clientele—and a very valuable clientele to advertisers—which hated yellow journalism constitutionally; but nineteen out of twenty metropolitan newspapers yielded to the influence in some degree. Not one daily newspaper in Chicago, not even the "News" and "Post," wholly escaped. In New York the resistance was greater. It changed the "Sun," "Times," and "Evening Post" only so lightly as to be almost imperceptible. The Kansas City "Star" went proudly on its way, a great commercial and professional success, and hardly yielded a line to yellow journalism. Conservative Philadelphia held pretty stiffly against the invasion, as did a great part of the South, especially Charleston and New Orleans. The San Francisco newspapers, which felt the Hearst influence earliest, fell universally. The conservative "Chronicle" struggled hardest; but it was printing a more or less yellow colored Sunday supplement by 1901, and comics within two years more, and its local reports grew louder all along the line. Denver presented a beautiful type-case. Tammen and Bonfils established the "Post" and began to out-Hearst Hearst. They had three rivals—the "Republican," a conservative, old-time journal, and the "News" (evening) and "Times" (morning), lively organs owned by Thomas M. Patterson, a fighter. The corporation-loving "Republican," by virtue of support from the "upper classes," was able to stand firm, though it made mild concessions in its Sunday supplement. But the "News" and "Times," comparatively free organs engaged in a desperate fight for popular liberties, trimmed and changed month by month until they howled nearly as loudly as the "Post," although—to my mind—they howled a different and a better message. So it went, the country over.

At the beginning of this century, or a decade after Goddard brought the "World" Sunday supplement to full bloom and Hearst invaded New York, the American press had undergone another transformation. Physically, it had increased immensely in size; the growth of advertising, the cheapening supply of wood-pulp paper, worked to that end more potently than Hearst. Headlines had swollen. Front pages, which in 1890 presented seven solid columns of print with short headlines a column wide, because by 1900 maps of boxes and pictures. Reporters went further than ever before in invading privacy, in finding the news which—conservatives would have us believe—is none of a newspaper's business. More and more also had the interest in news-writing come to depend on taking one picturesque fact and twisting it to the fore, to the destruction of a sane point of view. The scope of news publication had increased enormously. Replacing several old and imperfect press bureaus, the Associated Press had established itself and become the most enterprising, and—then—the fairest press bureau in the world. The composite character of news, on the other hand, had declined greatly. The personal note had come in with the Hearst newspapers and the great body of woman readers which they created. Year by year public affairs had sunken in importance, and gossip about public characters had correspondingly risen. "The debate on the McKinley tariff," says a veteran Washington correspondent, "drew four or five columns—mostly literal transcripts from the speeches. The report of the Payne tariff bill drew half-columns of condensation. But if Taft puts on a sweater and walks around the Washington Monument, *that's* worth a half-column."

The Merely Silly

ANOTHER class of news, so-called, had followed the Hearst idea into newspaper offices—the merely silly. This consists in taking some shallow and picturesque opinion, point of view, remark, in the day's news, and treating it with the solemnity due to a world philosophy. A professor advises a Radcliffe class to enjoy their girl-life—"dance, play, even flirt," he says. A twist, a little exaggeration of the fact, and newspapers are running "sob squadders'" symposiums, editorials, on the question: "Should girls flirt?" This method is at present the curse of New York journalism. The general standard of newspaper writing had improved; that came not from the

Nell Brinkley: She draws "suggestive and pleasing feminine hysterics"

Rudolph Dirks: Who created the india-rubber Katzenjammers

"Tad" Dorgan: Famous for his sporting and "Bunk" cartoons

yellows, however, but from the university men, who began to take journalism unto themselves in the nineties. The recognized intellectual activities of journalism had languished. Real criticism, for example: where in 1880 we had three clever literary, dramatic, and musical critics, in 1910 we had only one; and to-day not ten men in the country compare with the standard critics of European papers. The editorial page went still further back in standing and influence.

What I may call news efficiency had improved greatly. By that I mean getting the latest event to the furthermost reader in the shortest possible time. To this end the metropolitan papers perfected a wonderful and complicated system of transmission, bending press bureaus, city news associations, telephone exchanges, special trains, superb mechanical detail, to that object. This process, and the nervous public appetite for the very latest which it created, united with advertising considerations which I shall not discuss here to produce one curious result. **From ten o'clock in the morning to five or six in the evening is the best time for news;** far more events "break" in that period than in the remaining hours of the twenty-four. Indeed, by nine o'clock in the evening most of the day's news-making—except for a few crimes, night being the time for burglary and murder—is over and done. Interest in sporting news was growing; and all the great sporting events except prize-fights occur in the afternoon. **So the evening newspaper grew in financial importance,** absorbed more and more professional brains and energy. This quickened the whole current of American journalism, but swallowed it also. Given that most of the news has happened by six o'clock in the evening and most of the rest by nine: usually the first edition of a morning paper goes to press at half-past twelve A. M. and the final edition at half-past two or three. There remains, then, from three to eight hours for finish, during which reporters and editors correct facts, make shift at leisurely writing, go a little way toward second and sounder judgment on the event. In the evening papers the reporter is telephoning facts with the fire or the convention roaring about him, the "rewrite man" is "taking it off the phone" with his left hand and writing it with his right, while the printer snatches it away sheet by sheet. No time there for finish—only for the fact as it looks in the first flush of excitement.

"Bud" Fisher: Creator of the grotesque "Mutt and Jeff"

The Virtues of Yellow Journalism

TO THE European observer, blind to the kind of democracy which we know, all of these tendencies are bad, banal, vulgar. From the purely American point of view, something may be said for every one of them except the melodramatic cheapening of public intelligence.

The improved speed of news distribution helped to quicken the nervous force by which the American works his industrial marvels. All along, our press has been usher to progress in this respect. By informing us at lightning speed that gold had been discovered on the West Coast or in Alaska, that the inhabitants of a Territory on the fringe of the world were agitating for Statehood, that a new railroad was pushing into the coal district, that stocks were declining in Wall Street, that a blight had fallen on the crops of Nebraska, that the elevated line was tied up in a wreck, that just such business houses had been destroyed by a fire in Chicago, our newspapers saved a world of energy, ministered directly to the quick adaptation to an emergency which is our greatest practical gift. **In itself, the flaring headline, in nine cases out of ten the first feature which an Englishman criticizes, is entirely defensible. A nervous, busy people, characteristically extravagant, we want to know at a glance the most important fact of the last hour, and we do not grudge the cent which we pay for it.** Only when the big headline proclaims something false, evil or silly, or when it lies about the news beneath, is it fair game for general criticism. Even the invasion of privacy, the publication of private scandals, errors, and troubles of which the law has taken no cognizance, has its sincere advocates.

"Tom" Powers: Possessor of a queer but effective style of humorous drawing

James Swinnerton: A veteran among the Hearst "feature" illustrators

Further, and most important of all, the ruthless bravery of the yellow editors inspired journalism in general with a courage to make popular fights, to attack the high priests of privilege and advantage. The yellow spirit of going out and finding the evil ahead of the law, the yellow method of using news as a good advocate uses his facts, infused the entire profession. The commonwealth needed some such force in that period, when large social and economic abuses had gone ahead of deterrent laws. Apart from the galled jades in Philadelphia, all who know of it admire E. A. Van Valkenberg's "North American." When Van Valkenberg began to stir up Philadelphia, the old Quay spirit strangled politics, press, finance. The people who bought the Philadelphia newspapers bought not one which fought their fight or whole-heartedly pleaded their cause. Van Valkenberg has checked, converted, exposed abuse after abuse. For a moderate example: when he began to look into the kind of food which corner grocers were selling to his city, he found ninety-six per cent out of five hundred samples dangerously adulterated. When he finished with the great poisoners, only nine per cent out of eight hundred samples contained dishonest adulterants. This result, and many others like it, he achieved by methods which Pulitzer brought into journalism, and which Hearst extended. Half brigand, half loyal irregular, these crude fighters taught strategy, major and minor tactics, ballistics and logistics to the army of public good.

Forget not, either, that they themselves fought the good fight. No general of special privilege ever encountered so vigorous a general of the people as Collis P. Huntington met in Hearst. Again and again the presence of a Hearst reporter in Washington threw into confusion a strategic move of the Southern Pacific; almost alone the San Francisco "Examiner" killed the most vicious system of rebates which the West ever knew. That New York enjoys eighty-cent gas is due to Hearst. In the Boston gas fight he was the ally of the reformers against eight newspaper friends of the company. It was Hearst who found and presented the evidence of the coal roads' conspiracy. When Harrison Gray Otis, for a whimsy of his own, tried to defeat a just school-bond issue in Los Angeles, it was Hearst who arranged and carried through a "sentimental sale" which gave schoolhouses to the children of the city. It was Hearst who made it a newspaper's business to prosecute certain big oppressions not only with its right hand but with its left; not only with its news columns but with its paid attorneys. Forget this not in a period when Hearst is keeping silence about the Southern Pacific in California, and when, for hidden political motives of his own, he has been helping in his newspapers and magazines the Senatorial fight of John R. McLean, friend of the fattened.

Having changed the profession and business of publicity, yellow journalism suddenly went into a decline. This may be news to the general; but the extreme form which Hearst perfected for his newspapers and which commercialism copied in dilute form is numbered with yesterday. Compare to-day's New York "Journal" with the corresponding date in 1905 or, better, in 1903; you will find this but the dim tint of that.

The Change in Hearst

HEARST himself, probably, could not give the exact reasons for the change; they are intertwined in his singular, close psychology. With his political career we have nothing to do here, except as it affected his newspapers. But from the moment when he first ran for office he found it necessary, as politicians must, to compound with large interests to which he had been steadily inimical; from that time forth he could never show the courage of a simon-pure journalist. Also, marriage and a family are in no wise calculated to make a man more militant and reckless. And a veteran Hearst man gives one reason which may enter into the calculation. "It's profit-taking time," he says; by which he means that circulation is now established, and advertisers are slow in patronizing a newspaper which attacks what they believe to be their interests.

Yet a better reason remains: simple response to circulation demand. Sympathetic and nervous touch with circulation started both Pulitzer and Hearst on their way. Still, in the well-conducted Hearst office, the executives receive every day a statement of "stops" and "starts" from the whole city, arranged by districts. If the circulation falls off to-day, if it fell off in the gas-house ward yesterday, the executive must find the reason why. Conversely, he learns just what kind of news and features hit, and what class of population they hit most. This adjusts the editor admirably to the wants of his public. **Through the slow process of years, Hearst journalism responded to a sounder taste on the part of its public.**

The shrewdest of newspaper philosophers has said: "There's a darn sight more psychology than common sense in this newspaper business, anyhow." The changing demand was a matter of popular psychology. The taste for this melodrama is unnatural; and any unnatural appetite grows with what it feeds upon, demanding two grains of the drug this year where last year it craved only one. The essences of the yellow drug were lurid imagination and continual change. Imagination has its boundaries; yellow editors and reporters soon reached them. The time came, too, when all the changes on journalism were rung, when there was no new nor even second-hand thing which the public had not heard before.

Further, one faction of readers "read out," as I may express it, from the Hearst newspapers. In general, **the more a man reads the better he reads. The consistent novel reader satisfies himself at first with the story; he grows into a desire for something deeper,** demanding style, psychology, and illumination on life; and when he comes to enjoy Meredith and Hardy, Albert Ross and E. P. Roe satisfy him no more. The history of periodical publication points the larger public moral. In the youth of us middle-aged folk, the populace read the New York "Ledger," "Saturday Night," or the "Waverley Magazine," cheap, sensational dispensers of lurid, ungrammatical fiction, and obvious, bromidic fact. Munsey with "Munsey's" and Walker with the "Cosmopolitan" raised popular literature one notch; the public abandoned the "Ledger" and its kind, and these magazines took the circulation. Presently McClure started his magazine, bringing the standard a notch higher; Munsey and Walker had to improve in order to meet the demand. Now, the cheapest of those periodicals which hold the great national circulations are as gold to brass beside the popular periodicals which careful mothers hid from us in our youth.

The yellows had created new bodies of newspaper readers; first, women, then just entering the new era of feminine development which so quietly affects our present world; **and, secondly—**especially in New York**—the late immigrant in process of learning English and American public consciousness. All the time these people were reading up out of yellow journalism; shallow melodrama interested them no more.**

And its own exaggerations were sniping off subscribers in detail. The reader of the tenements was ready to believe that the world ran by such melodrama—until they even happened in his own block. In such case he knew that the little suicide was not a "pretty girl richly dressed" nor yet a "mystery which baffles the police"; he knew that she was just plain Kitty Smith, whose squalid tragedy all her world understood. He lost immediately a confidence in the yellow newspaper which he never regained. This equation entered curiously into Hearst's Boston experiment. New York, Chicago, even San Francisco, have the metropolitan characteristic of individual aloofness; circles of acquaintance are small, and generally one does not know the people in the flats below or above. Boston, more settled and leisurely, keeps a fine neighborhood flavor of interest and gossip. And a large part of Boston was able to see these lies of exaggeration. Other factors entered into Hearst's long struggle to make his Boston paper pay; but he had to modify this policy before he could gain so much as a foothold.

The New York "Journal" remains the one positively yellow newspaper in the Hearst string, though this also has greatly modified its policy. And concerning it the circulation experts of the other newspapers report one illuminating thing. "It changes its whole circulation," they say, "about once in six years." Just so long does it take the average reader to read himself out of the "Journal." In fact, the flow of new immigrants into New York is its blood and life. Were immigration stopped to-morrow, the "Journal" would have to modify or fail.

As the yellow attitude toward news evaporated, the Hearst newspapers found their main remaining strength in the Sunday supplement,

(*Concluded on page 36*)

"Kate Carew"

The most eminent woman caricaturist in America, with a style all her own

Arthur Brisbane

By all odds the best-known newspaper editorial writer of the period

"Alan Dale"

A popular "feature" dramatic critic who mixes his ink with vitriol

With the Insurrectos at Juarez

Orozco's Light-Opera Troupe, That Wasn't Altogether Comic

By ARTHUR RUHL

Collier's Special Correspondent. Photographs Copyright 1911 by Karl Halm

El Paso, Texas, February 15, 1911.

WHEN your correspondent stepped off the overland train at 6.38 last Wednesday morning, somewhat subdued by the hour and the slow asphyxiation of three days in a Pullman car, he was promptly warmed and encouraged by a fresh copy of the El Paso "Times" which a brown little Mexican newsboy thrust into his hand.

This veracious newspaper—with that stern reticence and sanity which so distinguish us Anglo-Saxons from the excitable and inferior Latin races—had adorned half its front page with a war map in which the town of Juarez (just across the river and the Mexican line from El Paso) was hemmed in by a semicircle of black rectangles, like dominoes, representing detachments of troops, exactly as if it were Gettysburg or Waterloo. From the six columns of quivering type spread over the rest of the page it was learned that Orozco and his men were at the city's gates ready to attack at dawn, that "never had there been a better opportunity to observe the movements of a small but important battle," but (and this was placed in a special box, headed: "WARNING!") no place would be safe except the top of a neighboring mountain, and citizens must keep off the streets and exercise the greatest caution until the battle had ended.

One's immediate impulse was to dash to the firing line—it was already well past dawn—but realizing, to quote a local *jeu d'esprit*, that "Juar-ez Hell," and that a correspondent, like a soldier, fights, as the saying goes, on his stomach, your representative swallowed a hasty but nourishing breakfast and boarded a trolley car for the front.

The front proved to be a line stretching for a mile or so along the river between the outskirts of the city and the smelter works. In the immediate foreground was the muddy Rio Grande, scarcely more than a brook at this season, with American soldiers policing its northern bank and beyond the parched arroyos and cactus-covered hills of Mexico. Straggling along the American side were many gigantic gentlemen with slightly slouching shoulders and broad-brimmed felt hats, who, were they to appear in a New York hotel, would at once be taken for millionaire cattlemen; a portion of the youth and beauty of El Paso in automobiles; tourists on their way to California; Mexican laborers, for the moment disengaged, and innumerable bright, dark-skinned little boys whose tattered shoes were invariably caked with yellowish mud from having tried to cross the lines one way or another by wading the Rio Grande.

Picking Out the Cone-Hat Rebels

ALSO there were all sorts of field-glasses. They ranged from battered brass telescopes to prism binoculars, and they were all directed toward the rocks and chaparral of the opposite shore. Following their direction, it was possible to descry in the low bushes which fringed the waters—like so many quail or prairie chicken half hidden in the grass—the tall conical tops of forty or fifty Mexican sombreros. More of these hats were presently apparent among the rocks farther up, and after I had climbed a little hill on one side and benefited from the experience and the opera-glass of two kindly elderly ladies who had left their housework to see how the battle raged, the insurrectos could be picked out in the most distant and interesting places—as part of a clump of cacti or of a bit of yellowish rock that just jutted above the soft blue mountain sky-line a mile or so away. There they lay with their guns beside them, and one got the interesting notion that it needed only a signal, a sentry's shot or something, and that whole blazing, barren mountainside would jump into life.

There were, in fact, a couple of shots, over the hills somewhere, and the fringe of spectators down below came scrambling up our little eminence with glad and hopeful cries. But the hats across the river never stirred, and the sentries on our side merely turned for a moment and then resumed their patrol.

About an hour later some little specks began to move down the distant mountainside just where a white scratch, like a chalk-mark, showed the trail, cutting over the shoulder into the valley beyond. It was the insurrectos' horses being brought down to drink. Quiet reigned. They were carefully studied through their slow zigzag progress down the trail and during the entire progress of their attempt to swallow enough of the Rio Grande to forget that there was nothing in the world for them to eat when they had climbed back to camp but disintegrated rock, and many profound conclusions were drawn as to the size, equipment, and courage of the hidden command. After the horses had disappeared, the air was again made electric (it having been rumored that the insurrectos were out of food) by the similar appearance and departure of several hundred goats. And so the day's battle ended, and the sun went down that night with Juarez still in the hands of the Federals, who stabled their horses in the bull-ring where tourists bound for California often see their first bull-fight, and, drawing their ladders up after them, slept the sleep of faithful retainers of Porfirio Diaz on the roof of the Juarez church.

Dissatisfied with the view from the audience, I determined to climb up on the stage with the actors, and the next morning I "penetrated" to the insurrectos' camp—a feat which consisted in getting

The American Newspaper

(Concluded from page 20)

which still holds strong on yellow lines, and in another activity which had been only secondary during its best days—what newspaper men call "feature stuff." Chief of these features is the comic supplement, which Goddard and Outcault began with "The Yellow Kid." Clever and genuinely humorous cartoonists like Opper, Dirks, and Swinnerton found the knockabout level of fun which the public wants, discovered also the general interest in the old friends of a series, and developed the form. The children helped in this: children, in the language of the old advertisement, cry for Happy Hooligan, Buster Brown, the Katzenjammers. And not only children; I have seen the laborers waiting on Sunday morning at the station of a Californian fruit camp, all hungry to get the latest from Happy Hooligan or Noah's Ark. In spite of imitators, the Hearst people, with their educated touch on the public pulse, have kept this feature first in popular esteem.

Hearst perceived early our growing interest in sport, mark of an Anglo-Saxon-Celtic people passing from the era of hand labor to that of machinery, and proceeded to cultivate the taste. Rough-and-ready cartoonists and writers like "Tad" Dorgan and Fisher gave the public the flippant, humorous, slangy view of sport which it liked. On the woman side of his activities, he found such people as Ella Wheeler Wilcox and Dorothy Dix, dispensers of feminine philosophy in sugar-coated form. Of late Nell Brinkley, who writes and draws pleasing and suggestive feminine hysterics, has come into her own. Here and there other newspapers have one feature writer or illustrator who equals in detail his Hearst rival. Nowhere has Robert Edgren of the New York "World" a superior on the sporting page; from both the popular and "high-brow" point of view, McCutcheon, cartoonist of the Chicago "Tribune," stands alone: in the comic supplement of the New York "Herald," McCay with his "Nemo in Slumberland" equals the best of his Hearst rivals. But nowhere else is there such an organized body of popular feature men. This matter, distributed through all the Hearst papers syndicate-fashion, is the real present backbone of their circulation.

With the evaporation of the vices in extreme yellow journalism, some of its virtues in keeping the social balance evaporated also. Here and there, and for various motives and reasons, Hearst has dropped popular causes. We find him in some districts the friend no longer of the powers that struggle and riot, but of the powers that rule and prey. He entered Los Angeles partly at the request of the labor unions, which had in the "Times" a sworn enemy. He found Los Angeles a hard soil for unionism. As I have said before, Otis, by reiteration in the news columns, had created general non-union sentiment in his city. Then, too, Los Angeles is a business community, prone—with one of those subtle distinctions which mark off one American city from another—to take the financier's view. While the Los Angeles "Examiner" fought and returned deficits, Hearst sent S. S. Chamberlain, his "wrecking crew," he of the wizard sense for public taste, to look over the field. Chamberlain studied and meditated for a week; and ended by choosing an un-Hearst-like course. He sent for Julian Hawthorne to write up the orange groves; for the district about Los Angeles is full of transplanted New Englanders, to whom oranges are a vital commercial fact and the Hawthornes a glorious tradition. It went; and on a similar policy he has run the "Examiner" ever since. In San Francisco his "Examiner" fights no longer against the Southern Pacific, the big tent under which the system in California has gathered all predatory interests. He entered Boston shouting for the people. Somehow that kind of exploitation of public interests appealed to Boston no more than did yellow news; least of all did it appeal to the Boston advertiser. The road to returns from the Boston "American" was very long; only last year did the paper begin to pay. He never turned into this road until he threw over labor unionism and assault on privileged interests.

The life has passed out of pure yellow journalism. Its spirit remains, however, in the universal influence which it had on the profession at large. Generally, the good that it did lived after it; the evil is becoming interred with its bones.

It may seem that I have followed one of his own reporting methods and twisted Hearst a little out of his proper place in the history of the last two decades of journalism. But his indirect influence has been far greater than his direct effect. He is the one great fact in newspaper history since Pulitzer, the one American journalist of our period whom the historian of the year 2000 can not ignore.

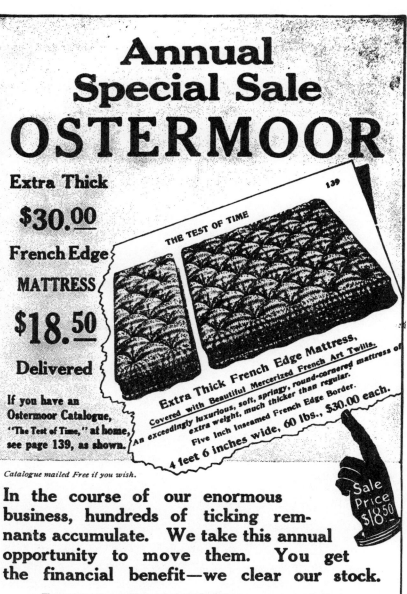

V

What Is News?

IRWIN HAD no greater success than any textbook writer or editor at defining that key ingredient of journalism—news. But he did realize that news itself is not so much a commodity subject to precise definition as it is an ethic, or way of looking at the world. He was able to describe the system at work and to illustrate how some events are of greater interest to newspapers (and, presumably, to newspaper readers) than other events. And his description of the news ethic of 1911 seems pertinent today, for it reveals the great dilemma of journalism. Very much committed to society's value system (indeed a product of that value system), journalism must, if it serves society in the highest sense, find the means to facilitate criticism of society. This task is almost unbearably difficult, and change comes very slowly. Today a top editor 50 years of age who learned his definition of news 25 years ago quite possibly had a mentor who, as a cub reporter, took the 1911 definition as gospel. Thus the news ethic evolves not year by year but generation by generation.

An illustration is the South's so-called "misdemeanor murder" (of a Negro by a Negro, with a light sentence resulting from that mild challenge to the value system of the society in power). Such events were rarely news because they contained nothing that even remotely touched the lives of most whites in the community. By the same assumption, most civil rights activity was ignored by the press until whites began to be directly involved, first in courts, then in sit-ins, then in violence. Only fairly recently, and then perhaps as much in response to competition from other media as from a perceived need to broaden the news ethic, have newspapers begun to define news in a way that allows the "departure from the established order," as Irwin puts it, to be reported before that departure has been completed.

The American Newspaper

A Study of Journalism in Its Relation to the Public

By WILL IRWIN

V.—What Is News?

This article attempts to define what Charles Dudley Warner called indefinable—news from the journalistic point of view. It shows that news-interest—"what the public wants"—rests, contrary to the opinions of most city editors, on certain well-defined principles. The next article in the series, which appears on April 1, is entitled "The Editor and the News," and is a discussion, with examples, of newspaper ethics. The photographs below illustrate the processes of gathering news

Roosevelt caught by the press bureaus as he emerges from the Jungle

John Hay pauses in his morning walk to grant an interview

The Outpost of Civilization — Peary telling the story of his North Pole discovery to the reporters

Correspondents under guard watching the battle of the Yalu River

NEWS is the main thing, the vital consideration to the American newspaper; it is both an intellectual craving and a commercial need to the modern world. In popular psychology, it has come to be a crying primal want of the mind, like hunger of the body. Tramp wind-jammers, taking on the pilot after a long cruise, ask for the papers before they ask, as formerly, for fresh fruit and vegetables. Whenever, in our later Western advance, we Americans set up a new mining camp, an editor, his type slung on burro-back, comes in with the missionaries, evangel himself of civilization. Most dramatically the San Francisco disaster illuminated this point. On the morning of April 20, 1906, the city's population huddled in parks and squares, their houses gone, death of famine or thirst a rumor and a possibility. The editors of the three morning newspapers, expressing the true soldier spirit which inspires this most devoted profession, had moved their staffs to the suburb of Oakland, and there, on the presses of the "Tribune," they had issued a combined "Call - Chronicle - Examiner." When, at dawn, the paper was printed, an editor and a reporter loaded the edition into an automobile and drove it through the parks of the disordered city, giving copies away. They were fairly mobbed; they had to drive at top speed, casting out the sheets as they went, to make any progress at all. No bread wagon, no supply of blankets, caused half so much stir as did the arrival of the news.

We need it, we crave it; this nerve of the modern world transmits thought and impulse from the brain of humanity to its muscles; the complex organism of modern society could no more move without it than a man could move without filaments and ganglia. On the commercial and practical side, the man of even small affairs must read news in the newspapers every day to keep informed on the thousand and one activities in the social structure which affect his business. On the intellectual and spiritual side, it is—save for the Church alone—our principal outlook on the higher intelligence. The thought of legislature, university, study, and pulpit comes to the common man first—and usually last—in the form of news. The tedious business of teaching reading in public schools has become chiefly a training to consume newspapers. We must go far up in the scale of culture before we find an intellectual equipment more a debtor to the formal education of school and college than to the haphazard education of news.

Axiomatically, then, the quality of news, its freedom from undue bias and taint, is supremely important. Could one slant or taint all news at its source, he would vitiate all public intelligence. Could one raise the standard of all news at its source, he would correspondingly elevate public intelligence. And since it is so vital, we must stop here to consider what news is, before we consider what, in the ideal, should be the attitude of writer and editor toward his product.

It looks simple at first sight. News is a report of just what occurs in the world, or rather what has just occurred. But a million billion things occur hourly in the world, from the movement of the finger by which I write this line to the surging of the crowd which is at this minute harrying strikebreakers along the Canadian border. The movement of this finger is not news, while the surge of that crowd is: and something more than importance divides them. My neighbor, John Smith, a virtuous man of well-conducted life, is just going to his office. He will do business honorably all day, come home, eat his dinner, enjoy the evening with his family, and go to bed. That, again, is not news. The world is working hard to-day on a million mighty labors. To-morrow will be Sunday; most of the million on million human units in it will listen to sermon or mass, and rest and be virtuous and reasonably happy. And that is not news, while the raging of a thousand men along our border is—decidedly. Tell the former fact to a man and he is bored; tell the latter, and he stops to listen.

Here lies the distinction, and it is also a definition: *The beating of strike-breakers is news because it is a departure from the established order.*

During all our formative years, from infancy to mature intelligence, we are learning that established order. Most formal education, still more of the education which a child gets from his environment, is nothing else. His first information concerning the old and fixed things about him is news to a child. He gets the news-interest, the catch in the breath, the quick widening of the eyes, when his mother tells him first about the world's shape or the Christian belief in judgment day. By the time his education takes final form, he has in his mind a set idea of his world, the details pretty definite. Statement and restatement of these details, as that John Smith and the other John Smiths work hard all day and eat dinner every evening, are superfluous and tiresome. But when man or nature violates the established order—there is news. The departure may work for good and progress or for evil and degeneracy; it makes no difference. Blériot's flight across the English Channel was news as much as the Thaw murder. One was a departure upward, the other downward. "Hinnissy," says Mr. Dooley, "ye might write th' doin's iv all th' convents iv the worruld on th' back iv a postage stamp, . . . while Scanlan's bad boy is good f'r a column anny time he goes dhrunk an' thries to kill a polisman." A convent, being the segregation of extremely good and obedient persons, follows the established order with great strictness; Scanlan's boy characteristically departs from it.

Yet if convents and the conventual life had not been, and were suddenly established among us, that

The woman reporter and Nicholas Longworth

The reporter puts a question to Viscount Maidstone

The news photographer at work from the twentieth story of an uncompleted skyscraper

News photographers lying in wait for their prey

fact would be news. Herein comes another distinction. With our education in established order we get the knowledge that mankind in bulk obeys its ideals of that order only imperfectly. When something brings to our attention an exceptional adhesion to religion, virtue, and truth, that becomes in itself a departure from regularity, and therefore news. The knowledge that most servants do their work conscientiously and many stay long in the same employ is not news. But when a committee of housewives presents a medal to a servant who has worked faithfully in one employ for fifty years, that becomes news, because it calls our attention to a case of exceptional fidelity to the ideals of established order. The fact that mankind will consume an undue amount of news about crime and disorder is only a proof that the average human being is optimistic, that he believes the world to be true, sound, and working upward. Crimes and scandals interest him most because they most disturb his picture of the established order.

That, then, is the basis of news. The mysterious news sense which is necessary to all good reporters rests on no other foundation than acquired or instinctive perception of this principle, together with a feeling for what the greatest number of people will regard as a departure from the established order. In Jesse Lynch Williams's newspaper play, "The Stolen Story," occurs this passage:

(Enter Very Young Reporter; comes down to city desk with air of excitement.)

VERY YOUNG REPORTER *(considerably impressed)*—"Big story. Three dagoes killed by that boiler explosion!"

THE CITY EDITOR *(reading copy. Doesn't look up)*—"Ten lines." *(Continues reading copy.)*

VERY YOUNG REPORTER *(looks surprised and hurt. Crosses over toward reporters' tables. Then turns back to city desk. Casual conversational tone)*—"By the way. Funny thing. There was a baby in a baby carriage within fifty feet of the explosion, but it wasn't upset."

THE CITY EDITOR *(looks up with professional interest)*—"That's worth a dozen dead dagoes. Write a half column."

(Very Young Reporter looks still more surprised, perplexed. Suddenly the idea dawns upon him. He crosses over to table, sits down, writes.)

Both saw news; but the editor went further than the reporter. For cases of Italians killed by a boiler explosion are so common as to approach the commonplace; but a freak of explosive chemistry which annihilates a strong man and does not disturb a baby departs from it widely.

Last year Porter Charlton, rich and well connected, murdered his wife, a woman who had given up "society" to go on the stage, crammed the body into a trunk which he sunk in Lake Como, and fled to America. In the same week several other men in humble circumstances murdered their wives. Why did the Charlton case get so much more attention and interest from writers and readers? Mainly because it departed further from the customs of the established order. The "upper class," having a better opportunity, is supposed to be less given to the greater crimes than the "lower." Women in "society" do not generally go on the stage. Wife murderers are not generally so hardened as to cram the body into a trunk and sink it in a lake. Of course, since mankind is complex, other factors entered into the case, such as that basic instinct of snobbery which makes us like to contemplate beings greater and more esteemed than ourselves. But the deepest reason for interest in the Charlton case was the wide departure which it presented from the normal.

This interest is in itself a progressive force; it lies close to the noblest practical activities of the human spirit. Invention, moral heroism, and genius in art are nothing but the discovery of something useful or fine apart from the established order.

The subject-matter of which it treats greatly modifies news interest in the masses and in the individual. First of all: *We prefer to read about the things we like.*

The chief business of a true yellow journalist is to find the class of news which will interest the greatest number of people; and to this end yellow journalism has made a formula: "Sport for the men, love and scandal for the women." "Money and politics for the men, love for the women," says an executive of the Scripps papers. "Power for the men, the affections for the women," expresses it better. Power is a man's business, his chief intellectual liking; politics, wealth, and sport are all different manifestations of it. Affection is a woman's business; love is affection at its height; scandal, affection gone wrong. Every trained journalist understands that no minor news succeeds better than a story about an animal—as the dog who rescued his master from fire or drowning. Aside from the basic news interest which they represent, their departure from the accepted order, these stories "go" because most people like animals; else we should have no cats but mousers and no dogs but hunters. The rule holds with stories about little children and, especially, those about beautiful women. Herein the yellow editor who sprinkles his pages with the phrase "pretty girl," lays hold on the universal, since both sexes, from different causes, glory in the beauty of woman. As I have hinted before, interest in the doings of high society, which get so much space in our sensational publications, and so much more in the English press, proceeds from that instinct of snobbery which democracy can not cure. The under stratum yearns to reach these heights of fortune and esteem; it likes those brighter beings and would like to resemble them. Even when it envies, it pays tribute to the principle, since envy is only liking and disappointment mixed in bad chemical combination.

Theatrical managers are still citing, for amusement and instruction, the great interest which New York took in the third act of Denman Thompson's "Old Homestead." The scene was the thing; it represented the exterior of Grace Church at night. Every New Yorker had seen the real Grace Church, yet people crowded the theater to witness its canvas counterfeit. Their motive introduces the second factor which intensifies news interest in the individual:

Our interest in news increases in direct ratio to our familiarity with its subject, its setting, and its dramatis personæ.

Nor is this an outgrowth of the first principle, that liking governs news interest. While by nature we characteristically like our relatives, and by association and man's free choice our friends and environment, this principle goes deeper. For example, we do not love our enemies, in spite of Christianity's two thousand years; and yet a piece of news which relates either the good fortune or the disaster of an enemy is most important to any normal man.

The interest in familiar things, people, and places —publications have waxed greater on no other policy. To-morrow you may open your newspaper and discover that your next door neighbor has been ar-

The Call-Chronicle-Examiner

SAN FRANCISCO, THURSDAY, APRIL 19, 1906.

EARTHQUAKE AND FIRE: SAN FRANCISCO IN RUINS

The combined "Call-Chronicle-Examiner" printed by the San Francisco newspapers on the morning after the earthquake. This is one of the heroic episodes in American journalism. It is notable, also, as probably the only newspaper issued both free and without advertisements

The Chicago reporters waiting for Paul Stensland

The "City Room" at night

The birthplace of modern slang—The baseball reporters at a League game

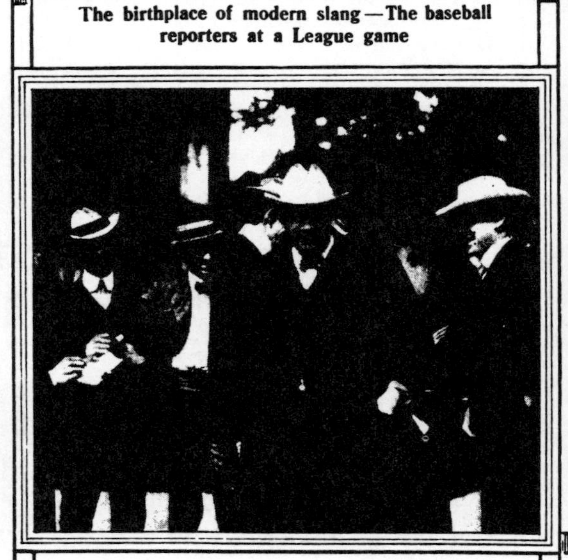

Mark Hanna in the act of refusing an interview

Newspaper telegraphers flashing news of the Thaw case from the Criminal Courts Building in New York to the five continents

rested for speeding his automobile or has fallen from a scaffold and broken his leg. Though the item occupy only an inch in the column, it will probably cause more discussion at the breakfast table than two columns about an earthquake in Peru, a famine in Russia, or a rebellion in the Sudan. Of course, with increase of intelligence and education, with mental broadening, the circle of familiarity widens; the man of culture may care as much to read of the Russian famine as of his neighbor's arrest; but that is because he has read of Russia or studied the wheat supply.

The Small Change of News

THIS special interest in familiar things explains a freak of newspaper making which puzzles publishers. The Boston "Globe" has grown great and rich through small bits of local news from Boston and the suburbs. Nearly every day it prints pages, and every Sunday whole sections, of notes from Wareham, North Scituate, Nahant, Marblehead, and the like. It has been said, half in joke, that the "Globe" "tries to publish the name of every inhabitant of Massachusetts twice every year." Herein General Taylor, the publisher, plays on the weakness for familiar things. New England is old, settled, and stable. The units of population have generally traveled but little; their interest remains in Boston and in the near-by communities from which they sprang, at which they summer, or in which their kinsmen live. So, where the editor to shifting populations like New York searches for great stories which, by appeal to the news principle and to some universal instinct for power or love, will grip the whole population, Taylor's men are finding two-line items, each of which will interest only a dozen people, but interest them more than almost any large general story.

The New York "World" and the Chicago "Tribune" mow subscribers down in battalions with artillery; the Boston "Globe" picks them off in detail with small arms. Nor is the human vanity in seeing one's own name pleasantly mentioned the main factor in Taylor's success, as some believe. For the same method succeeds in South Carolina, different by a world from Massachusetts except for the fact that it is a stable and settled community. And the Charleston gentility, which sets fashions of thought for South Carolina, dislikes personal mention, holding that no gentleman will tolerate "newspaper notoriety." In fact, experts have discovered, in the last two decades of systematic study, that mere personal mention without some news interest behind it does not pay, as a circulation getter, for the space which it occupies. The kernel of the "Globe's" success with this policy lies in attracting ten people here and twenty there with a short, mild bit of news which by familiarity greatly interests them, as that Mrs. Jones—"the Mrs. Jones we know, my dear"—has given a high tea, Miss Jones is engaged, Willie Jones has been confirmed, Mr. Jones has built a house.

The Selfish Interest

NEWS is a commercial necessity as well as an intellectual satisfaction, part of our business as well as part of our thought. And so:

Our interest in news is in direct ratio to its effect on our personal concerns.

The fact that Reading common stock has dropped two points is hardly news at all in the absolute, so slight a variation from the regular and accepted does it proclaim. To the man who holds ten thousand shares of Reading common, it may be the most important news in any paper. The Leadville "Herald-Democrat" and the Butte "Miner" publish daily columns of "notes from the mines," just as the New York "Sun" publishes a Wall Street edition. Not once a week does anything happen in the mines which rises to news in the absolute by presenting a striking departure from routine and custom. Unilluminated by personality or color, these notes make little appeal to that interest in familiar things which the Boston "Globe's" suburban notes satisfy. The people of Leadville and Butte want them because mining, their only industry, affects the fortunes of all, and the slightest change in the policy or conduct of a mine may take away the individual's employment or increase the receipts of his grocery.

The Sense of Proportion

FINALLY comes the most obvious factor of all, but by no means the least influential.

Our interest in news increases in direct ratio to the general importance of the persons or activities which it affects.

This principle is hardly worth examples. News about President Taft is more interesting than news about John Smith, because Taft is more important in the world than Smith. So Taft's sore throat is "worth" a paragraph to every newspaper in the United States, while Smith's broken leg draws scarcely a line in his country weekly. A dramatic change in the fortunes of the Standard Oil Company is supremely interesting; the unexpected foreclosure on Baccigalupi's corner grocery gets rightly no space in the newspapers. This is merely the working of man's sense of proportion.

The Feeling for the Dramatic

THESE are not the only factors that intensify news interest, but they are the chief ones. Sense for the clash and adjustment of character and incident which we call drama is a factor. That a woman finds her long-lost child after ten years' search is mild news; that she finds him in the next hospital cot, fellow victim of a train wreck, is great news. So with the sense of humor. Such newspapers as the Kansas City "Star," the New York "Sun," and the Chicago "Tribune," daily print stories which have only slight interest through departure from the accepted order, through popular liking for their subject-matter, through self-interest, or through the importance of the persons and interests involved. But they fall naturally into such form, or the skilful reporter casts them in such form, that they amuse. Charles Lynch's stories of Rosey the Lawyer and the Duke of Essex Street had scarcely an inch of news to the page; yet some people took the "Sun" for these stories alone. In fact, a hundred activities of the mind attract or repel the reader to or from a given bit of news; but none so powerfully as the intellectual factors on which I have laid special stress above.

The New York "Times" puts a question to Roosevelt

VI

The Editor and the News

This article now seems incorrectly titled, because it deals almost exclusively not with the editor but with the publisher of the newspaper. Yet there is significance even here. The publisher of Irwin's time was still likely to be the editor of his paper, or at least he called himself such and exercised much direction of the paper. Thus Irwin speaks of Scripps, Hearst, Ochs, Pulitzer, Watterson, Bonfils, and Tammen in terms that leave no doubt that these men were more than owners of business properties. Although the newspaper was becoming a large business enterprise in 1911, it was not too large for the owner to retain direct control of editorial content. Irwin talks of the editor's influence on the news, and of how the paper takes its ideological coloration from the chief directing officer. And he finds nothing remarkable in the fact that the editor-in-chief happens to be the owner. Newhouse, Thomson, and others with their view of newspapers as strictly business endeavors, had yet to come. The corporate owner of the newspaper, like that of other key American businesses, was in reality in the embryo stage.

The phenomenon that sociologists today call social control of the newsroom Irwin clearly recognized and described: the viewpoints of the chief made themselves known in various ways and filtered downward through the editorial staff. Irwin, in his day of 2,600 daily newspapers (compared to 1,700-plus today), accepted that fact calmly, with none of the concern that attends its discussion in an era of monopoly newspapers. He not only assumed that truth would prevail over falsehood, he was still able to assume that the encounter would be free and open. Today we are not so sure.

The American Newspaper

A Study of Journalism in Its Relation to the Public

By WILL IRWIN

VI.—The Editor and the News

The Ethics of News-Publication; the Commercial Attitude Toward Journalism; the Cases of the New York "Times" and the Denver "Post"

EVERY night there happen in New York, Philadelphia, and Chicago a thousand events which fit the definition of news; and information on most of them reaches the newspaper offices. Not one-tenth of them, however, get into print. The editor's work, therefore, is always selective. According to his point of view as transmitted through the trained men under him, he prints certain things and omits certain things, uses one item as a "front-page feature" and another as a "filler." If you live in the radius of four or five big city newspapers, compare, to-morrow, the right-hand or "outside" column of their front pages. This column, by the immemorial custom of American journalism, holds the day's most important piece of news, as the editor sees news. Unless there is something exceptionally important afoot, you will find one printing in that column a social scandal or an episode which drags in society by the heels; another a political story; another a movement in high finance. A Scripps newspaper, with the Scripps outlook on economic and social questions, has in that preferred position an account of a working man's strike in Sweden, a Hearst newspaper a breach of promise suit, an Ochs newspaper a railway merger.

The Quandary of the Editor

NOW, in making this selection, two lights guide the honest editor. In the first place, he must sell his newspaper. He, like any one else not wholly an artist who ministers to the intellectual needs of the populace, must consider not only what he would give the public, but what the public will take. He himself may be scholarly in his tastes; the discovery of a Sapphic ode in a Greek excavation, or the fact that Professor Wallace has found another document concerning the life of Shakespeare, may be to him the most highly important news of the day. He knows, however, that a hundred potential readers will be far more interested in the latest picturesque murder. Editors exist who have naturally the popular point of view, whose interests are those of the man in the street. They are the born commercial successes of the craft; of such, for example, are many of the best Hearst editors—like Andrew Lawrence.

The other light to his feet is his conception of what the public should want; and there are men in the profession who are guided by this light alone. They will make no concessions to popularity for revenue's sake. Such men, if they manage to remain in the business, never achieve heavy financial success, although they may, through their limited circulations among highly intelligent people, have great personal and professional influence.

These are the poles. On the one extreme is the business attitude. We are here to supply a commodity—news—and, to a certain extent, views upon that news. We are responsible for furnishing sound news. That is, we will not lie, exaggerate, nor pad, any more than we would, if we were manufacturing linens, cheapen our product with cotton threads. But we will give the public exactly what it wants, without bothering to elevate the commonwealth. If we find that people prefer murders, then murders they shall have. Of course there are certain obscene and improper things which they might like, but which we will not give them, on account of our own reputation as gentlemen—just as a firm manufacturing shoes or stockings or dress goods will not push its sales by means of obscene advertising. Besides, that kind of thing is bad business in the end. But up to that limit our only responsibility is honest news—our nearest approximation to truth as we see truth.

Adolph Ochs

Publisher of the New York "Times," and perhaps the best and highest example of the "commercial" publisher

To such publishers the newspaper is a private enterprise and its proprietor responsible only to his own conscience. They forget, probably, that the extraordinary freedom granted our press is a tacit franchise; and that the payment expected by American society for this franchise is leadership by means of light.

The Professional View-Point

ON THE other hand is the professional attitude, assumed, whether they admit it or no, by such men as Bowles of the Springfield "Republican," the Gonzales brothers of the Columbia "State," and Villard and Ogden of the New York "Evening Post." We are here to help lead the world and to improve it, such being the distinction between business and the so-called learned professions—spite of the fact that business, in this age, is sometimes more highly ethical than the so-called learned professions. It is an article of agreement in our franchise from the people that we shall lead them up; that we shall give them not so much what they are clamoring to hear as the things which we consider it best for democracy to know. Although forty men on the street will read an intimate interview with Mamie Jones, the murderess, to one who will read a bare statement of the murder, we will not give them that interview; it is better for the people to have something else in their heads. Later, I hope to show the incidental dangers in that highly logical attitude. Let me here, however, illustrate the obvious and inherent dangers in the commercial attitude.

Best, perhaps, among our great practitioners of commercial journalism is Adolph Ochs, publisher and proprietor of the New York "Times." Certainly he will do for a type of the rest. He took the "Times" in 1896. It was then the wreck of a glorious newspaper—the shade of that journal which Raymond used so effectually in war time. Ochs, a good business man, a keen judge of public taste, reduced his price to one cent, thereby cutting into the circulation of the two and three cent "Sun" and "Herald," whose clientele he was after. He began to give the news—straight, uncolored, essentially truthful. "All the news that's fit to print" was his motto; and he nearly lived up to it. His guide was what the public wanted to know; and he satisfied that want. His newspaper is not clever, and it is not especially illuminating. But it comes nearest of any newspaper in New York to presenting a truthful daily picture of life in New York and the world at large. Being new in the field, Ochs was comparatively unhampered by association and influence. He was able even to talk about a few "sacred cows" which the other newspapers left alone. The "Times" prospered in its field. It passed the "Sun" and "Herald" in circulation; it began to rival even the yellows. Advertisers who like respectability came his way; and the "Times" became a dazzling commercial success.

The "Times" Idea

OCHS, in short, made it fulfil his picture of a newspaper. His news is a sound product, with few shoddy threads. In general, it may be said of any New York news story unconnected with politics or Wall Street that the "Times," the "Sun," and the "Post"—when it takes notice—are most likely to give an accurate report; but the "Times" is in a position to go further with truth than the "Sun." (I should add the morning "World" to this enumeration did it not retain some of the yellow habit of exaggeration.) The "Times" has fewer towers of silence than most; usually it dares, when the news blows in that direction, to tell the truth about its sources of income. To draw on COLLIER'S own experience: The verdict of $50,000 in the libel suit of Collier *vs.* Postum Cereal Co., Ltd., was a "good story." In the first place, this was the largest libel verdict ever given in New York State and possibly in the United States, and the public loves a superlative. In the second place, it was a most entertaining trial, full of humorous episodes. Nearly all the New York newspapers, including the "Times," were beholden to C. W. Post for page after page of advertising, and all had a reasonable expectation of future favors from that direction. The other New York newspapers ignored the case, or dismissed it with short paragraphs; the "Times" reported it fully. A sound product—"all the news that's fit to print"—

H. H. Tammen

Half-owner of the Denver "Post"—"The flamboyant and picturesque Harry Tammen has caught Denver's fancy"—"a clever man with a rich tongue"

Fred G. Bonfils

Half-owner of the Denver "Post"—"The worst to be said of the 'Post' is that it runs on . . . the kind of business that flourished in the days of Hannaism"

what the public wants to know—such is Ochs's ideal. He fails to live up to that ideal in an important particular; but so do all other "commercial" publishers. For if one abide strictly by the rule, "what the public wants to know," he must recognize that the man in the street is as eager to read about a public robbery as a private burglary; that legitimate muckraking is a news-need as much as criminal court reports. But that fault is common to his kind of publisher. Again, news centering about high finance attracts the "Times" unduly. That also is a fault of the breed.

Ochs does not halve his ethics, either; he recognizes that clean advertising columns are as much the business of an honest newspaper as clean news columns. There his standards are exceptionally high. He excludes most patent medicines—though he has let down the bars a little of late—all obscene matter, all financial offers known to be unsound. If, occasionally, a bit of "fake" financial advertising gets by the censorship, Ochs himself is not necessarily to blame—any more than he is to blame when an unsound piece of news written by an irresponsible reporter slips past the copy readers. The perfect newspaper would require not only a perfect man for head, but a perfect staff.

Ochs, in short, takes the attitude that the newspaper business *is* a business; that he is manufacturing a product; that he is responsible for making a sound product and distributing it honestly. And his New York "Times" is as high an expression of that attitude toward journalism as we have in the United States.

The Flaw in the "Times"

YET something which we have the right to expect from a newspaper is lacking from the "Times." Believing in no responsibility further than telling the news truthfully and giving an intelligent direction to the opinions of his readers, he does not go out of his way, as he might, to expose the filthy corners of a city which piles up considerable dirt now and then. He opposes special privilege in his editorial page; but special privilege might ride rough-shod over New York, for all the notice he would take in the news. When the reformers got their case before court or commission, he would report the proceedings fairly and accurately, would comment upon them intelligently; but until the case did come before court or commission, thus becoming news in the conventional sense, he would consider that the matter was no affair of the "Times."

"So act that thy action might become a universal law" is, I believe, the essence of Kant's ethics. Apply this rule to the case of the New York "Times" and Adolph Ochs. Were his rule the universal law of journalism, we should have a soberer and straighter thinking people, doubtless. We should also have the guerrillas of special privilege raiding private right almost unhampered; for we freed our press from the restrictions of the English common libel laws that it might perform a function which the law can not—defending the body social from the perverters of laws. Against these evils we have no other sentinel. To gather and publish news freely, without serving the commonwealth by means of that news, is to take without paying. Yet Adolph Ochs, with his New York "Times," is the best we may reasonably expect from the commercial attitude toward journalism.

And, indeed, this attitude toward news-journalism becomes an absurdity as we go further down the line, and approach the commercial publishers who hold those business ethics so wofully common in the palmy days before the Spanish War—"Anything goes so long as you stay inside the law and pay your debts." Omit from the enumeration the blackmailers—and it is a solemn fact that a few metropolitan newspapers in America do get advertising by means of suppressed information. They are operating without the law. Omit the newspapers, even less uncommon, which exist to further "special interests." They violate the letter, if not the spirit, of the law against obtaining money under false pretenses. Let us confine ourselves to the newspapers conducted on the principle "anything legal for business." And far down toward the bottom of that list we reach—the Denver "Post." Read Ben B. Lindsey's "The Beast and the Jungle" and learn how ill such a newspaper serves its community. Yet in the last analysis the worst to be said of the "Post" is that it runs on "big business" lines—the kind of business which flourished in the great, bloated days of Hannaism.

H. H. Tammen, a waif and a pedler at the age of seven, really began life when a bartender of Philadelphia advertised for a boy assistant to the porter. Tammen applied for the job because a saloon is always warm, and there is always free lunch to eat. The bartender took Tammen because he looked little and hungry, and wore outlandish Dutch homespun clothes. Literally, he was brought up behind a bar; he learned to read from the newspapers which patrons left on the tables. A clever man with a rich tongue, a despiser of his own wares, he rose to the very heights of bartending. "I was the best in the world," he says. He was head of the bar at the Palmer House in Chicago before he came of age; and in 1880 the new Windsor Hotel at Denver sent for this supreme artist. Here he saw and embraced his first chance at fortune. Colorado is rich in attractive mineral specimens. Tammen began to pack assortments in cigar-boxes and sell them for twenty-five cents a box to tourists. This business prospered; he replaced the cigar-boxes by showy cases, moved from a cellar to a store, left the bar, and persuaded an advertising agency to back "Tammen's Rocky Mountain Specimens." With minor variations from British ideals, this reads so far like a Samuel Smiles "Self-Help" story; indeed, such rise of a waif in a barroom to wealth and power in an honored calling is one of those triumphs in which democracy glories.

The Building of the Denver "Post"

Tammen and Bonfils found in a Missouri court-house the motto: "O Justice, when expelled from all other habitations, make this thy dwelling-place," and had it painted over their own door. When the sapient citizen of Denver raises his eyes to it, he smiles

The Partners Meet

TAMMEN, type of the Western hustler with forty enterprises in mind, went to Chicago in 1893 to market a portfolio of World's Fair views. There, because they employed the same printer, he heard of Fred Bonfils and his fortune. Bonfils, who came from beginnings different from those of Tammen, had been running a Little Louisiana Lottery in Kansas City, Kansas. He had $800,000 put away in storage vaults. "I knew I could use that money," said Tammen. On impulse he went down to see Bonfils. He could have talked his way through the gates of Paradise, this Tammen. Bonfils showed him the cash in vault; and forthwith promised to back Tammen in his ventures. The first projects failed; then the old Denver "Post," a fly-by-night sheet, gave up the struggle, and offered itself for sale at $12,500. Tammen got Bonfils to advance the sum, and to double it for running expenses; and when the "Post" turned the corner they became joint owners.

To make the "Post" circulate, and to transmute that circulation into money—it would seem that they never had any other intention. First they attracted notice by tearing into anything and every one. Hearst and the yellows came along, showing the short cut to great subscription lists. Tammen and Bonfils sent for some of the best-advertised Hearst writers, and began to out-yellow Hearst. They raked kitchens and boudoirs for scandal and gossip; they browbeat, they bullied, they wrote from the ethical heights on subjects which did not affect their interests, that they might have a reputation for fairness when they came unfairly to advocate causes which did. They made the "Post" a special advocate of business projects in which they were interested. Affecting to oppose corporation privileges, they nevertheless helped the financial and political game of certain predatory corporations—see again "The Beast and the Jungle." Reviled and insulted and shot, they buffeted and ferreted it through to amazing profits in view of Denver's size. No one can fairly call the "Post" good journalism as a whole. Except for a certain education in the emotions which has set off this "newspaper with a heart and soul," it tends to disintegrate public intelligence. By a false picture of the world, it subverts the public power of judgment. Its uncertain advocacy of good causes, along with bad, bewilders the public mind. But it has "gone" like wildfire; it has made money; it has been good business; and, on the other hand, it has seldom, if ever, done anything which the law could touch.

Both the partners are good "newspaper men" with a lively news sense, or they could not have done it. Bonfils has his own quieter powers, but the flamboyant and picturesque Tammen has caught Denver's fancy. He has said: "If you're going to be a faker, be an honest faker. Tell 'em what you're like, then touch it up a bit, so they'll be surprised when they find how good you really are." Proceeding on that principle, Tammen has said, both publicly and privately: "Sure! I'm a crook! I'm a blackmailer! What are you going to do about it?" He does not mean that, as he shows when he takes off his showman's front and talks his real thought. But even in those sincere moments he tells, as meritorious examples of good business, such instances of these:

"Good Business"

THE owners of the "Post" own also the Sells-Floto Circus, second-rate in size. The Ringling Circus, first-rate in size, approached Denver. The Sells-Floto wanted that territory exclusively for itself. By raising a side-issue in print, by using private influence with the city officials, part of whom the "Post" had supported for election, Tammen and Bonfils got Ringling's license fee raised to an impossible figure. Ringling had to show at a loss outside of the city limits. This, of course, was "good business"—helping the by-product with the reputation of the main product. Overland Park was the race-track of Denver. Tammen and Bonfils "wanted in" on the controlling company. Refused, they started a campaign to prohibit racing in Colorado. And that was "good business"—showing the teeth of your corporation, that the next small firm offered an advantageous alliance might hesitate before refusing. So Harry Tammen has only reduced to an absurdity the opinion that collecting and selecting news, combining it with editorial opinion, and putting it out to the masses, should be regarded by the editor as a business, not a profession.

But Tammen and Bonfils of the Denver "Post" are an exception in one direction just as Bowles of the Springfield "Republican" is an exception in the other. Between them is a regiment of conscientious editors whose idea of news-publication is to blend what the public wants and what it *should* want. They publish enough sensation, enough highly seasoned matter, to keep up circulation; but they publish also more than the public really wants of "uplift" matter, of news touching on intellectual affairs. The mere, passing, human news of the day is the sugar on the pill. Not that they despise good reports of the latest murder or disaster or disappearance. No man could be a successful newspaper man without taking delight in the stories of this class, which enable him to exercise the sharpest technique of his craft. But they hesitate to "overplay" crime, disaster, and scandal for a little increase of circulation. They recognize, in short, the obligations of a newspaper, the payment which American society requires under its franchise.

This being allowed, what, finally, is the kernel of editorial ethics? One word, I think, expresses it—"truth." Or better, perhaps, four words—"the search for truth."

(Continued on page 2)

The American Newspaper

(*Continued from page 19*)

Understood in the broadest sense, that bounds the editor's professional morality. But what is truth? Something like the Fourth Dimension, which the finite mind can state but not grasp; something seen differently by each beholder. And what a laborious process is that of arriving at the final human approximation to truth in any one of the fifty stories which a newspaper publishes every day! William Smith is murdered; it seems most likely that Robert Jones did it. The next morning, in fact, the newspapers are so sure of it that they accuse Jones. Detectives must find and sift evidence, coroner's juries sit, grand juries return indictments, petit juries listen to evidence and summings-up, before man creeps so near to truth in action as to determine that Robert Jones should die. But by the demand of his public, the editor must publish the fact that Smith was killed, with the probable fact that Jones killed him, on the very day of the murder—nay, at its very hour. In this case the ideal of truth becomes a desperate impossibility; yet the instance typifies three-quarters of the news which daily journalism must handle.

Fact or Gossip?

"MOST news," says Tiffany Blake, "is not fact, anyway. *It is gossip about facts.*" In this, I think, he has said a wise and final word. News, as it works out in newspaper practise, amounts to gossip, the impressionist picture of truth. It is gossip organized to our uses, subdued to our hand, and raised to both a science and an art. For before journalism was, the town or tribal gossip discharged in irregular and primitive fashion most lower functions of a newspaper and some higher ones. He "mixed," he found by force of his prying curiosity the things which were his business as a member of the tribe, and the things which were no one's business. After that, he circulated through town or settlement, telling. And I conceive of one gossip, expressing most closely the bad sense we have come to feel in that word, whose tongue wagged on the hinges of malice and vanity, who spread no good thing about his enemies, and who made a mountain of rumor from a mole-hill of fact for the satisfaction of attracting attention. To him tribe or town listened, though they despised. He was a curse to his world. Foolish rumor and baseless report play a large part in the history of all ages down to the one which brought accurate journalism, and the springs of destructive rumor were such tribal gossips.

Another kind of gossip there must have been. I imagine a man of ready speech, rolling and curious eye and attractive manner, an ornament at any fireside, who came with his mouth full of greater and better things. The chiefs and the council had decided to change the spring planting from the east field to the west; that was a good thing; he had dug into the land and found it rich. Rab had wounded Ush and stolen away his wife; that was a pity, and Rab had his hands full with her, which served him right. A sickness was on the cattle in the northern fold; let those in other parts of the village keep their cows away lest the devil get them also. The chief's counselor had been caught stealing. Many thought that the tribe should exercise its immemorial right of deposing the unfit leader. I imagine him telling these tales of the day with the narrative gift, but also with a ripe philosophy and a point of view as high and progressive as the age knew. I think of him as ignoring the trivial things, the mere surmises, the facts which, spread abroad, would have injured individuals without benefiting the tribe. Such as he helped the upward march from tool to machinery, tribe to nation.

The Point of View

EACH of these gossips had the eager curiosity and the burning desire to communicate its results which mark the real journalist. The difference between them consisted partly in moral intention, but mainly in point of view. And that necessity for approaching truth from a point of view rules us of the twentieth century A. D. as it did them of the twentieth century B. C., though they spoke simple things by word of mouth to one full fireside, and we complex things by word of pen and type and lightning press to a hundred thousand firesides. Nothing above a market report, or a tabulation of stock fluctuations, but shows the point of view of him who wrote.

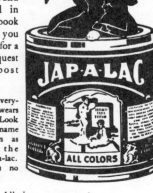

Picking at random, as a Scotch soothsayer pricks his Bible for a sign, I lay my finger on a piece of news in this morning's Boston "Post." It is an item, a "stick" long, from Lynn; it relates to a young girl who went to sleep with a re-

volver under her pillow. The revolver exploded in the night, wounding her in the shoulder. As you read it, you find the reporter's point of view. It was a "regrettable accident." "Restlessness in sleep" was the probable cause. A reader sympathizes with the young woman. I imagine its treatment from other points of view. First, the flippant and jocular—the girl who went "heeled" for that old fetish of humor, the man under the bed, and shot only herself. Then the sensational, hinting, by a twist here and a turn of phrase there, that there was more in the case than the girl told. Then the heavy monitory, implying—if only by inserting the adverb "carelessly"—that the girls should not keep revolvers under their pillows. Be a journalist anything more than a clod, anything less than an archangel, he must have a human point of view; be his work any warm expression of himself, anything beyond a dry, unreadable lump, he must throw on it that light which is an expression of character and belief.

The old editor, feeling about for proper use of the news-force, either overemphasized this factor or ignored it. The blatant old party organ published, if Democratic, only the Democratic rallies and speeches, ignoring the Republican or sneering at their meetings in little ten-line reports. The point of view was there, but bigoted, narrow, and unfair. Another kind of editor, who left no descendants to this generation, held, as the fettered English do, that news should be colorless, that all expression should come in the editorial columns. So he killed art in reporting, reducing it to a mechanical formula, thereby dulling the minds of his readers and forfeiting some of his hold on his public.

The Editor Leads

PART of our inheritance from the yellows has been a blending of news and editorial; a recognition that the paper's policy, if consistent, must infuse both—a color which is a tint in the news columns and deepens in the editorial. Since the individual, by the spirit of the age, is coming more and more to form judgments on public affairs from the raw data, the editor's statement of facts is more important in forming public opinion than his opinion on the facts. Also, bald, colorless relation of important news about an institution or a person that the editor is madly denouncing on his editorial page is really an inconsistency. Suppose his editorials declare that the local political gang is a band of robbers. When news "breaks" that the city auditor has vindicated prophecy by stealing a million dollars, shall the reporter who writes it withhold his hand? Is not the paper inconsistent if he does?

Now it is the directing editor or publisher who most potently sets this point of view for the whole paper. By all the laws of popular psychology, he can not be effective unless he does this. Even the simplest new idea is not inserted into the public mind by a single thrust, but by continual hammering. He can not give every reporter his head, allowing him his own point of view. This would produce only a fabric of stitched things. Moreover, reporting involves so much "leg work," requires so much spurring from the buoying sense of adventure, that, as a rule, only very young men do it successfully. A reporter's useful life is about contemporary with that of an athlete. Men so young have, of themselves, a point of view too immature for final trust with important affairs. The editor must guide them in this, must educate his "cubs" and instruct his older acquisitions in his own attitude toward life and the news.

Two Front Pages

NEWSPAPERS, in fact, tend always to take on the character of their directing hands; it is a trade saying that "a paper can not rise higher than its source." Every journal of ripe age acquires personality like an individual; that is the point of view at work. In New York the Hearst "American" is fighting the Pulitzer "World" for circulation. They are of the same type. Each has abandoned the extreme yellow policy; each is after the wide appeal. They often interchange men, so that an "American" executive may have worked last year on the "World," or vice versa. Yet they differ widely in their selection from the same news supply. Says an editor of the "American": "Often in looking over the news of the day, deciding what stories we shall run on the front page, I think of the 'World,' try to pick the stories which *they* think most important. I can usually do it, too. I don't know why; but this is a first-rate 'American' story and only a second-rate 'World' story, and that a great feature for them, and only a mild one for us." And this difference only expresses the varying viewpoints of Hearst and Pulitzer, as they make their way downward through the editorial staff.

VII

The Reporter and the News

THE REPORTER is the sensory antenna of the newspaper. As Irwin realized, much of the real power of a newspaper resides in the reporting staff, through its organization, deployment, and skill.

By 1911 the press was already approaching top efficiency in news gathering by means of the "beat system," which allocated reporters to regular coverage of the city's main centers of news. Irwin estimates in this article that probably nine-tenths of the day's news was gathered in that way. The news tip, which sometimes permitted competitors to be scooped or beaten, accounted for the remaining tenth. Even during those years when competing newspapers were most numerous, Irwin seems to be saying, the scoop was of little real use in building a modern newspaper. His comment is all the more interesting in view of today's rather widely held assumption that a strength of the monopoly newspaper situation is the scoop's de-emphasis, which theoretically helps prevent hasty publishing of incomplete stories. If the scoop was of so little real importance in a competitive situation, why is its absence so beneficial in today's noncompetitive world?

The beat technique of systematic news gathering is still retained, of course, though better newspapers have come to recognize certain inherent weaknesses and try to compensate for them. Perhaps the chief weakness of the beat method is that it tends to give what may be an unreal or artificial shape to the news. Thus the police reporter may see his product as police beat news (so many crimes, so many arrests, so much progress on this or that investigation) and in the day-to-day writing of these stories may miss the significance of trends over time, or may even reject worthwhile stories because they do not fit within the usual framework he employs. This rigidity in viewing the news can become invested with "tradition" to the extent that the original reason for adopting the beat system (efficiency in news gathering) is no longer the chief consideration in its retention or modification. For it is obvious that today's system of news gathering must be different from the 1911 system. The tremendous growth of the federal government, to cite one example, shows the need for different organization. The federal beat of Irwin's day was infinitely less complex than it now is. Indeed, with the great increase in federal spending at all levels of government, each level—state, county, local, and metropolitan—is now a federal beat. A story written from facts obtained only from the federal building will give only part of the picture. Hence the increase today of news beats that are more topical than geographical: civil rights, higher education, urban affairs, and so on.

Despite the very real differences between today's reporting and that of Irwin's time, the emphasis on artfulness remains. The half-century intervening has seen a stress on "objective" reporting begin, grow to the point where demagogic assertions which assassinated character were printed and then the printing defended as "objective" reporting, and finally diminish in favor of "interpretation." The labels may change, but when Irwin speaks of the need to stalk truth from a point of view, he seems indeed very modern.

The American Newspaper

A Study of Journalism in Its Relation to the Public

By WILL IRWIN

VII.—The Reporter and the News

This article deals with the art of reporting, as first worked out by Charles A. Dana. It shows where journalism blends with literature, and where it stands apart. It shows how necessary is the faculty of accurate and minute observation in artistic reporting, and how the yellow reporter conceals his lack of art by melodrama and faking

IN CONSIDERING the editor's relation to the news, we have seen how the supreme head of a newspaper sets the major point of view for his writing gentlemen, is keeper of their larger ethics. He determines, in his functions of selection and training, whether his newspaper as a whole shall be radical or conservative on public questions, shall treat money and property with exaggerated respect or with scant courtesy, shall make man more important than wealth or wealth than man, shall appeal to the head, the heart, or the lower nervous centers. He can not, however, set for his writers their minor points of view on the little things which come under their notice. If he tries to do so, he tends to destroy all originality and individuality in the product of his force.

What now of the reporter, the newest arm of this newest power in civilization? Here is a young man sent out among the million complexities of the day to find the facts which will interest his world, to see truth for the home-stayers, as truth presents itself to his point of view. "He wields," said Dana, "the real power of the press." This is only measurably true, since the editor or publisher should, and generally does, lay out the larger scheme for his reporters. But the fact remains that this prying, romantic individual, wholly an outgrowth of modern life, is a more vital member of the social organism than the philosophers have let themselves admit. Through the glass which he holds up before us, most of us see our times. His product is daily bread of the minds to three-quarters of the population. He is to the individual reader the most important functionary in a newspaper organization, just as the police power is to the humble private citizen the most important function of law. If he write sanely, truthfully, with good taste and art, he cultivates sanity, truth, taste, and sense of proportion in his readers. If he write narrowly, cynically, loosely, and without taste, he correspondingly lowers the intellectual standard of his time. He furnishes the raw material for public opinion. If the strand be shoddy, how can the finished fabric be sound?

There is a craft in reporting and an art; the reporter must first get his material, by burrowing as far as he can through the wrappings which hide fact and truth, and then write it. Each of these activities calls for a separate faculty not always united in the individual. The experienced city editor has this dual function in mind when he speaks of his "break-in reporters" and his "artists" or "writing men." The man who possessed merely the faculty of getting news was all-important in the times which followed Bennett and preceded Dana. Later he divided importance with the news-artist. Yet he who is merely a writer, with no "nose for news" and no knack of getting it, is still less vitally important than the reporter with the mere sense and skill of news-gathering. The supreme reporters are those in whom the two faculties blend. Such were "Jersey" Chamberlin, Stephen Crane, Julian Ralph, John P. Dunning, and Harry Stevens of the last generation; such are Clifford Raymond, the late "Nick" Biddle, E. H. Hamilton, and Frank Ward O'Malley of this.

The first personal question which a layman asks a reporter is usually: "What do you do? Just go out and hang around until you find a piece of news?" That was exactly the method of the earliest reporters, and is still of the country editor. But expansion has brought system into metropolitan journalism. A city is now "covered" by a machine as fine and complicated as a rotary press. The city editor keeps men day and night at the police station and emergency hospitals, these being the points where news of crime and disaster first manifests itself. He has a man or a bureau at the local financial center, whether it be a stock exchange or a banking district. "Routine men" watch the local centers of government, as the City Hall, the courts, and the Federal Building. Others visit daily such institutions as the Public Library, the Chamber of Commerce, and the bureaus of charity. If it be a seaport, each newspaper has a marine specialist at the water-front. Specialists keep in touch with the churches, the labor unions, "society," and the women's clubs. By a similar system the press bureaus keep watch of the wider world.

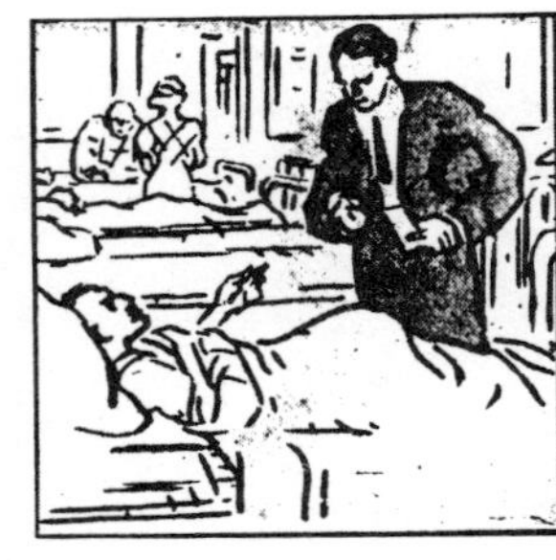

Probably nine-tenths of the news, and on most days all of it, comes originally from one or another of these sources. For the rest, the original information—the "tip," in trade slang—proceeds generally from some private source, as a gossipy friend of the city editor or of a reporter. In the scope of that narrow tenth lies the "beat" or "scoop," the exclusive piece of news so cherished and esteemed by the older generation and of so little real use to modern newspaper building.

Why Don't Our Newspapers Tell the Truth?

IN THE larger and more advanced cities these routine activities are taken off the individual newspaper's hands by a news agency, which "covers" the regular sources and rushes the bare information to all its clients at once. Then from his own staff the city editor sends a reporter to look further into the matter and to write the story. Little remains to chance; the machine for news-gathering is as well-ordered as it can be, considering that it must constantly encounter emergencies.

Truth, fogged by the imperfections of human sight, hidden under the wrappings of lies, stands the final aim of a reporter when he goes out on a news tip. It is the working hypothesis of a reporter. "Why don't our newspapers tell the truth?" ask politicians and excellent ladies of women's clubs. Could they only know the difficulty of reaching an approximation to the hidden fact! Accurate perception of the event which has just happened before the eyes of flesh is so exceptional as to be almost unknown. Hugo Münsterberg tried an experiment once before his Harvard class in psychology. As the students settled themselves to the lecture, two men rose from the front seat and started to fight. Others joined in to separate or to assist them. A minute of lively action followed. "Gentlemen," said Dr. Münsterberg, when the disturbance was quelled, "we have only been acting for your benefit, a little drama, rehearsed beforehand. We know, for we followed our lines, just what happened. Please write down all you saw." The resultant papers differed ridiculously from each other; and all differed materially from fact. Later, Münsterberg produced another such drama, this time warning the class, asking them in advance to observe, and to write out their observations. The results were only a little less inaccurate. A professor at a Kansas university, imitating the Münsterberg experiment, staged a pretended "shooting scrape." One of the actors sprang into the mêlée flourishing a monkey-wrench. Not a member of the class but saw it as a pistol. The steamer *Rio de Janeiro* struck the reef off Fort Point in the Golden Gate, ran out toward the sea in the darkness and ebb tide, and sank, blowing her whistle until the water drowned her steam. In the subsequent inquiry the duration of her whistle blasts became important. A company of soldiers was quartered just above Fort Point; most of them heard the blasts. Part of their drill in soldiering had consisted in counting off seconds. Yet some said that the blasts were ten seconds long, some two minutes, and some that there was just one continuous blast.

Now the reporter really approaches accuracy of perception. Daily training has made him so. Had Professor Münsterberg produced his drama before a body of journalists, I venture that their reports would have varied but little in statement of fact; I venture that certain individuals among a body of reporters watching the Kansas experiment, would have detected the monkey-wrench, and that had there been a trained journalist in the barracks over Fort Point we should know more than the Government ever learned about the means the *Rio* took to save herself.

But the reporter sees few of his comedies, tragedies, dramas, and little novels of the street first-hand. He is not there when the trains collide, the maniac shoots, or the thief escapes. He must take his information second-hand from witnesses with untrained and imperfect eyes. The courts, when they come to adjudicate these matters, will have trouble enough and to spare in getting at the probable truth; yet lawyers and detectives have weeks to weigh, sift, and correct by that circumstantial evidence which is often the best evidence, where reporters have but minutes.

This would be difficult enough were all the witnesses of the events which he sets about to chronicle disingenuous and truthful. But no one is so beset by the falsity of man as this same reporter. "Half the population," some one says, "is trying to keep out of the newspapers and half trying to get in." And both these classes lie consistently, or employ press-agents to do the lying for them. In unraveling these tangled things, in arriving at his results—marvel of accuracy in view of his difficulties—the reporter's feet, like Patrick Henry's, are guided by the one lamp of experience. Roughly acquainted with all classes of men, all kinds of human institutions—for each day brings him in contact with a fresh aspect of life—he develops an intuition, which is only crystallized experience, for the probable fact hidden under human contradictions and lies. You, reader, as a consumer of newspapers, do not often see a newspaper story about a little girl lured away from home and imprisoned in a dark cellar by a villain. Yet cases of that kind are commonly reported to the police. Now experience has shown that a certain kind of hysterical girl who has played truant from home for a day or so usually falls back on her Laura Jean Libbey and invents such an excuse to her family. The girl's assertion is uncontradicted; but the reporter, remembering previous cases, does not accept the story unless it has strong circumstantial corroboration. Here we have an obvious case of experience in action.

In this elemental function of finding just what happened, reporters and those editors in most immediate touch with them are, by and large, about as sincere as we may expect imperfect humanity to be. The untruth in our journalism resides elsewhere. William Jennings Bryan once raised the question: "Have we an honest press?" Were news investigation all of journalism, the answer would need be a strong affirmative. Excepting for the very "yellow" reporter, who has lost his sense of truth and proportion, these men are after the fact and nothing else. Indeed, reporting is an unsurpassed training in sincerity. And where news results seem untruthful, the fault lies often with the reporter's judgment, not his intentions. He may accept, in the first excitement following a disaster, the statement of some hysterical official that twenty people are dead, may telephone in this estimate for an extra, and may find later that the victims number only two or three. Here the public is partly to blame, since it demands immediate information. News editors, in throwing out extras while the event is still fresh, generally make allowance for this tendency and cut down the first figures. "Halve 'em," is the rule of a great press bureau. And in late years the roster of victims grows rather than diminishes with succeeding extras.

Again, the layman criticizes, as the reporter writes, from a point of view. Given that Mr. Bryan, for example, is in a political campaign. His picture of himself and of the Democratic cause is not quite that of an unbiased outsider. If a company of archangels, absolute in virtue and holding knowledge of absolute truth, were to become incarnate and write the running story of his campaign, still neither Mr. Bryan nor his partizans would be satisfied; any report which did not lean toward their side would seem to them unfair and dishonest. I have heard the same news report of a political or sporting event criticized as "unfair to us" by both sides. Still more does this apply when the critic is a galled jade. In the height of the Roosevelt war on corporations, I encountered a stranger who denounced with violence and some profanity the "lies" of the American press concerning corporations. To the Washington "Post," I believe, he paid the tribute of exception. For the rest—lies, all lies! "Why, they make you think Roosevelt is a well-intentioned man!" he said. "Why don't they tell the truth and show him up for a demagogue?"

"What is his name again?" I asked when the stranger had gone.

"—— of the Salt Trust," came the answer.

Unaware, as most men are, that truth must be stalked from a point of view, he took the variant point of view for deliberate falsehood. The criminal on trial believes that he is "getting the short end of it" from the newspapers, when they are trying fairly to present both sides of the evidence. With much just criticism of the truth in newspapers is mixed always this unjust carping.

Curiously, the falsity in newspaper presentation of the world increases as it rises to the top. It is, in fact, when he passes up from news-gathering to writing, when he sits down to tell in his most interesting fashion the story which he has found, that the reporter meets his greatest temptation to depart from truth. As he reviews the facts on his way to the office, they may seem bare, unilluminating. An imaginary detail here and there, a conjunction of this remote fact with that, a remark taken from its context and thrown to the fore, would give it, he feels, more dramatic, pathetic, or comic force. Few newspaper writers are so conscientious as never to have yielded to this temptation. Yet truth, illumined by a point of view, is the very kernel of the reporter's art, as it is that of his ethics. And this introduces the fact that reporting—contrary to the opinion of Robert Louis Stevenson and his kind—may be dressed out with ornament; that an art akin to Stevenson's own distinguishes the great, smashing, effective news stories from the mere dull tabulation of events. The craft is like to furniture-making and interior decoration. A trade in its mediocrity, it becomes an art at its best. This art is a reporter's special province, as keeping major ethics is that of an editor.

Some Great News Stories

EVEN in the academic definition of that hazy word, journalism blends with "literature." Living between book covers, passed on from generation to generation, is a great body of English letters written solely for the need of the day. It includes most essays by Addison and Steele, a good part of De Foe, the Junius letters. De Foe wrote "Sunday stuff"; Addison, "features"; Junius, editorial. Further back than that, Pliny's story of the Pompeiian disaster was a news story supremely done. Charles A. Dana used to say with all reverence that the story of the crucifixion in the Gospel according to St. Matthew was the greatest of all news stories. Xenophon wrought but as a reporter when he wrote the immortal "Anabasis" to tell the Athenians what account their ten thousand had given of themselves in Persia. Had Athens possessed daily newspapers, doubtless Xenophon would have published his story in them, instead of on papyrus. In our own time, Mark Twain laid his hand to little more worthy of preservation in his complete works than the news story, done first for a Sacramento daily, of the shipwrecked crew which he found in Hawaii; and Hazlitt's "The Fight" is a sporting report.

Though journalism reaches these immortal heights but seldom, we have produced in this country volumes of matter for the daily press much better by any literary standard than most which we preserve in magazines or embalm in books and call literature. Of such are the unhappy John P. Dunning's account of the Samoan disaster and Lindsay Denison's story of the struggle to rescue Bill Hoar the diver—both lost now in old files, their very dates forgotten.

The Requirements of News Writing

ONE principal canon governs the art of news writing—severe plainness. The novelist writes to tell an imaginative tale for the reader's leisure; perhaps, going deeper, he writes also to illuminate, criticize, and explain life in bulk. The poet writes to conjure beauty. Seemly for each of these is all proportionate decoration of style and philosophical digression. The reporter is telling a story of the day. He writes in haste; in like haste his patron reads. A swift, rushing narrative, whose movement to an end no ornament dams or delays, should be his aim. He may catch the reader's attention by a trick of style or a turn of wit in the opening sentence, he may carry it on from stage to stage by similar devices, but he can not stop long to moralize or to describe. In the first place, it clogs the story; and the rush of narrative is more important to him than even to the fiction writer. In the second, he has no time to struggle for those decorations which come spontaneously only with leisure. If he follow the right method, this haste need not make him a mere stringer of stock phrases—"still smoking revolver," "mad panic," "prominent citizen"—as so many mechanical reporters are.

Within these seeming narrow limits is room nevertheless for art—wit, humor, pathos, drama—so long as it abides by the journalist's chief ethical canon of truth, and is not merely an invention. A man in New Jersey sat on a hickory limb and sawed between himself and the trunk. He fell forty feet on his head. "Having the kind of head which goes with that kind of trick, he was uninjured," wrote the reporter. That play of wit lay within the canons of his art, even though he showed a brutal attitude toward the victim. A woman left her baby in its carriage at the door of a department store. A policeman found it there, apparently abandoned, and wheeled it to the station. As he passed down the street, a gamin yelled: "What's the kid done?" The reporter put that in; and here again he was within the limits.

Curiously enough, if one look only on the surface, but naturally if one but look deeper, the more artistic a story is, the more it squares with the facts, with the event as it happened—which is perhaps only a fashion of saying that good journalistic writing lies in finding the art in truth.

For imagined details seldom quite fit in a news story. Somehow they stand crudely out from the picture. Critical writers of fiction have observed this principle at work in the reverse process. An actual and remembered incident, incorporated in an imaginary story, usually remains an insoluble lump in the finished product; it is the first thing on which a clever critic lays his finger, saying: "This is incongruous." Just so, imagined detail lumps and mars a good news story. For fiction is the art of lies—often true lies paradoxically—and reporting the art of truth. The greatest reporters, such as Julian Ralph, Harry Stevens, and Stephen Crane, have got their effects from details which they perceived in the event.

How poor, indeed, is the imagining of any ordinary man compared to the detail which surrounds the event itself! If it be great enough to get into the newspapers, it must have personality, atmosphere, a background. Behind every tragedy lies a whole novel, behind every movement for human good a poem. No story so dull, so commonplace, that the writer can not get the incident he needs from what he sees.

What he sees—there is the point, there the difference between the mechanic of news and the artist. Those very perceptions which make the good news-getter, applied to a different purpose, make the news artist. Forty reporters met Mrs. Maybrick at New York after her release. One, a woman, saw that she was wearing a ready-made gown. No one else noticed that. Another, a man, saw that for all her nervously erect carriage she showed the stiffening and coarsening of the back which hard labor imprints on woman—mark of her scrubbing at Woking Jail. No one else saw *that*. A man and a woman of my acquaintance, both writing journalists, visited a cheap vaudeville team in their dressing-room. It was a new experience for them both. "What struck you most vividly?" asked the woman afterward.

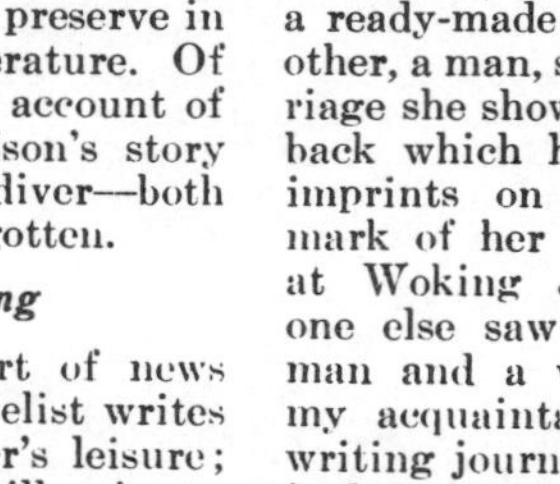

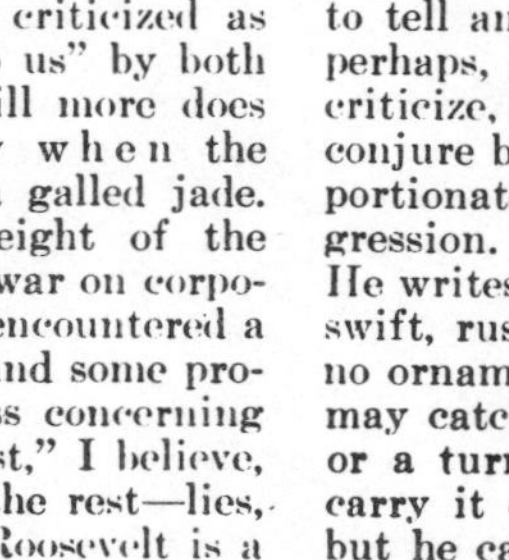

"The way that stage mother was maneuvering to keep between me and her daughter," he said, "it's a pathetic commentary—shows what they expect of life."

"I didn't notice that," said the woman. "But did you see the baby asleep in the suit-case under the dressing-table?"

"No, I didn't notice that!"

Here was good detail—that of the suit-case almost beyond imagination of the novelist—yet these two pairs of trained eyes saw differently.

In fact, most false, yellow, and unduly sensational newspaper writing is only a confession of lack of art. Let us go back to the type-story which I have used already as illustrating the yellow method with news—the servant girl in cheap clothing who has

(Continued on page 35)

The American Newspaper

(*Continued from page 22*)

committed suicide by the park lake. Put an artist in reporting on that. If it strike him on his sympathetic nerve, he will observe the poor, worn hands, the cheap clothes, imagine the struggle against poverty, scorn, and vice to which she has succumbed, and make a story whose pathos will carry it to every one. It is the yellow reporter, untrained to do this, who makes it a "Mystery of the Park," a "Pretty Girl Richly Dressed." By a lie he tries to match the other's skill in truth.

Weddoc of the Chicago "Tribune" had a story one morning about a girl who had gone the easiest way—and turned on the gas. It was a "plain suicide," good for an inch-long item in every other Chicago newspaper except one, which tried to make it a mystery. Weddoc marked the knot of white crape on the tenement-house door, listened to what the neighboring women, gossiping palm to face on the steps, had to say about her case, and wrote a classic. The knot of white crape ran through it like a refrain, as he traced her course from the tough public dance to the gas-chamber. And he never once threw in a word to bring his own point of view to the surface—never once raised his voice. Buried in the dusty old files of the "Tribune," it lingers in the memory of Chicago. A child, lost for an afternoon, was found dead in an alley—she had fallen from a roof. That happens commonly in the tenement district of New York. E. C. Hill told exactly what happened, with skilful management of the little details. And what old reader of the "Sun" has forgotten "A Little Child in the Dark"?

The Qualities of a Good Reporter

IT may seem that I am treating only of the exceptional man; it may be argued that the rank and file can not hope to be artists. As a matter of fact, such abilities lie hidden in nearly every man who has the sense of romance, the thrill of life and the power of expression which made him a journalist in the beginning. Ignorant, mechanical copy-reading, and a false view of news, have spoiled good reporters by regiments. Dana himself said that he produced his great results with pretty ordinary material. It was not that he got exceptional men, but that by intelligent handling, knowing where to curb the point of view and where to give individuality its head, he made the most of material little above the ordinary. He had unusual assistance in this; Amos Cummings and Chester S. Lord were artists in news, and Selah Merrill Clark, chief schoolmaster to the "Sun," has put genius into the ungrateful task of copy-reading. William R. Nelson of the Kansas City "Star," whose ideas on the journalistic mission differ from those of the "Sun," but whose view on the art in his craft is about the same, makes like comment on his own staff.

"Any one who can write an interesting letter," said Julian Ralph, "has it in him to be a good writer for the newspapers." And any one with that faculty is amenable to training in seeing and recording details. Above that, of course, lies capacity, the qualities of mind and heart which approach greatness; these set off the exceptional reporter. But none who is capable of holding a place on a newspaper need be a mere mechanic.

The Effect of the Atlantic Cable

ON his way to Europe after the Civil War, that great old correspondent George Alfred Townsend ("Gath") sighted the steamer which was laying the first Atlantic cable. "There's the end of newspaper writing," he said. Gath was wrong; we were hardly at the beginning of good newspaper writing, for Dana had not yet acquired the "Sun." But the cable, and succeeding forms of swift transmission, have vindicated his back-thought. For they have introduced a uniformity, a kind of monotony, into the literary form of newspapers. In Gath's time the New York "Herald," the Cincinnati "Enquirer," the Chicago "Tribune," and whatever other great newspaper of the period you may name, sent its own correspondents to the seat of important news, no matter how far away. After the Atlantic cable had finished the application of Morse's invention to journalistic needs, the general press bureaus appeared. Even the greatest newspapers came to rely on them for all but the most important news outside of their own territory; and a press bureau, ministering to all kinds of organs, tries to keep its writing bald and colorless. Telegraph editors can go only so far in rewriting the bare statements of the Associated Press or the United Press, and even then the rewriting avails little, since it is second-hand work. Where the city has a local news bureau, the same tendency is at work with local reports. The best editors and the smartest staffs regard this agency only as a dispenser of "tips," sending their own men to do the investigation and writing. But the more slipshod workmen print the minor news about as the press bureau sends it; and this is another tool bending the newspaper toward standard gage.

The Press Bureaus

In fact, editors are everywhere trying all devices to beat this tendency. The Associated Press and the United Press are the leading news bureaus. The United Press, younger and lesser of the two, runs only an "evening wire." All over the country, editors of important evening papers take both services, for the sake of variety. The New York "Sun," through its Laffan Press Bureau, farms out its own news; this matter, being especially well written, is valuable for enriching interest. The seven English Hearst newspapers have only two Associated Press franchises between them; Hearst has been forced to create a press bureau of his own; and he rents the service to other newspapers outside his territories. Of late, the New York "World," "Herald," and "Times" have taken to farming out their best news stories; they have long syndicated their "features." By picking and choosing among these syndicates, the news editor may create, in stiff mosaic, a picture of his times a little different from that presented by his rival across the street.

So it goes with "features." Once city newspapers outside of the metropolis had their own exclusive humorists and comic artists; the Denver "Tribune" and the Chicago "News" cherished Eugene Field as their property. Except for the cartoonists, who exercise a political function and can not be passed around with apparent sincerity, the "feature-man" appears nowadays only to be swallowed up by a syndicate which sends out his work to twenty, fifty, a hundred newspapers. Such was the early fate of Finley Peter Dunne ("Mr. Dooley"). "Walt Mason" appeared but two or three years since on the Emporia "Gazette." Already, he is in a syndicate. The fine flavor of locality is gone from most city newspapers; one must look far down the scale of population before he finds something which stands out, a distinct personality, like William Allen White's Emporia "Gazette," or Chester Rowell's Fresno "Republican." This but follows the modern industrial law; machine production and easy transportation tend to erode all local customs and peculiarities.

This movement of the times makes against good newspaper writing. It concentrates a few high-priced stars on the press bureaus, where art is limited through the necessary limitation of the point of view, or on such great metropolitan newspapers as farm out their matter syndicate-fashion. And it tends to make the rank and file in the smaller cities mere news machines.

The Effect of the Syndicates

However, another and opposing tendency is at work. As we grow great in wealth, as, having finished the all-absorbing task of breaking industrial ground, we begin to take our industrial leisure, a taste for art and all other fine things inevitably follows. Behold Chicago. Twenty years ago, when she was still plowing new industrial fields, her hideous rawness, her insensibility to the finer life, were a standard American joke. But Chicago established herself, pushed business development to a point near to diminishing returns. "Culture" followed; at first culture by main force, with the teeth clenched, then a dawning appreciation of the gracious and beautiful; and now Chicago is both producing and appreciating her craftsmen and artists. It is no accident—getting back to our own ground—that the Chicago newspapers are technically the best in the United States, and that their local reports are, by and large, the best written.

A Letter and a Reply on the Servant Question

DEAR COLLIER'S:

I ENCLOSE the letter from the domestic servant of which I spoke. The postmark was Chicago.

The incidents which the writer mentions illustrate the lack of system under which the private household is run. A chambermaid in a hotel works under a business arrangement; she is hired by the management to perform designated work, usually during designated hours. The hotel guest understands that she is under no obligation to give extra service.

When this chambermaid goes into a private household to work the arrangement between employer and employed becomes a confusion of business and personal relations.

Her duties are seldom accurately defined. A hotel chambermaid is not expected to run the risk of taking diphtheria from a hotel guest, but a private chambermaid is considered an ungrateful girl if she objects to doing for her sick mistress who has been so kind to her.

Yet a maid who relies too much on kind personal relations is held presuming. The telephone incident illustrates that. The telephone is the source of trouble in thousands of homes to-day, because the mistress makes no definite statement concerning its use. She says neither, "You may be called up on the telephone," nor "You may not be called up on the telephone." I have heard that telephone story from several mistresses. They tell it something like this:

"This morning the telephone bell rang and I answered it, and a man's voice said: 'Is that you, Katey?' I replied, rather coldly: 'This is Mrs. Johnson.' 'Oh,' he said, 'can I speak to Katey?' Now I'm not going to have Katey called away from her work in the middle of the morning like that. It's happened before, and I decided I'd put my foot down then and there. I just hung up the receiver, and when he rang again I didn't answer. When I went out in the kitchen I said casually: 'Oh, Kittie, some one called you up this morning. I don't know who it was.' She didn't say anything, and I didn't say anything more either, but she knew what I meant all right."

Unhappy mistress! Unhappy maid!

Sincerely yours,

MARY ALDEN HOPKINS.

MARY ALDEN HOPKINS, New York City.

DEAR MADAM:

LOOKING over COLLIER'S of January 14, I read with interest your answer to "Housekeeper" and also your views as to how servants' positions differ widely in different households. Maybe they do, but I have never been fortunate enough to secure any of the different ones. The women I have worked for have been arrogant, selfish, and wise in their own conceits. I am a domestic, having worked as such for twelve years, and can truthfully say domestic service is the lowest and most degrading work a girl can do.

I must say you have the best idea of service of anybody I know of outside of a servant, for, as you say, girls in laundries and factories work hard, but they have their hours, and that is all that is required of them.

Work as a chambermaid in a hotel, and the guests will treat you with consideration, and those same guests in their own homes will look on their servants as so much trash.

Some time ago I read an article in "Everybody's Magazine" by Roy McCardell, in which he stated one did not need intelligence to be a domestic. Why? I have worked in every capacity, from kitchen-maid to lady's-maid, and found it needed intelligence to scrub the kitchen floor. Let us come to the treatment of servants. I worked for three and a half years in a fashionable suburb of Chicago. I gave that family the best service I could give. I even washed the walls of their house—a man's work—served late suppers and early breakfasts, and had to put on the father's shoes, help him with his overcoat, and all the other little attentions that go to make a lazy life. When I left her I referred to her for a reference, and the one she gave me was that age did not improve my temper. Was not that appreciation for three and a half years hard labor?

I next secured a position as waitress with a family of six, four children included. On their dinner-table they used candles. Well, I have seen those children get up on the table and spit on the candles to put them out; and their father just laughed, because he thought it such a clever idea of theirs. One day their nurse came to me crying. "What is the trouble?" I cried. She told me the oldest son, who was then fourteen years old, had spit in her face. And, mind you, the mother of those four children boasts she never allows her servants to correct her children, so this will give you another idea of what servants have to take from untrained cubs.

So the housekeeper who can not understand why girls prefer laundry or factory work to domestic service in private families should go out and do service for three weeks, and in doing so could very easily solve the problem. I only wish I were educated enough to write a book on millionaires, their wives, and children. I would give them a view of themselves through the eyes of a servant.

A. O. C.

VIII

"All the News That's Fit to Print"

In describing the state of ethical practices in the journalism of his time, Irwin at first reading seems almost quaint. The exemption from publicity of the genteel class, even the existence of such a class, may seem today to be curiosities from the past. But the article foreshadows a number of developments which have come on strongly during the ensuing half-century. Right of privacy questions, the tabloid tastelessness of the 1920s, the efficaciousness of publicity in deterring law violation, codes of ethics seeking to professionalize journalists, and propriety of certain kinds of presumably antisocial news have become strong elements under today's general heading of social responsibility of the press.

"The newspaper should be a gentleman," Irwin writes. How simple, how Victorian that sounds. Perhaps there is no more precise code of behavior than this. Irwin could find none; and the motto of the New York *Times,* which he took for the title of his article, still stands today. Irwin the muckraker realized, however, that the concept was not nearly so simple in practice. "It is never gentlemanly to knock a man down," he adds, "but sometimes a gentleman must do it." The ethics of the press certainly have received much attention in the past fifty years, but the question still is open whether there has been progress in the moral state of the press, any more than in any other segments of society.

The American Newspaper

A Study of Journalism in Its Relation to the Public

By WILL IRWIN

VIII.—"All the News That's Fit to Print"

The present article deals with the ethics of news and news-writing. It points out the danger of too great delicacy in telling the scandalous truth, and the equal danger of too little delicacy. It discusses the question of private right as opposed to public curiosity and suggests the formula—"a newspaper, like the man who owns it, should be a gentleman." Finally, the author shows that there is an ethical code which governs all good reporters

THE St. Cecilia Society, oldest social organization in the United States, comes near to governing Charleston, South Carolina, citadel of venerable Southern manners. It does absolutely govern "polite society" in Charleston. He—or she—who belongs to the St. Cecilia is "in"; all others are "out." Wealth, power, and social position all group together, even in Charleston, which professes to set blood above all the other social qualifications. It follows that the class of people who create most of the best news, as modern journalism defines news, belong to this circle.

Charleston gentility has in its unwritten code an article concerning newspapers. It crystallizes that sentiment of Southern chivalry which Henry Watterson expressed when, in his criticism of American journalism, he made transgression of private right the main indictment against our press. Journalism must keep its hands off a gentleman. When he gets into public affairs—as when his bank changes management—he will tolerate brief and pleasant mention. But the reporter must not move a step beyond the borders of his home. The newspaper must not mention his wife, his daughter, or his guest. The St. Cecilia publishes, at the beginning of each season, a one-inch advertising notice of its assemblies. Further, this, the most important institution in Charleston, must not be mentioned in type. No social disturbance is so violent as to drag the name of a St. Cecilia woman into print. "What would happen," I once asked a Charlestonian, "if a young woman of the St. Cecilia set should elope with her father's coachman?" "In the first place," he answered, "it would not happen, sir. In the second, it would not be printed—not if the editor valued his standing in the community." The Pinckney murder strained these ethics to the breaking-point. Thomas Pinckney, Jr., was secretary of the St. Cecilia. He had called on a young woman and started home; the next thing seen of him was when a neighbor heard a pistol shot, and found him sitting on the pavement, wounded unto death. He died without telling who did it, and the case remains a mystery.

How Charleston Handled the Case

NO SUCH news had "broken" in Charleston since the war. The press bureaus sent columns of fact and conjecture to the remote corners of the country. The city talked of nothing else. In face of that the local papers could not quite keep silence. They published, British fashion, just what came out in the coroner's inquest—no more. Of late, one Charlestonian newspaper has kept up a society column, differing from similar departments in Northern newspapers in the fact that real "society," as viewed by Charleston, does not appear therein. In fact, reporters and editors keep lists on their desks of the St. Cecilia members and their families, lest they transgress the unwritten law.

Cut off from most of the local matter which feeds Northern journals, the "News and Courier" and "Post" have let their power flow into the editorial page, precisely as did the old newspapers in the period before Bennett discovered news. In no small city is there a pair of more able editorial writers than Major J. C. Hemphill—just now, after twenty years in Charleston, transferred to Richmond—and Thomas Waring. Further, the journalist occupies a position of personal power and high esteem. To take on full dignity, a public meeting must have an editor on the platform.

This system protects a class and not the mass. That is the first and most obvious criticism. Mr. Biddle of the St. Cecilia keeps his daughter's suicide, his son's wild escapade, out of the newspapers; little Giuseppe Baccigalupi can not claim like immunity.

The reporter may be a servant of truth, dragging evil to the light—

Or he may be this

Two Methods with News
Cartoons by Art Young

But suppose the system were universally applied, to Mr. Baccigalupi as well as Mr. Biddle? Suppose we carried it to other cities, larger than Charleston, and without the private system of social regulation which she has brought over from the ante-bellum period? Would it be best for society as a whole were this to become a universal rule?

Before we try to answer that, let us take another example and put another question. The New York "Evening Post" has stood for half a century as an exemplar and model to a certain kind of American journalist. Godkin, whose soul goes marching on in its pages, had the highest professional ideals. He believed in journalism as a mission and a trust. His idea of journalistic technique was modified British. He kept out of his pages scandals and most events which disgraced the individual. In one period the "Post" never mentioned murders at all. Now it usually keeps them down to paragraphs. By little more space than a bare paragraph it reported even the Thaw murder, which filled pages next morning in all the other New York dailies. In its treatment of polite society, it approximates the Charlestonian standard, only it draws no line between the Biddles and the Baccigalupis. What of such an attitude toward the news? Could this also, with best result for the commonwealth, become a universal rule?

Yes, if legislation were the only regulator of society, if man were made for the laws and not the laws for man. But law is only the last resort in creating and preserving social order. Without it has stood always public opinion, the legislator, judge, and jury, and gossip the executioner, furnishing an extra-judicial regulation of offenses which the slow, formal law can not reach. Gossip, it is true, was a cruel and capricious executioner, striking down the innocent with the guilty, blasting and slaying often at the caprice of a wicked tongue. The newspaper, which has absorbed and made systematic many things that went by rule of thumb in cruder stages of society, has generally taken over this legislative power of public opinion, this executive power of gossip. We are good not only through love of God and fear of the law, not only because it pays to be good, but also because we are afraid of publicity.

The Power of Gossip

"IT WILL all be in the papers!" is the first baleful afterthought of his family when the criminal is arrested. In assuming this higher function of gossip, journalism has made it not only systematic, but also somewhat responsible. The printed word remains. The written law provides remedy for both slander, which is false detraction by word of mouth, and libel, which is false detraction by word of print; but libel is more easily proved than slander. So, while this public gossip gets a larger audience than the fireside gossip, it is forced to be much more accurate, much nearer the truth.

I state a platitude when I say that government by the people is the essence of democracy. In theory, the people watch and know; when, in the process of social and industrial evolution, they see a new evil becoming important, they found institutions to regulate it or laws to repress it. They can not watch without light, know without teachers. The newspaper, or some force like it, must daily inform them of things which are shocking and unpleasant in order that democracy, in its slow, wobbling motion upward, may perceive and correct. It is good for us to know that John Smith, made crazy by drink, came home and killed his wife. Startled and shocked, but interested, we may follow the case of John Smith, see that justice in his case is not delayed by his pull with Tammany. Perhaps, when there are enough cases of John Smith, we shall look into the first causes and restrain the groggeries that made him momentarily mad or the industrial oppression that made him permanently an undernourished, overnerved defective. It is good to know that John Jones, a clerk, forged a check, and went to jail. For not only shall we watch justice in his case, but some day we shall watch also the fraudulent race-track gambling that tempted him to theft. If every day we read of those crimes which grow from the misery of New York's East Side and Chicago's Levee, some day democracy may get at the ultimate causes for overwork, underfeeding, tenement crowding.

No other method is so forcible with the public as driving home the instance which points the moral. General description of bad conditions fails, somehow, to impress the average mind. One might have shouted to Shreveport day after day that low dives make dangerous negroes, and created no sentiment against saloons. But when a negro, drunk on bad gin which he got at such a dive, assaulted and killed Margaret Lear, a schoolgirl, Shreveport voted out the saloon.

The Regulator of Society

So far I have mentioned only instances which come within the formal law. Over those offenses which violate the spirit of social order and yet break no statute, the newspaper, in its news-function, is even more powerful. Divorce, for example. Though views on the basic morality of divorce differ widely, the better part of our public believes that the application of the law, if not the law itself, is too lax; and certain divorces obtained within the law are shameful from any point of view. He or she who sets about to get such a divorce knows that the fact itself and, most likely, the underlying causes, will get into the newspapers. In all circles is the man or woman restrained from divorce not by religion nor kindness nor respect for the ultimate ends of social order, but just by fear of public opinion—a public opinion informed and guided through the newspapers. This power which helps keep the submerged tenth from picking and stealing also keeps the exalted hundredth from excessive vices, vanities, and follies. And it can not do this if it follow the Charlestonian rule of journalism nor yet the "Evening Post" rule. The question which I asked in the beginning answers itself: it would not be best for democracy were these to become universal rules.

In the case of the "Evening Post," one may argue that it is a class organ, not a popular one; that it looks for its limited circulation to people of education and culture, capable of abstract thinking; and that general statement of civic and social evils is enough to keep them vigilant. On the contrary, few even of this exalted class are so much moved by abstract theory as by concrete example. And these people, furthest removed from the scenes of disorder, are most in need of information. A blind, careless "upper class," with a prettified view of the world, may be a pleasant thing to artistic contemplation. It is not a good symptom for democracy. The New York woman who boasts that she has never been south of Fourteenth Street nor east of Fourth Avenue in her life is nearly as dangerous to our ultimate aims as the very criminal. One must write from a point of view; from my point of view this very overrefinement of the "Evening Post," this stretching of decency, is the great flaw in a newspaper which is otherwise almost a model of ethics.

Yet, after all these concessions, the fact remains that Watterson has right on his side. Ever since Bennett entered the field, our newspapers, an uncontrolled power, have continually trampled on the right of privacy. Even when they have served the ends of higher justice, they have generally done it not with those ends in view, but with the sole object of ministering to curiosity. This indictment holds, of course, chiefly against the sensational and yellow newspapers. They have published, for the purpose of gratifying unhealthy curiosity, the very things which we consider scandal and unfair gossip when uttered by word of mouth. Through those means of extracting information which are part of a newsgatherer's craft, they have worried intimate private details from reluctant witnesses. While the suicide lay newly dead in the chamber, the reporters have bullied and brow-beaten the family in the hall. Going further toward the depths, certain yellow newspapers have habitually approached actual crime in news-gathering methods. Stealing from wastebaskets, prying open desks, taking photographs from the wall when left alone in the reception-room, impersonating coroner's deputies—all this stands against the account of yellow journalism.

Within the law, but without all rules of good taste and seemly conduct, are other habitual yellow methods. I have known the whole family of a "star" criminal, nay, the very criminal himself, to draw a salary from a newspaper from the day he was arrested to the day of his execution. The salary was earned by giving up exclusive information and an intimate view of family affairs. I have known a police reporter to apply third-degree methods to a woman until he drove her into hysterics. I am acquainted with a man who owed his position on a newspaper solely to his skill in obtaining photographs by stealth. These methods, it is true, are all employed by detectives; and the law yields to detectives the right to use them. But the supplementary law which the newspaper enforces is not so well recognized that we yield the same right to reporters and editors.

Further, the addition of intimate details imagined by reporter or "rewrite man" was a regular method of yellow journalism in its wildest days. These imaginations almost always hurt; usually they made the subject of the story seem ridiculous and cheap. Knowing how far to go was one of the tricks.

Harmless Libel Laws

Libel is a curious law in its practical application. Few others fail so signally in accomplishing their object. For the most sensitive, and therefore the most deeply injured, are the least people to bring suit. They fear not only the appearance in court, but also the raking over of their private affairs, the resurrection of their family skeletons, by which the yellow journal often replies to a libel suit. In fact, those who demand and recover libel damages are usually those least damaged.

I have known an all-round criminal to get a ten-thousand-dollar award because a newspaper called him an "ex-convict," whereas he had simply served in the House of Detention. Few of our editors have ever been convicted for criminal libel. Yet one who nearly went to jail, and did pay a fine, merely committed the error of slipping an unproved crime into the record of a "crooked" saloon-keeper whose dive was a center for municipal corruption and gang-rule—a man whom the editor was fighting from the high motive of reforming city politics. Laws will hardly serve to correct this abuse.

Now there must be a line somewhere between refusing to cast light on dark places and walking over human rights. Neither you nor I, nor yet any editor who ever lived, can draw that line exactly. The fact is that it comes down to a matter of personal conduct. The newspaper, like the man who makes it, should be a gentleman. No one is able exactly to say what a gentleman is, though every one thinks that he knows a gentleman when he sees one. For manners are an art, not a code.

The Golden Rule of Journalism

I have compared a newspaper to a highly organized, highly specialized gossip. A gentleman, setting out to investigate the affairs of his village and relate them to his neighbors, would know what is fair and decent to repeat and what to keep secret as of no real importance; what questions he should ask in getting his information and what he should not ask. No other rule guides those newspapers which approximate the motto of the New York "Times"—"All the news that's fit to print."

And no other rule guides the best reporters—such men as the corps of Washington correspondents—who are bringing their craft from low esteem to something like professional standing.

In character, as in efficiency, the man who "works the street" has improved greatly during this generation—that in spite of the yellow flood. Journalists do not blink the fact that this department sprang from bad beginnings. The typical reporter of Bennett's generation, who hammered the news-cog into the world-machine, was not an exalted human being. O. Henry's Jeff Peters describes the older type—"Reporters always pull out a pencil and tablet on you, and tell you a story you've heard, and strike you for the drinks." Atterbury, Jeff's accomplice, adds: "A man about half shabby, with an eye like a gimlet, smoking cut plug, with dandruff on his coat collar, and knowing more than Shakespeare and J. P. Morgan put together." Typically, he was shabby within and without, a disrespecter of all persons, a grafter of small privileges such as theater tickets and railroad passes, frequently dissipated, almost always "bohemian." Indeed, an ancient trade superstition taught that the most brilliant man was

The Truth and John Billington

From the Newark (N. J.) Evening News, December 30, 1909

JOHN BILLINGTON was a leader of thought in a city proud and great,
And Billington's busy goose-quill was a pillar in the State,
And Billington's fame had borne his name to the country's furthest ends.
A powerful man was Billington, with powerful men for friends.

A SPIRIT stood by Billington's bed, one howling wintry night,
And Billington lifted a startled head and stared at the Thing in White.
"Away with you! To the devil with you!" he gasped, in a sleepy dread.
"You have sent me thither a thousand times; I am tired of the trip," it said;
"A thousand times you have heard me pray for half a chance and the light,
A thousand times you have turned me away—you shall hear me out to-night.
Though you waved me away with your pen to-day, you shall listen now, forsooth;
You shall harken well to the tale I tell. I am the Spirit of Truth."

A PHANTOM picture flashed in air at the foot of Billington's bed,
And Billington gazed with mild amaze, and his eyes grew big in his head.
He looked at a home of poverty. He saw a dying child.
He saw a young girl, sunk in shame, and a mother who never smiled;
A son bowed down and sullen, bearing the brand of a thief,
And a father hopeless and helpless, too sodden with rum for grief.
And over the picture, in letters of fire, "Want" was the word he read,
And Billington scowled to the Spirit. "What business of mine?" he said.

HE looked and saw where, overtime, women and children toiled
Till worthless human hands grew weak and precious goods were spoiled.
He saw a boss with ugly eyes threaten a woman there
Whose hollow cheek foretold too well the end of her struggle and care.
Again he looked, and he saw the death in a driven workman's face,
While a hungry man stood waiting near to enter the empty place.
He turned once more to the Spirit of Truth, and "Bother your show!" said he;
"Scenes like this are common enough. What do they mean to me?"

"LOOK again," spoke the Spirit of Truth, and spread before his eyes
A smiling land of abundance that stretched to the circling skies,
A land o'erheaped with richness, a kingdom of corn and wine,
Where bounty waited, enough for all, in forest and field and mine.
But cunning and craft had seized the wealth with greedy talon and claw
And set it aside for their private gain, and fenced it round with the Law.
"Look well," the Spirit commanded, and Billington answered flat,
"A threadbare subject, my shadowy friend. Where is a story in that?"

"GOD pity your stubborn blindness, man, and forgive you the chance you miss!
Away with your dead traditions! Is there never a story in this,
That Greed would garner the harvest, leaving the owner gaunt;
That the servants would sell to the master and thrive on the master's want?"
Then Billington spoke of property rights and of customs hoar and old,
And argued his dread of a flag blood-red that would rise if the Truth were told.
"Oh, fool!" the Spirit in anguish cried, "must history make it clear
That yours is the hand that sows the seed of the pestilence you fear?

"FOR ages long I have striven and toiled to free mankind from wrong,
I have pleaded and prayed for human aid to save the weak from the strong,
I have starved and fought and watched and wrought that the light might enter in
To end the sway of falsehood and banish the curse of sin.
And men have gone to the stake for me, and scorched in the cannon's breath,
And women have writhed in the torture and welcomed the arms of death
That the Truth might live to serve the world—and then, when the fight seemed won,
I gave the standard to you to guard—to you, John Billington!

"I TRUSTED you with my work to do, I gave you a charge to keep,
I placed in your hand a shepherd's staff to comfort my hunted sheep.
But now you turn it against me, and the Truth must go untold
While you devote your stewardship to the will of the power of gold,
To the pleasure of those who burden the poor, to the greed that fosters crime,
Oh! turn you again, John Billington; be true while there yet is time.
For this is the cry of a thousand souls that down to the Pit have trod—
Who keeps the Truth from the people stands in the way of God!"

BUT Billington slowly shook his head with a look disconsolate,
For his was a mighty goose-quill, a pillar strong in the State,
And his was a fame that had borne his name to the country's furthest ends.
A powerful man was Billington—with powerful men for friends.

LEONARD H. ROBBINS

he who drank most. Only recently have executives insisted on temperance as a practical virtue in reporters. Following the most romantic and adventurous craft which modern industry knows, he looked on public privilege and private rights as most adventurers do.

Perhaps it was the university man who changed all this. Greeley used to announce profanely that he would not have a college graduate in the basement—not if he knew it. Most of his colleagues held with him. But in the seventies the Bachelors of Arts began to invade newspaper offices, in the eighties they arrived in numbers, and in the nineties they took the profession unto themselves. Guessing roughly, I should say that half of the reporters on our metropolitan newspapers and three-quarters of the editors, are now college or university men. Is it intellectual snobbery to say that the university man in bulk brings to his work not only a better equipped mind, but a finer sense of personal conduct? Then, too, with the organization of news as a force in society appeared a conviction that writing for a daily paper is a worthy career. The older generation held differently; still under the belief that the power of the press must reside in editorial opinion, the great editors regarded news-gathering as a necessary nuisance. They looked down on their reporting staffs—and picked their men accordingly.

The Code of Ethics

NOW, strangely, these men at the bottom of the profession—if we measure standing by salary and public esteem—have come nearest of all American journalists to forming a professional spirit and formulating an ethical code. Not all reporters hold that code, of course, but the best, the directing journalists of to-morrow, do. These are its main articles:

First—Never, without special permission, print information which you learn at your friend's house, or in your club. In short, draw a strict line between your social and professional life. The journalist must keep such a line if he is to be anything but a pariah. The layman generally does not understand this. The remark, thrown at him across a dinner-table, "Of course, this is not for publication," offends the very young reporter; later, iteration breeds indifference.

Second—Except in the case of criminals, publish nothing without full permission of your informant. The caution, "But this is not for publication," stands between every experienced reporter and a world of live, sensational matter. As a rule, reporters and their directing editors abide by this article of the code to the last item. It is a question not so much of morals as of convenience. In news-gathering, acquaintance is half the battle. (*Concluded on page 30*)

The Latest in Alaska

Controller Bay and Its Control of the Alaskan Situation

By M. F. ABBOTT

ON JANUARY 28 COLLIER'S published an editorial in which it quoted a certain opinion to this effect: "Although the people of Alaska do not know to whom they ought to be thankful for their deliverance from the clutches of the Guggenheims, they know that theirs was a narrow escape." It then added: "Have they escaped? It is not yet time to sleep."

Was COLLIER'S correct in that warning?

On April 20 Robert M. La Follette introduced in the Senate of the United States the following resolution:

"*Resolved*, That the Secretary of the Interior be, and is hereby, directed to transmit to the Senate a list of all claims, locations, filings, or entries made upon lands withdrawn from the Chugach National Forest in Alaska, and restored to the public domain by the executive order of October 28, 1910 (No. 1260), giving the date of each claim, location, filing, or entry, and the name of the person or persons who made the same, and any and all action taken thereon, and if soldiers' additional homestead scrip was used in acquiring any right therein, to give the name of the soldier to whom each scrip certificate so used was issued, the amount of land taken under such certificate, and the name of each claimant or entryman who used the scrip certificate. Also what, if any, assignments of any such claims, locations, filings, or entries have been made, and to whom?"

The questions lying behind Senator La Follette's resolution were various. For instance:

Why in this case did the President use the executive order and not the usual public form of proclamation?

Why did practically no one even in the Forestry Service know about the executive order?

Who is the Richard Ryan at whose instance the President took this step?

Were Mr. Roosevelt and Mr. Garfield justified in taking the protective measures which Mr. Taft so quietly and conclusively overturned?

These are the essential questions which will perhaps for a long time have to be thrashed out. The answers to them may come too late to keep Controller Bay from passing to the Morgan-Guggenheim interests, but they will even then be worth answering, because the whole future of Alaska is still undecided.

Look at this map. The numbers 1, 2, 3, and 4, on the right-hand side, indicate the four most important groups of coal claims. Along the coast are seen three bays—Cordova on the west, next Katalla Bay, and, lastly, Controller Bay. *These three bays form the only possible outlets to tide-water—the only practicable shipping terminals for the coal, Cordova requiring too long a haul* (see sworn testimony of Stephen Birch before the Investigating Committee; Record, page 2148), *and Katalla having been proved impracticable after the Morgan-Guggenheim syndicate had spent one million dollars on a terminal plant there, only to have it washed away by the sea.* (See sworn testimony of same Birch, the managing director of the Morgan-Guggenheim syndicate; Record, pages 2150-5.)

The coal lands, a water-front on Controller Bay (see map), and a railroad between, therefore, constitute the three factors of the Alaska coal industry. Under the Roosevelt Administration the coal lands were all withdrawn from entry; the Controller Bay country was included in the Chugach National Forest; special agents (Louis R. Glavis and others) were borrowed by the Land Office from the Secret Service to watch developments; plans were made to resist the growth of monopoly and lock up the country temporarily until the Government could have a chance to mature its own plans for development. There were those in the Administration who believed that such sources of life as coal should not be given for nothing and forever, and that some form of leasing should be established in place of permanent alienation.

Coal Claims—1, Christopher-Simonds group, consisting of 77 claims, indicted for fraud; 2, English or Stracey group with 39 Claims. There are indictments against this group, but a decision adverse to the Government was rendered by Judge Hanford in March, 1911; 3, Cunningham group, 33 claims. NO indictments against this group; 4, Greene-White group, consisting of 130 claims, with indictments against them. ------ Proposed railroad from Chilkat, on Controller Bay, to the coal claims. Three railway lines are planned over this route—the Lippy-Davis, Cunningham, and Greene-White

Area eliminated from Chugach National Forest, around Controller Bay, by executive order, October 28, 1910

The Ballinger-Pinchot investigation showed that the time had come to decide on a comprehensive policy.

The key to the situation was the ownership or control of the coal land and the water-front of Controller Bay.

If before Congress should have a chance to act the title to any of these lands should become alienated, how would that alter the situation?

The Cunningham claims have not passed to patent, but a strategic site has been eliminated from the Chugach National Forest on the shores of Controller Bay.

Among other invitations to obtain land from the Government is that of the elimination of lands within a National Forest. They are being made every day under the act of June 4, 1897. But there are eliminations and eliminations. It has been the custom and general practise of this Administration and the last Administration to eliminate from National Forests by proclamation and not by executive order. Proclamations are of one sort, public in character; executive orders may be either private or public in character. It is incumbent upon the President to decide which shall be the method employed.

Mr. Taft having signed, between July 1 and January 1, some forty-six proclamations of eliminations from National Forests, and having proclaimed them in the usual way, *why should an exception be made in this lone case of elimination from the Chugach?*

Now the question of the final disposition of Controller Bay may be answered by the reader as his experience and his sense of humor shall dictate. He should realize that Mr. Ryan, who induced the President to take this remarkable procedure, has been a well-known factor in Morgan-Guggenheim development.

As to the coal claims, which are so closely related to the railroad situation, a very important question is now before the United States Supreme Court on an appeal from the ruling of District Judge Hanford at Seattle, made on April 4, quashing the indictments against members of the Stracey or English group of claims. Judge Hanford is a well-known opponent of the whole conservation movement. The appeal is likely to be argued before the Supreme Court within a few days. If the decision is favorable to the contention of the Government, all of the six hundred and forty coal land entries in Alaska, covering land valued at more than one billion dollars, will be canceled. If the decision is the other way, some of the claimants will receive patents and others will not.

The Morgan-Guggenheim Syndicate owns outright, controls, or has an interest in the following named companies, *among others:*

Northwestern Commercial Company, Northern Commercial Company, Northwestern Development Company, Katalla Company, North Coast Lighterage Company, Northwestern Fisheries Company, Kennicott Mine Company, Yukon Gold Company, Yukon Coal Company, Alaska Steamship Company, Alaska Central Railway Company, Seward Peninsula Railway Company, Alaska Steamship and Railway Company, Copper River Railway Company, Copper River and Northwestern Railway Company.

When Stephen Birch, managing director of the Morgan-Guggenheim Syndicate, was before the Ballinger-Pinchot Investigating Committee, March 25, 1910 (see Record, pages 2123-2214), Representative Madison said:

"So that they have gone into the coal business up there, and they have gone into the copper business, and they have gone into the fisheries business; they have the biggest steamship line running there; they have control, either directly or indirectly, of the only two railroads that are actually operated or capable of being operated; and the whole business, boiled down, means a great big plan and scheme upon the part of that Alaska syndicate *to control and maintain and own a very large portion of Alaska and its industries.*"

Mr. Birch—That is your inference.

Mr. Madison—But from the evidence can any intelligent man draw any other conclusion? (See Record, page 2192.)

The American Newspaper

(Concluded from page 19)

A man once betrayed goes forever off your calling list; continue the process, and you lose all acquaintance. Politicians, popular clergymen, police officials, and others who have daily contact with reporters understand this working agreement. The Washington corps has called Theodore Roosevelt "the greatest journalist of us all." He showed this in his confidences to the newspaper men. Again and again he told the reporters, at his daily interviews, the whole secret of a blind event. "This is for your own information. Don't print it until I tell you," he would say. And wo to the wight who did it! Seldom was Roosevelt betrayed, and then only on minor points.

Not only convenience holds good reporters to this article of faith, but also real sense of morals. I know a reporter who was ostracized for years by his fellows because he published matter after the admonition of secrecy from his informants. The breaking-point came when seven men from as many newspapers went to interview a politician under fire. He gave them the formal news, and later the story of his private relation to the event. "But you won't print *that*, of course," he added. "Oh, no!" responded all the reporters except this one. He published it; the story was a fine beat. "You didn't notice that I didn't say 'No,'" he said in extenuation. This read him out of the craft.

"Keyhole Reporting" Taboo

THIRD—Never sail under false colors. State who you are, what newspaper you represent, and whether or no your informant is talking for publication. If there is keyhole work to be done, leave that to the detectives, who work inside the law.

Fourth (and to Henry Watterson, the cardinal article in the code)—Keep this side of the home boundary. Remember that when the suicide lies dead in the chamber there are wretched hearts in the hall, that when the son is newly in jail intrusion is torment to the mother. Nearly all reporters who expect to remain in the business respect articles one and two. Articles three and four most of them would like to respect. They can not do so, however, without permission of their directing editors and of the publisher, a court of last resort. Half the reporting staffs are forced to do distasteful things because the publisher needs the news and does not care how the mere agent gets it. Yet with the passing of yellow journalism, and the contemporaneous passing of the craze for beats, publishers begin to see that enlightened self-interest may demand observance of even these articles. The reporter is, to the plain citizen, the visible representative of his newspaper. A violated home becomes a hostile home; and certain journals owe their special facilities for news-getting to the decency and acceptability of their reporters. There are city editors as scrupulous about the methods of their men as any reporter could wish. On the New York "Sun" and "Post," the Kansas City "Star," the Chicago "Post," the Boston "Transcript," and the Washington "Star," the reporter who presented information plucked from a waste-basket, or bullied from a woman at the back door, would be presenting an application for discharge. Most of these newspapers have their shortcomings; in some, the vices may be more harmful to the body politic and social than any lapse in manners. But they do insist on decent relations between the reporter and his public.

The Limits of Gentility

THE newspaper should be a gentleman—such is the whole formula. However, some arbiter of manners has said: "It is never gentlemanly to knock a man down, but sometimes a gentleman must do it, nevertheless." When the law is not the regulator of society but its disturber, not the protector of the weak but the bulwark of the brutal strong, then the newspaper, chief expression of public opinion, becomes agent of a justice higher than formal law. Justice is grim business; its processes from arrest to execution are not pretty. And in such a fight as that with the Quay gang in Philadelphia or Tammany in New York, a few breaches of mere manners count for little beside the ultimate object. When Watterson made his criticism of our press, several American editors expressed themselves in approval or opposition. Ernest S. Simpson, editor of the San Francisco "Call," stated the other side:

"It is a well-recognized function of American journalism," he said, "to play the part of an electric light in a dark alley. The light exposes ugliness, and until it is exposed ugliness will not be cleaned up. The people who most fear publicity talk most of sensational journalism. Let Colonel Watterson take care that he is not charged hereafter with trying to turn off the electric light in the dark alley."

IX

The Advertising Influence

For Will Irwin, the muckraker very much committed to notions common to most of the writers who formed that movement, it was essential to be alert for and to pinpoint a *bête noire* of the newspaper industry. If the beast existed, it was the undue influence of advertisers on the editorial content of newspapers. In this article Irwin cites numerous examples of instances where large advertisers were able to play off one paper against another under threat of withholding advertising or granting larger contracts. Do such attempts at influencing news coverage occur today? Undoubtedly they do; but undoubtedly, too, they are far less widespread than once they were. The main reason has to do with the strengthened economic position of the sole survivor in the one-newspaper town, and reflects perhaps the chief strength of the monopoly situation. Today, instead of the newspaper desperately needing its advertisers in order to survive, the roles are reversed. Radio and television cannot carry by themselves the entire advertising program of a large department store or a supermarket chain. The newspaper, with its extra sections on Thursdays and before holidays, is considered essential. Both publisher and advertiser recognize this, and the newspaper's position is stronger for it.

Two important developments affecting the newspaper occurred within two years after 1911. Irwin writes of the ethical practice followed by reputable publishers of clearly distinguishing matter inserted by advertisers from editorial matter. The postal act of 1912 made this practice law as one of its requirements for obtaining second-class mailing privileges. The law also required publication twice a year of a sworn statement of ownership, management, and circulation. Many publishers vigorously opposed this law as an infringement on a free press. In some cases, it has subsequently become clear, publishers were falsifying circulation claims in order to charge advertisers higher rates. This aspect of the situation Irwin does not go into, though he must have been aware of it. In 1913 the Audit Bureau of Circulations was established by advertisers, advertising agents, and publishers for the purpose of certifying newspaper circulations. These two events, passage of the law and formation of the ABC, did much to put the advertiser-newspaper relationship on a sounder footing.

The American Newspaper

A Study of Journalism in Its Relation to the Public

By WILL IRWIN

IX.—The Advertising Influence

In this article begins a discussion of the influences which hamper free journalism in the United States. It describes the system of publication through which the advertiser, not the reader, pays for the newspaper. By the example of Boston, a city of fairly high journalistic ideals, it proves that the constant demands of these advertisers for special favors may weaken the use and influence of the press. The next article will discuss the advertiser's side of the question

FROM these last ten years of so-called muck-raking we have evolved a phrase—"the system." Like most new phrases, it has behind it meaning and history. In the complex organization of modern society grow large and rooted injustices, often the fault of no one man, at worst the fault of only a few. The agents of these systems may be above the ordinary in private virtue. They are but operatives, each tending, oiling, and repairing one little wheel in a great machine. Or, if they work directly and personally for evil, as does the ward boss in a political system, they may do it without any searing of the inner soul. They found the system at their birth into affairs; they absorbed it with their business education; they have never seen it through virginal eyes. The modern specialization of industry beats souls into tortured forms, as it does minds and bodies.

The main handicap on American journalism in its search for truth, in its presentation of that truth to its times, is precisely such a system. And, curiously, this one—unlike the Wall Street system, the Standard Oil system, or the system of ward politics—did not owe its inception to moral turpitude on the part of its founders. No Rockefeller or Gould, Quay or Croker, built it up; on the contrary, it grew from the editorial and business policy not only of the ruthless Bennett and Hearst, but of the conscientious Greeley and Medill. It arose with the growth of the times; but it is no less a perplexity and a danger.

The Advertiser Pays

THE "system" in the American newspaper proceeds from the fact that the subscriber, who buys the newspaper that it may teach him about his times and fight his battles against privilege, is not paying for that newspaper. *The advertisers are paying*—about one per cent of the population, and often the very one per cent united, in the present condition of American society, with the powers most dangerous to the common weal.

That, however, is not quite the taproot of the trouble. The American newspaper has become a great commercial enterprise. A million dollars—yard-stick of big business—seems like a pauper's purse beside the fictitious or actual value of many metropolitan journals. The possibilities of profit and loss vary between the Chicago "News'" net earnings of $800,000 per annum and the $400,000 dropped in one year to establish a new kind of journalism in Boston. Men and companies controlling such funds look at business in the business way. It has followed inevitably that the controlling head of most newspapers, the so-called publisher, is not an editor with the professional point of view, but a business man. When the American Newspaper Publishers' Association meets in national convention, it does not discuss methods of news-gathering nor editorial problems. The addresses treat of the price of white paper, of new machinery, of organization for extending circulation, of the advertising rate.

The old "sixpenny" newspaper, which flourished before the time of Bennett, took advertisements, though it did not really need them. Its editorial running expenses were low; it could make profits on its sales alone. From the moment when the New York "Sun" and "Herald"—now, it happens, two and three cent papers—entered the field at a price of one cent, advertising became a vital necessity. Hudson, the old newspaper historian, stops for a moment his consideration of evaporated issues to record that Bennett systematized advertising, put it on a cash basis, and established a regular corps of solicitors. He had to do it in order to live. So did the old editors of high purpose who followed him. For after Day and Bennett cheapened the price on the street, the six-cent metropolitan newspaper departed this life. Only New Orleans and the Pacific Coast held to a price even as high as five cents—New Orleans because it proceeds in everything by ways of its own, the Pacific Coast because it would not recognize a coin smaller than a nickel. The Cincinnati "Enquirer" is the one subexception to this rule. One or two cents became the law; and the drift was toward the smaller price. Within six months all the Chicago newspapers have dropped to one cent. True, a few publications with special clienteles hold out to this day for a higher price. The New York "Herald," for example, circulates mainly among the wealthy, easy-spending class of the lavish metropolis; so is it able to charge three cents. Yet many experts believe that greater circulation and advertising receipts, and in the end greater profits, would follow a lower sales rate. Reduction from two cents to one was the beginning of its present prosperity for the New York "Times." The New York "Evening Post" and the Boston "Transcript," three-cent newspapers, have their confessedly limited circulation among readers who do not weigh pennies. The Springfield "Republican" has been able to keep the three-cent rate because of its excellence and its place in the affection of western Massachusetts. Nevertheless, its one-cent rival across the street makes claim to nearly double its circulation.

The Presence in the Sanctum

A Change of Base

THE newspaper whose subscribers paid for it died with the birth of the news. In the period between 1850 and 1880, if the advertiser's money did not do the paying a baser influence did. For we have lost along the way one excrescence of journalism. Time was when many newspapers "took their graft" from politics, and accepted regular subsidies from candidates or central committees. Generally, though not wholly, that passed. The business became systematized. The advertiser paid. Following the law of commerce, the newspapers organized their salesmen of advertising, and sent them forth to cajole business away from their rivals. The department store arrived with its enormous contracts—sometimes $50,000 a year to one publication—and its news-advertising, liked by housewives and therefore a builder of circulation. He who got most advertising was the most successful business manager. The rush for this kind of revenue became a craze. Many merely commercial publishers seemed to forget circulation, the product which they were selling to advertisers, in the rush for customers, as though a weaver should neglect his factory and his wool-supply and look only to his sales-agency. In the eighties all were issuing such proclamations as this: "Circulation 73,000, 20 per cent above that of our nearest morning rival." By the early years of this century newspapers were bawling: "We published 554,000 inches of advertising in this period against 448,000 by our nearest rival."

Slowly at first, then with increasing momentum, advertisers learned their power. Indeed, in certain quarters, the advertising solicitors helped to teach them. For the less conscientious and solidly-run newspapers began offering comforts and immunities as a bonus to attract customers. Advertisers got into the way of asking for these special privileges; often, in communities where the newspapers were timid and mushy, for every privilege, even to dictating policies. The extent of their demands varied with the local custom of their communities.

But finally, in cities like Philadelphia and Boston, an impossible state of affairs confronted even that publisher who cared more to be an editor than a money-maker. The system had grown so set that he must make concession or fail. For if he did not, his rival would get "the business." And without "the business" he could not pay the high editorial salaries, the press bureau fees, the telegraph tolls, the heavy wages to mechanics, which first-class journalism demands. So must he cheapen product, lose circulation, and fade away.

Hardly can one blame the advertiser. His is the business view. Modern business demands mutual favors. With whom do department stores spend more of their earnings than with the publishers? Have they not, as business men, a right to ask not only slight favors but also policies favorable to their interests? And indeed we can not blame the publisher, if we concede that he is merely manufacturing a commodity, that a newspaper is just a commercial institution. In the strictest business ethics, the manufacturer holds to nothing beyond making the product which will honestly please and satisfy his purchasers. And the chief purchaser of newspaper wares is, after all, not the reader but the advertiser. This consideration, if no other, reduces to an absurdity the business attitude toward journalism: "I am manufacturing a commodity. I am responsible for turning out a sound article—no more."

The Proportion of Ad Revenue

HOW much the advertiser pays, how little the subscriber, is shown by one unit of measurement employed in the business offices. The publishers of one-cent newspapers try to make the revenue derived from subscriptions and street sales pay for the white paper on which they print. If they achieve that result, they consider that they are doing exceptionally well; if, in addition, they pay for the cost of circulation—paper-wagons and carriers—they call themselves marvels. All other expenses, as rent, the upkeep of a great mechanical plant, salaries and wages to one, two, or three hundred employees, ink, power, and incidentals, the advertiser pays. More pertinently, he pays interest and profits.

Estimating from what exact knowledge we have, I should say that the advertiser turns about three and a half to four dollars into the average metropolitan newspaper to one dollar paid by subscription and street sales. The proportion varies greatly; practically, it is always on the side of the advertiser. One New York newspaper confesses that the proportion is 9 to 1. The Scripps League has an important member which makes a profit at 2 to 1. But Scripps is a genius at newspaper economies. In New Orleans alone is the balance on the other scale. Until recently the "Times-Democrat" got nearly two dollars from sales to one from advertisers. But New Orleans is a "five-cent town," and the "Times-Democrat" charges nine dollars a year to its regular subscribers, where a one-cent Northern newspaper with a five-cent Sunday edition charges six dollars or less. Besides, New Orleans, as I have said, is a law unto herself. And the "Item," which has entered the city with new methods, more nearly approaches the Northern ratio.

News Suppression

WHAT does the advertiser ask as bonus in return for his business favor? Sometimes a whole change of editorial policy—as when the Pittsburg newspapers were forced to support a candidate for the bench chosen by the department stores; more often the insertion of personal matter of no news value in itself; most often the suppression of news harmful to himself, his family, or his business associates.

Taking one small and general example, I have never seen a story about a shoplifting case in which the name of the store was mentioned. It has occurred, I believe, in certain favored corners of the country, but not in my horizon. Usually the item reads: "In an uptown department store," "In a Fourteenth Street emporium." The department store exists for and by women; they like respectability and safety; news that criminals are at large among its counters may frighten them away. So reasons the store manager, and doubtless he is right. 'Tis but a small favor to a customer, the denaturing of such news. Publishers who show considerable backbone concerning advertising control of larger policies generally grant this favor to the department stores.

Carried further, the advertiser asks, and often gets, suppression of scandals and disgraces affecting his family, or disasters injurious to his business. Here the harm begins; for if the justification for newspaper publication of scandal and disaster is the extra-judicial justice which it evokes, this is class discrimination and special privilege.

THE NEW YORK HERALD.
RODGERS & ORR BROS
EHRICH'S
EDLER'S
FURS
FURS
CLOAKS
O'NEILL & CO
PARISIAN
HAIR

THE NEW YORK HERALD.
First May Sale of White
$150,000 Worth of French and American Lingerie
GIMBEL BROTHERS

The Growth in Advertising

Above, the "Dry-Goods-Store" page of the New York "Herald" in 1875. Ehrich's, the largest advertisement, occupies three-quarters of one column. Below, a typical one-page department store advertisement in the "Herald" of 1911

For example—and a type-example at that—an elevator in Henry Siegel's Boston store came down to the first floor, behaving curiously. The operator investigated. He found the mangled and dead body of a woman—Jeanne Goulet of Marlboro, Massachusetts. How it happened no one exactly knew; it is only certain that Miss Goulet's death was an accident, not a crime. There was a good sensation. The Boston newspapers ignored the event—just as they had ignored an escalator accident in the same store a few years before. It is true that the Goulet case happened at the time of the Chelsea fire, when the newspapers were "cutting everything to the bone." But on that same day several of them carried a story about a little boy killed by a log at Dexter, Maine.

In fact, if one looks for a large general example, he can do no better than consider the present state of the Boston press. Like any one who is about to say something detrimental, I begin by stating the virtues of Boston journalism. For decency in drawing the line between silence and invasion of privacy, it is quite satisfactory. Much of it has a kind of intellectual cast which squares with Boston's best old ideals. The "Globe" satisfies the New England liking for small and pleasant personal gossip, and does it smoothly and sanely. The "Post" has taken the "Globe's" policy and supplemented it with a large view—if a somewhat sensational one—on the larger world. It has achieved the miracle of appealing to both the Back Bay and the gas-house district. The "Transcript" justly regards itself as a beacon-light of journalism. Not even the New York "Evening Post" gives more real education on the "higher life," publishes such a mass of well-written advices concerning social and intellectual movements. The "American" is least yellow, and probably most truthful, of all the Hearst evening organs.

Yet Boston has all but universally fallen into an attitude of subserviency toward the advertiser. From his first cub assignment, the typical Boston journalist has been taught that the price of journalistic silence is a two-inch advertisement. Here and there throughout the country are newspapers just as respectful to their source of revenue; but in no other city is this system so frankly accepted as a necessary part of the business. Let us see how it works in practise.

The Beer Cases

HEARST had entered Boston in 1905; was struggling, Hearst-fashion, for circulation, and he began with the best device of yellow journalism, the war on special privilege. Later, he used that sword more sparingly. At about this time Dr. Charles Harrington, an admirable health officer, turned his attention to the Massachusetts breweries. He found by analysis that much of the beer and ale sold in his State was adulterated, contrary to law, with salicylic or fluoric acid. In the course of six weeks the grand jury indicted a dozen brewery companies and many bottling-houses for this offense. It was important news, as any newspaper man knows; Hearst used it for one of his loud campaigns. But did the "Transcript" or the "Globe" or the "Post" publish the fact? They did not. Red Fox Ale, made by the Massachusetts Breweries, was on the list of indictments. Red Fox Ale had a small advertisement in the "Transcript." When the grand jury returned its finding in that case the "Transcript" published a list of the day's indictments, but omitted this highly important one. The grind of justice reached Harvard Beer, a heavy advertiser on billboards and in newspapers. Most of the other brands changed their names after the exposé; Harvard Beer decided to give up adulteration and to go on with its name and advertising.

What the "Transcript" Published

THE Harvard Brewing Company was indicted on Saturday, April 8. Most of the evening papers, including the "Transcript," ignored this important piece of news. The "Transcript" published in its issue of April 8 the fact that a workman had fallen from a tree, that an aged pauper had been found dead in bed, that the Harvard Shooting Club was about to hold a meet, but not the fact that Harvard Beer, known to every consumer of malt liquors in Massachusetts, was in peril of the law for adulteration. Neither was the fact noted on Monday, April 10. But on Tuesday, April 11, "Harvard Beer, 1,000 Pure," appeared in the pages of the "Transcript"—as a half-page advertisement. This advertisement shrunk in the issue of April 13 to three columns, in which form it continued through ten issues. But for the "American" and the "Traveler" the adulteration of Harvard Beer would have escaped the Boston public. If any other newspaper noted the fact, it concealed it in a far corner of an obscure page. I regret that this special and glaring instance, so useful in proving the rule of Boston journalism, hits the

(*Continued on page 22*)

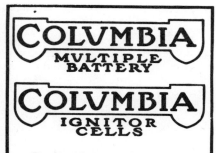

The American Newspaper

(*Continued from page 16*)

"Transcript" so hard. For in a great many instances it has been the one Boston newspaper which has shown a disposition to sacrifice advertising for news. It fell in this case, however; and this is not the only case.

The "Transcript's" Independence

THE "Transcript," indeed, has just given striking proof of its general independence. The Jordan Marsh department store is perhaps the heaviest single advertiser in Boston. In the spring of 1910 they built an annex across Avon Street from their main building; and they wanted permission for an overhead bridge connecting the two structures. By the law of Massachusetts, a municipal permit was not enough in this case; it was necessary to get a bill through the Legislature. This was not in itself a harmful measure; the bridge would have been a real convenience to the public. But the precedent was rather dangerous. Jordan Marsh, apparently, feared opposition; and they "requested" the newspapers to keep silence. The bill came up for hearing before the regular committee. The "Transcript" noticed this hearing, thereby making itself offensive to Jordan Marsh. The committee passed the bill over to the Attorney-General for an opinion on its constitutionality. He reported on March 31 that it was undoubtedly unconstitutional. Now that decision was news—first, because it denied to Boston a public convenience, and, second, because it was a precedent for other firms which wished special favors in the use of the streets. As a matter of fact, it was the most important piece of State House news on that day. The "Transcript" printed it at its news value—three-quarters of a column. One or two of the others guarded themselves by brief mention. Silence from the rest. I do not know what contracts or arrangements the "Transcript" has with the Jordan Marsh Company; but I do notice that Jordan Marsh has not advertised in the "Transcript" since early in April. Apparently the "Boston Bible" is paying for its impious presumption.

Boston went through several fights with the gas company before it got a fair rate. The company, realizing on what side its bread is buttered, is an advertiser—and it is allied with other advertisers. And the reformers, in successive battles, had to fight not only against the company and its allied interests, but against the thick, heavy silence of the newspapers —though Hearst, it is true, took their side in the last battle.

A Dollar a Line!

IT was in one of the early skirmishes that the attorneys for the people and the company introduced their arguments on the same day. Next morning most of the newspapers printed the company's argument in full, and the argument of Louis Brandeis, attorney-at-large for the people, in brief synopsis. That night a reformer, himself an advertiser and therefore a privileged person, approached a Boston publisher.

"Why don't you give us a fair shake?" he asked. "Here's seven columns of gas argument and only half a column of Brandeis's reply."

"Well, sir," replied the publisher, "I'd really like to accommodate you. But we're publishing a newspaper, and we can't make it all gas fight. The company paid a dollar a line in good money for that speech, so we just had to publish it in full; and we were forced to cut down on Mr. Brandeis."

The instances are too many for mention in detail. The following, rightly understood, are just funny:

A. Shuman, clothing dealer and philanthropist, is a liberal advertiser. He is also a director of the City Hospital. The Boston City Hospital is rather better than most; but in the best of such institutions arise from time to time cases of carelessness in diagnosis or treatment. When the "station man" reports such a case to a Boston newspaper, it goes into the waste-basket—automatically. I can not find that Mr. Shuman ever asked this favor. The trained mind of the Boston copy-reader says: "City Hospital—Shuman—Shuman — advertiser — out with this." There was a divorce in a department store family. The proceedings occurred in open court. All the reporters had access to the records, and the family did not ask to have the fact suppressed. Perhaps they reasoned, as many do in like cases, that if a marriage be made public so should its dissolution. Nevertheless, the "Traveler" alone published the fact. That month the other newspapers had dozens of divorce stories, each affecting persons of lower social position, and there-

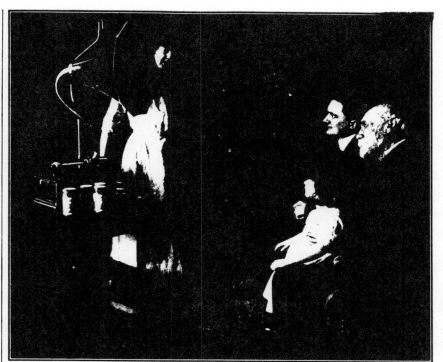

IN ANSWERING THIS ADVERTISEMENT PLEASE MENTION COLLIER'S

fore of smaller news value, than these. Again: the process was automatic, instinctive, in the mind of the Boston journalist.

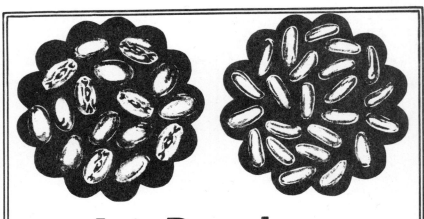

Two excellent examples came out in 1910. Mrs. Minnie M. Akers entered Houghton & Dutton's department store in the Christmas rush of 1907. She was in a delicate condition. A store detective mistook her for a shoplifter; had her detained and searched. He made a great mistake; not only did he discover no evidence, but he gave her such a shock that she all but died. She and her husband brought a suit, which came to trial on May 16, 1910, and obtained a verdict of $8,400. Now note: there were seven jury sessions going on at the time; this was in the "fourth session." It was the most important case tried in all seven sessions on that date. The "Herald" and the "Advertiser" run a court column for the benefit of lawyers—a brief synopsis of all cases. The "Advertiser" gave a three-line, colorless record of the verdict; the "Herald" dropped the case out of its record. It reported sessions one, two, three, five, six and seven, but not session four—while that case was on! When, next day, a small personal damage case came up in four, the "Herald" resumed its full report. The "Herald" was then near bankruptcy, and was inclined to eat out of every hand that dipped into gold. At this period, indeed, it put forth for the benefit of its editors a "keep-out book," listing those persons and firms who must be "extended every courtesy." But the other papers were just as subservient. For this unusual case, this heavy verdict, was fair news matter in the general columns, outside of the legal department. Had the defendant been a saloon-keeper, for example, it would have been good for an item anywhere.

Publicity and the Department Store

THE Boston "Traveler" changed management last year, after the episode of Fahey *vs.* The National Shawmut Bank, to be mentioned later. Cleveland capital bought it; Cleveland newspaper men took the management. And the Cleveland newspapers in general are fairly free from advertising control. The new editors started, apparently, with the same "square-deal-to-all" rule which Hearst followed when he invaded Boston. An ammonia tank blew up in the basement of Henry Siegel's department store at about four o'clock one afternoon last July. The "Traveler" and the "American" are the only Boston evening newspapers which publish a late "baseball extra." All the others had sent their last edition to press by four o'clock. The Hearst "American" ignored it. The "Traveler" sent a reporter. He found the condition of affairs picturesque, though not dangerous. The fumes had rolled up into the store, driving the shoppers and store-girls before them. A few of the girls had gone back for their hats; fumes had overcome them. When the "Traveler" reporter arrived, men employees were assisting them out.

The "Traveler" published this story on the front page. The morning newspapers passed it over without a line. The Associated Press sent it out. The New York newspapers proved their appreciation of its absolute value by giving it space—many on the front page. The Boston "Transcript" next afternoon showed better backbone than it did in the Harvard Beer case by printing the Associated Press story. And that was all the publicity which this "live news matter" got in Boston. In the same summer a hot bolt dropped into a barrel of tar at the Charleston Navy Yard. The barrel blazed, and the workmen heaved it overboard; whereupon the episode was closed. But that made space in all the Boston newspapers—the "American" gave it a "five-column display" on the front page. The navy does not advertise.

Another Influence

ANOTHER and more subtle influence spreads from the advertiser to asphyxiate free journalism in Boston. Before I attack that point I must digress to lay before the newspaper reader a distinction which every newspaper maker understands. If your journal is to preserve even the appearance of frankness, it must make some physical distinction between voluntary statement of the truth and paid matter. Generally, the distinction is set by the character and "face" of the type. The reader should know it at a glance, usually does know, whether this or that item is paid matter, or genuine news written untrammeled from the point of view of the reporter. The advertiser pays his tribute to the power of the press by his eagerness to get a "type-display" identical with that of the news columns. So appears the so-called "reading notice," whose price is from two to ten times that of corresponding space in advertising type. Fair newspapers generally accept such matter, but

"Ah, cook knows what *I* like!"

So exclaim all her favorites when she serves the delicious, appetizing

As they come from the can, they are whole, rich in color, and, especially when hot, laden with an aroma irresistible.

As a food, their nutritive value is very high. They are concentrated nutrition. In the process of digestion, beans are almost entirely absorbed, containing very little waste.

The smacking zest of Snider's is due to the perfect seasoning sauce, made from Snider's Tomato Catsup. The daintiest of the pork, a bit of jowl, makes them luscious.

Snider's are good food and good economy.

"It's the Process"

Try Snider's Chili Sauce upon roasts, chops, steaks, and all fish.

The T. A. Snider Preserve Co.
Cincinnati, U. S. A.

All Snider Products comply with all Pure Food Laws of the world.

"The Best of All"

THE young bride will appreciate no present so much as a Tyden Locked Dining Table. For it will be as beautiful, strong and rigid in ten years as the day it came into the new home.

THE Tyden Lock is a simple device hidden in the pedestal, which holds the halves of the pedestal tightly together preventing sag and gap. It centers the top and allows the insertion of up to three leaves without pedestal division.

YOUR dealer will gladly show you a Tyden Locked Table, as there are over sixty of the best makes so equipped. We will send on request "Tables Beautiful," a handsome little booklet that tells of table decorations for special occasions.

TYDEN LOCK

TYDEN LOCK ADV. BUREAU
661-B Monadnock Bldg., Chicago

Make Stained Glass Out of Plain Glass by using

Windowphanie

which is a thin, translucent material perfectly reproducing all the rich coloring of the most beautiful stained glass. Easily applied by anyone to ordinary windows, without removing them from the sash. Costs very little. Practically indestructible. Made in conventional patterns, also appropriate designs for any purpose. Suitable for doors, transoms, and windows in private houses, as well as in churches, hotels, etc. Send for free samples and catalog showing borders, panels, centerpieces and filling-in colors. Dealers wanted.

D. E. HALE, 19 E. 14th St., New York

state its purpose by printing at the end "Advt." or the three stars (⁂), which have come, in the perception of most readers, to mean the same thing. Between those three stars and blank space lies the difference between truth and falsehood. When he makes a "reader" appear like news, the editor adulterates his product. It may be quite harmless adulteration, as when he gives news of a millinery opening in a department store. It may be poisonous adulteration, as when newspapers here and there throughout the country publish "dollar-a-line" Smith's paid despatches lying about the situation in the corrupt insurance companies. It is always, in greater or smaller degree, a violation of the newspaper's tacit contract with its readers.

Reading Notices as a Bonus

NOW "reading notices," published without star or distinguishing mark, have been a constant source of revenue to most Boston newspapers. Boston has recently improved a little in this respect; a new law is at the bottom of the reformation. By common consent, however, the department stores still expect reading notices as a bonus. "How many readers will you give us?" asks the store advertising manager of the solicitor. Unless he desire something contrary to obvious public morals or to the newspaper's policy, any one, until recently, could insert nearly anything in most Boston newspapers at a dollar a line. The Boston Elevated, for example, wishes to make an example of conductors convicted of "knocking-down" fares. These cases are merely petty larceny; the amount of the theft is seldom more than ten or fifteen dollars; they are hardly worth the attention of a metropolitan newspaper. But until recently the Elevated Company has paid certain newspapers a dollar a line to publish these items as news. Go back and compare these ten-dollar larcenies, published in full, with the $8,400 Houghton & Dutton verdict, absolutely suppressed! If the conductors also were advertisers, doubtless their crimes would not be published—not though they stole a whole railroad.

Much mere "stuff," crowding out more valuable matter, gets into the Boston newspapers through this cringing attitude. If the management ask favors, so may the chiefs of departments. The sister-in-law of a head buyer belongs to the Little Busy Bees of the Tenth Unitarian Church, which is about to give a lawn party. The head buyer is likely to ask, and the newspaper to grant, extended advance notice of this mildly thrilling event. So, in preferred position, occupying three columns with pictures, we find the lawn party noticed, not as news, but merely as something about to happen. How much padding and "fluff" has appeared concerning the Boston Opera House only the Boston news editors know. For the department story family of Jordan is heavily interested in this philanthropic enterprise; and much of this matter comes from the press agency, not of the opera-house but of the Jordan-Marsh Company. The process is harmless adulteration—not poison, only a little water. But when it becomes too common it distorts the picture of this world which the newspaper presents its readers.

The Effect of Boston Journalism

DECENT of speech, cowardly of heart, a prophet when the cause does not touch its own pocket, a dumb thing when it does—by such journalism is Boston served. Has its half-hearted policy affected the public intelligence of its city? I believe that it has. For the social and intellectual caste of Boston is curious. The ancient New England spirit of stern virtue remains; the second generation from the fiery Abolitionists have kept their idealism, if not their fire. Boston orders its saloons closed on Sundays, and sees that they remain closed; it enforces strict decency of public conduct; it is the last American word on good taste in municipal architecture. And notice this parallel: on conventional personal morals, on merely physical municipal improvements, its newspapers are strong. In no other American city is so great a proportion of people who want to do the right thing. But they wobble ineffectually, while the gang and allied interests go straight to what they want. For in few other American cities do the people so dimly understand what is the right thing socially and politically. That the moral face of the world has changed in this generation; that the great issues are no longer political but economic; that new conditions have brought new sins—Boston as an entity knows not these things. And I for one believe that Boston is so not because she is Boston, but because her newspapers have withheld the light that never was in university or college—the light of a sane, broad, truthful point of view on the daily flow of the times.

Send for our free Portfolio of exterior color schemes, showing 15 attractive color combinations

It is always difficult to select pleasing color combinations from color cards. It is also difficult to select the paint, varnish or stain best suited to the surface it is to cover.

This Portfolio, "Color Schemes for Exterior House Painting," not only suggests many harmonious combinations, showing them in colors on actual houses, but also contains complete specifications for securing the results shown, naming the particular paint, varnish or stain which will make these pleasing results permanent.

Are you going to build, remodel or decorate?

Then you want our Portfolio, "A Cottage Bungalow," which gives the complete plans for interior decorations. Each room in the house is shown in colors, with complete specifications for producing the effects shown. Even the rugs, draperies, hangings and furniture are included.

Send for both of these free Portfolios today. You incur no obligation by doing so.

The Sherwin-Williams' Brighten Up Line is your guide in getting just the right paint, stain or varnish for all surfaces in and around your home. A booklet telling what each is, what each is for and how each is applied, sent free on request.

COVER THE EARTH

SHERWIN-WILLIAMS PAINTS & VARNISHES

Sold by dealers everywhere. Ask your local dealer for color cards and full information.
For the Special Home Decoration Service write to
The Sherwin-Williams Co., Decorative Dept., 615 Canal Road, N.W., Cleveland, Ohio

X

The Unhealthy Alliance

UNCONCERNED with anything so relatively subtle as a publisher claiming more circulation than he actually had in order to charge higher advertising rates, Irwin here documents the practice of charging advertisers for favorable news coverage. Although there is no way to discover how widespread the practice was, Irwin demonstrates that it did exist in at least two large cities, New York and Boston. Perhaps his description is somewhat extreme; doubtless the majority of American editorial writers in 1911 were incensed that Arthur Brisbane, noted for his innovations but never for his scruples, should be proposed as typifying their kind. Nevertheless, a good deal of research—from the Revolutionary period when the British subvened certain Colonial editors, to the present day, when editorial pages sometimes carry as the paper's own effort editorials written and distributed by national pressure groups—has shown conclusively that newspapermen's morals are no better than those of the citizenry at large.

In these two articles on the influence of advertising, Irwin was treating the major problem facing the mass media of the day. Even as he wrote, the trade journal *Printer's Ink* was advocating adoption of a model law to make fraudulent advertising a misdemeanor, and since that time most states have adopted some form of the law. Eventually publishers themselves adopted advertising regulations for their own papers and began to scrutinize advertising copy for truthfulness and honest presentation. Establishment in 1906 of the Food and Drug Administration, and in 1914 of the Federal Trade Commission, laid the basis for increasing government regulation in this area, and the private sector at about the same time set up better business bureaus across the country. To the extent that such efforts brought relief, muckraking articles such as Irwin's must be given a share of the credit.

The American Newspaper

A Study of Journalism in Its Relation to the Public

By WILL IRWIN

X.—The Unhealthy Alliance

This article shows that many newspapers slant or tint their editorial columns of their own accord in order to attract or to stimulate advertising; and it reveals the system once prevalent in the New York "Journal" whereby a thousand dollars would buy indirectly an editorial by Arthur Brisbane. It shows further that sound business policy as well as public weal demands a general clean-up in the advertising columns of the American newspapers. The next article, which will appear June 17, will deal with the control of newspapers by "Big Business" through the Advertiser

THE business of newspaper making is at present in the involved and disorganized condition which always follows a period of expansion. None of its perplexities is greater than this one of advertising and the relation of advertising to editorial and news policies. So far as one can draw generalizations regarding anything so involved, this rule holds: the relations between newspapers and their advertisers tend naturally to become unhealthy; and publishers of a certain commercial, get-rich-quick class are primarily to blame.

The Craze for Advertisements

THE ultimate profits of journalism—so it would appear to the shallow-minded—have lain in advertising revenue. In the decade which followed the establishment of yellow journalism the rush for advertisements became a madness. The shrewdest practical economist in the business of newspaper making once spread out for me on his study table a newspaper which, although of large circulation and good advertising patronage, was nevertheless in financial trouble. By pure arithmetic, he showed how this and that plethoric advertisement was published at apparent profit but actual loss—owing to the "overhead" cost of getting the business. "Enough advertising, you see, and the sheet would go into bankruptcy," he said. And if business sense so easily goes by the board for the pride and prestige of announcing, "We published 100,000 more inches than our nearest rival," how much more easily may journalistic ethics! "Anything to get advertising," is the tacit motto among publishers of this wildcat variety. For this they publish dangerous and obscene "medical display," containing words and ideas which the editors would not permit nor the public countenance in the news columns; for this they exploit enterprises which every man in the office, from the solicitor who takes the advertisement to the circulation manager who sends it forth, knows to be fraudulent; for this, finally, they barter the honor of their editorial staffs. And once such a publisher begins to set the pace for a city, his weaker competitors, however much they dislike it, are often forced to imitate his methods or fail.

Where Combination Fails

WE HAVE already considered the influence of the advertiser in suppressing news. I took Boston for an example. Boston is "overnewspapered." Business managers in that city must calculate closely, and they must be cautious about changes which may affect their revenue in the slightest degree. Yet even in Boston, organization among the publishers would cure the suppression habit, and cure it with ultimate financial gain and little immediate loss. The bona fide advertiser needs the newspaper as much as the newspaper needs him. In no other manner could department stores, theaters, and clothing houses reach their patrons so cheaply and so efficiently. But the business manager, real head of many modern journals, will not put the shoe on the other foot. For if he should throw away the advertising club over the news columns, he would be throwing away a weapon of competition. The newspapers can be brought together for common causes. They unite to suppress news of one another's libel suits, to bring down the price of white paper, to resist labor unions, to facilitate the means of circulation. On the policy of resistance, so necessary to free journalism, publishers have seldom united—first, because each dislikes to give up a means of beating the other, and, second, because many of them see no good reason for trying to be independent.

Brisbane's editorial on "Constructive Criticism," and C. F. Zittel, vaudeville manager

1075 HAMMERSTEIN'S TRACK

WINNERS AT A GLANCE...
1. MATHEWSON, MEYERS & TULLY
2. MACK & WALKER
3. BLACK BROS. } Dead
PRIMROSE FOUR } Heat

Selections made Monday matinee. Weather clear. Track fair. Going fair. Off at 2:15 P. M. Starter—George May. Timer—Mike Simons. Trainer—Harry Mock. Betting Commissioner—Brady Greer. Sheet Writer—Chas. Jones. Patrol Judge—Aaron Kessler. Judge—William Hammerstein.

THE SUMMARIES

Entries.	Pos.	Kind of Act.	Co.	Songs	Start.	Finish.	Bows	Ran.
Matty, Meyers & Tully.....	5	"Curves"..............	3	1	Big	Big	7	1
Mack & Walker............	4	Songs & Comedy......	2	3	Sweet	Sweet	4	2
Black Bros................	2	Banjo & Dances........	2	0	Good	Big	4	3
Primrose Four.............	9	Quartette..............	4	All	Late	Late	2	3
"The Code Book".........	8	Dramatic...............	4	0	Good	Good	3	4
Avery & Hart..............	7	Col. Comedians........	2	3	Good	Good	3	5
Van Hoven................	6	Dippy Magician........	1	0	Good	Good	2	6
Sprague & McNeece.......	1	Roller Skaters..........	2	0	Good	Good	1	7
The Salvaggis.............	3	Dancers................	5	0	Pose	Good	1	8

Any way you want to take it, Christy Mathewson, Chief Meyers & May Tully simply walked away with the show. What a great satisfaction it must be to Miss Tully after 6 weeks of hard work (with two angel face ball players) to have nothing but praise bestowed upon her act. May Tully is a big girl, and the two boys are big men, but May Tully is going to be an awfully big actress some of these days. Mack & Walker. Well, what's the use of going into ecstasies. Isn't their offering dainty? Black Bros. (only in name) can dance for my money. A delightful 12 minutes are the Black Bros. "The Code Book" is a harmless dramatic playlet, with the laurels going to Mr. Allen Arwell. The little skit will never do any harm, and at the same time will never set the world afire. (Chorus by Co.—We never intended it should.) Van Hoven is a cross between Frank Tinney and James J. Morton, but nevertheless, pleased in his offering. Primrose Four. Any time a quartette must close a show, I will apologize for them. Sprague & McNeece prettily set the pace with a neat roller skating act. The Salvaggis comprise 4 big girls and a man. The work is all done by the leading lady and the man, the other 3 salvationists could be beautifully preserved in alcohol (wood).

A sample section of "Zit's Racing Chart"

No, if we had the whole truth, we should understand that the custom of suppressing news, of slanting news policies, at the request or command of the advertiser, originated not so much with the advertiser himself as with the solicitor of the newspaper. It is easy, in the rush and competition for advertising, to fall into the habit of getting business by hinting that "the 'Bazoo' takes care of its friends." It is almost as easy for the business office, guardian of the proprietor's revenue, to cajole or drive the editors into suppressing this piece of news, abandoning that policy. Again I say: blame not the advertiser. He sees his business attacked; perhaps he sees his family on the edge of disgrace. Being human, he is not likely to consider the remote consequences to the public of this or that specific act in defense of his own. The newspapers—if not the one in immediate question, then others in the past—have given the idea that advertising brings special favors. He "puts down the screws" with sincere conviction of his rights in the matter.

To show who was usually party of the first part in this unhealthy alliance, let us take an aspect of the relations between the newspapers and the theaters in New York. From certain instances the public has gained the impression that the dailies of the metropolis are forced to trim their dramatic criticism to suit advertisers. That is not generally true of New York, although it is the case in some smaller American cities. Daily dramatic criticism in New York is shallow; but so, generally, is all American criticism, whether of the drama, literature, or art. That branch is the last to sprout on the tree of culture; it has hardly budded in America. But New York criticism is usually free from business control; most managers understand that their theatrical advertising will not buy favorable notices. Yet, on the other hand, Hearst's "Evening Journal" has of late been offering the influence of its editorial page as a bonus to theatrical advertisers—so illustrating as in cross-section where the primary responsibility frequently lies.

In Fairness to Hearst

BEFORE I proceed we must set ourselves right toward William Randolph Hearst. There is a kind of muckraking, much in vogue of late, which consists in massing all the invidious facts about a man or an institution, and, by ignoring the sense of proportion, proving what appears a black case. Such work is accurate, but not truthful. Nothing were easier than to muckrake Hearst in this fashion. He is a strange, complex creature, touched by genius if not wholly of the genius type. His acts and his influence have been as curiously mixed as his character. If he has tended to lower the tone of American news reporting, to make it more sensational and less accurate, he has also helped, more than any other man, to revive the newspaper's tribunate of the people. If in his fighting years he trampled brutally, often unjustly, upon private feelings, he also carried the standard of public rights—carried it for a time with little support. If he lowered popular taste, he also spread the great, necessary ideas among those who would never have grasped knowledge in any form other than the one he offered; he was a kind of plowman for culture. And if he was unethical, even unmoral, in many of his methods, he was also an inspirer of the larger public morals. I write this parenthetical paragraph not because COLLIER'S fears his rather ridiculous threat of arrest for criminal libel, but just that we may keep our sense of proportion. For the instance which I am about to cite to illustrate my point is one of his little tricks which can be defended only by reviewing his larger career.

Until the year 1907 the "Journal" was considered a poor "medium" for the theaters. In spite of its immense circulation, it did not reach, the managers felt, the easy-spending class of people who constitute Broadway audiences. Its theatrical advertising was, therefore, inconsiderable. On the editorial end, it had never printed any regular theatrical criticism. Late in 1907 the "Journal" determined on a new policy. Hearst transferred Ashton Stevens, a clever writer of light dramatic criticism, from the San Francisco "Examiner," and set him to work doing reviews and interviews for the "Journal." He founded a dramatic department in that newspaper; but apparently he was never a party to the remarkable harmonizing of news and advertising which followed during the next three years.

Enter "Constructive Criticism"

IN THE holiday season of 1907-1908 the New York "Journal" made two interesting departures. It published a brace of editorials on Arthur Brisbane's page, announcing a new policy regarding the theaters; and started C. F. Zittel's "Vaudeville Racing Chart." The first editorial appeared on December 13, 1907. "How to Criticize Men, Actors, Children, All Workers," was the head. The "Journal," declared this editorial, had determined to adopt a new policy—"Constructive Criticism." It would not tear down, merely to show its own cleverness, it would build up. "It is the intention of this newspaper," said Brisbane, "in criticizing books or plays to tell the public about those that are GOOD AND WORTH SEEING, and leave the others to their natural fate WITHOUT KICKING AN UNHAPPY FAILING, MAN OR WOMAN. . . . We want (our readers) to know that if they read extended criticism of a play in this newspaper, IT IS BECAUSE IT IS A GOOD PLAY AND ONE THAT, FOR REASONS STATED, WOULD AMUSE THEM OR INSTRUCT THEM. Why do we not imitate the sun, that warms, develops, and brings out what is good?" On January 8, 1908, Mr. Brisbane reiterated, saying among other things: "The criticism that encourages and stimulates good work is GOOD criticism. . . . We want, and we propose to print, only CONSTRUCTIVE CRITICISM."

On January 18, ten days later, appeared in the "Journal" the first number of "Zit's Vaudeville Racing Chart." Incidentally, we behold therein this piece of constructive criticism:

"Mlle. Agoust and Co. give one the cramps. Of all the Kosher cheese acts ever offered in vaudeville, some parts of this one should be sent to the Board of Health."

Zittel had been a press agent. His chart is simply an original method of reviewing vaudeville performances. It consists in a kind of burlesque of the regular form sheets or charts of horse-racing which appear in the sporting pages. The theaters are the "tracks," the performers the horses: and every Saturday "Zit" arranges the numbers at each house into winners of first, second, and third places, and "also rans." A sample of this method is shown with the inventor's portrait on the preceding page.

This was a bid for vaudeville advertising; and it succeeded. Within a month the "racing-chart page" was filled out with "cards" and announcements of vaudeville headliners.

On November 6, 1908, Arthur Brisbane began to play his part in constructive criticism. The leading editorial that day was headed: "A Great Play —Two Powerful Men Collaborate." The play was Gillette's "Samson"—"At present at the Criterion Theater," to quote Mr. Brisbane. "Go to see it," he advised. "It will make you think! . . . It contains a lesson for husbands, wives, and others."

On November 7—the next day—the "Journal" carried a full-page advertisement of "Samson."

And Still More!

THE next Brisbane editorial regarding a theater appeared on December 30, 1908. "The Battle —Ingenious Play Ingeniously Advertised," ran the headlines. That no one might make a mistake about what play was meant, the editorial began: "At the Savoy Theater, in New York, Wilton Lackaye, a powerful actor—" Mr. Brisbane commended "The Battle" as a play that made people think. "It is an interesting, startling, highly dramatic performance, drawing great crowds . . . highbrowed, prosperous dilettants are buying boxes, and lower brows, perhaps a little more thoughtful, cheer from the galleries."

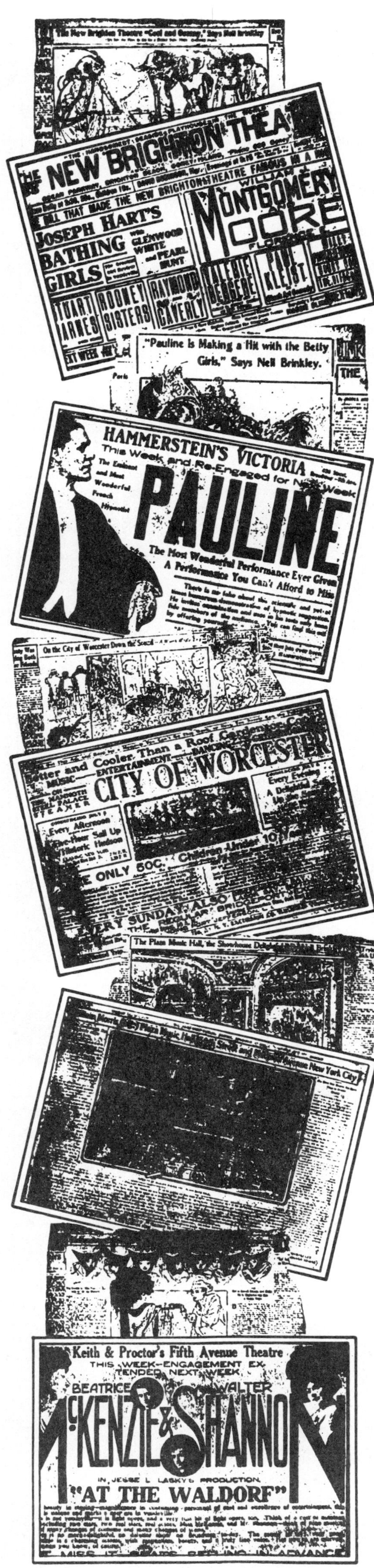

Nell Brinkley's Part — Some of the coincidences between her work in the "Journal" and half-page advertisements

Three days later, on January 2, 1909, a full-page advertisement of "The Battle" appeared in the "Journal."

An editorial headed "A GENTLEMAN FROM MISSISSIPPI—This is One of the Plays that Has a PURPOSE—May its success breed Imitators," led off the editorial page on January 29. It advised all readers interested in American Government and fond of a good, exciting play, to see "A Gentleman from Mississippi"—"Now running at the Bijou Theater on Broadway between Thirtieth and Thirty-first Streets," to borrow the language of the "Journal." "An amusing play"—"Makes you think"—"A play that will last for years"—"Deserves to succeed and its success is great"—I quote at random.

The next day page seven of the "Journal" was filled with an advertisement of "The Gentleman from Mississippi."

The One Exception

THE "Journal" carried, on February 6, 1909, a full-page advertisement of "The Girl from Rector's," a comedy with music which almost holds the American record for salaciousness. On February 8 Nell Brinkley, on the "feature" page, had a seven-column illustration and story headed "Mighty Scrumptious Frocks in 'The Girl from Rector's.'" This is notable as the only full-page theatrical advertisement appearing in the "Journal" between November, 1908, and October, 1909, which was not recognized by an editorial.

However, on February 14, the editorial page resumed constructive criticism. "The Dawn of a To-morrow" was the head, and it was also the name of the play, "which is at the Lyceum Theater, on Forty-fifth Street near Broadway," said the editorial. "It is a good play for all people to see . . . if you want an immediate, pleasant, and touching Dawn of a To-morrow, go up to the Lyceum Theater and see Eleanor Robson act, and shed tears—if that is your way of expressing emotion."

The full-page advertisement of "The Dawn of a To-morrow" appeared on February 20, 1909, on page seven.

"Fighting to Keep a Husband" was the headline on the leading editorial of February 26. It related to Thompson Buchanan's "A Woman's Way," in which Grace George was starring. "For three reasons we invite our readers who like light comedy and excellent dramatic work by an excellent actress to see Grace George in her new play at the Hackett Theater in Forty-second Street," said the "Journal."

The full-page advertisement for "A Woman's Way" appeared on page seven of the next issue.

"Don't Fail to See 'The Fortune Hunter'" announced Mr. Brisbane in the headline of his leading editorial on September 22, 1909. This play, "Now running at the Gaiety Theater, on the corner of Broadway and Forty-sixth Street," to quote again, was packing the house. "Go to see 'The Fortune Hunter' NOW. In a few weeks you will probably find it impossible to get seats unless you take them a month ahead. If you can't get seats in the orchestra, get them in the gallery. The Gaiety Theater is admirably ventilated and the gallery seats are exactly as good as the orchestra seats for sensible people. . . . We predict for this excellent, moral play a success so overwhelming as to prove that a GOOD play is the thing that good citizens want, and that a majority of the citizens are good."

The full-page advertisement for "The Fortune-Hunter" appeared on September 25, page four.

The Direct Evidence

FINALLY, reversing the former order, on October 9, 1909, appeared an advertisement for "On the Eve" with Hedwig Reicher, and two days later came the editorial: "A Play for Thoughtful Men and Women." Then, for a time, Mr. Brisbane ceased to write editorials about plays which had bought full-page advertisements. To recapitulate: in the period between November, 1908, and October, 1909, eight new plays advertised in this manner. Seven of these were specially commended by Mr. Brisbane in two-column editorials. Three other plays, which bought no special advertising, were treated on the editorial page in that period—"What Every Woman Knows," "An Englishman's Home," and "Israel." The first of these was written by J. M. Barrie and performed by Maude Adams; it was important enough therefore to deserve attention from any editorial page. "An Englishman's Home" was a play of special political interest, dealing as it did with national defense; most American and English newspapers discussed it editorially. And "Israel" furnished a text for a discourse on Jew-baiting—always a favorite theme with Brisbane. He advised his readers, especially the young girls among them, not to see "Israel," because it was improper. All three were Frohman productions.

This evidence is so far merely circumstantial. As a matter of fact, there is plenty of direct evidence. The new advertising policy of the "Journal" was public property in the theatrical district, where gossip travels as in a little village. Every manager

(Continued on page 28)

One Year of "Constructive Criticism" *in the* New York "Journal"

Have You Seen "Samson" at the Criterion Theatre?

A Story of Hatred, Money and Love. Money Is Weakest

EDITORIAL PAGE OF THE EV
THE NEW YORK EVENING JOURNAL.

A Great Play; Two Powerful Men Collaborate

SAVOY THEATRE

WILTON LACKAYE IN "THE BATTLE"

And the Following Editorial from the N. Y. Evening Journal:

FOUR WEEKS IN ADVANCE

EDITORIAL PAGE OF THE EV
THE NEW YORK EVENING JOURNAL.

"The Battle"—Ingenious Play, Ingeniously Advertised.

A GENTLEMAN FROM MISSISSIPPI

Brady & Grismer's Production

BIJOU THEATRE

Broadway, Bet. 30th and 31st Sts.

All men have their price, But honor is the price of some men

Story of the Play

EDITORIAL PAGE OF THE EV
THE NEW YORK EVENING JOURNAL.

"A Gentleman from Mississippi"

RESERVES CALLED OUT TO WD IN LINE AT BOX OFFICE

Verdict of All: "BEST FRENCH COMEDY EVER SEEN IN NEW YORK"

4 WEEKS IN ADVANCE

Holiday Matinees Lincoln's and Washington's Birthday

DON'T MISS IT! THE SEASON'S GREATEST HIT

Mighty Scrumptious Frocks in "The Girl from Rector's"

LYCEUM THEATRE

"Miss Robson's 'Glad' stands out as the most striking ..." —Eve. World.

ELEANOR ROBSON

Liebler & Co., Managers

in Mrs. Frances Hodgson Burnett's Play of Christian Optimism

"THE DAWN OF A TO-MORROW"

THE NEW YORK EVENING JOURNAL IN A LEADING EDITORIAL SAID:

EDITORIAL PAGE OF THE EV
THE NEW YORK EVENING JOURNAL.

"The Dawn of a To-morrow."

EDITORIAL PAGE OF THE EV
THE NEW YORK EVENING JOURNAL.

Fighting to Keep a Husband

GRACE GEORGE

Assisted by FRANK WORTHING

in "A WOMAN'S WAY"

By THOMPSON BUCHANAN

Hackett Theatre, 42d Street, Near Broadway, New York

World's Greatest Family of Actors

ETHEL BARRYMORE

JOHN BARRYMORE

Messrs. Cohan & Harris to the Public

GEORGE M. COHAN

SAM H. HARRIS

EDITORIAL PAGE OF THE
THE NEW YORK EVENING JOURNAL

Don't Fail to See "The Fortune Hunter"

A NEW and GREAT ACTRESS, A POWERFUL PLAY

THE PLAY

"ON THE EVE," a Story of Russia's Great Tragedy

SEE "ON THE EVE" AT THE HUDSON THEATRE

A Play for Thoughtful Men and Women.

All the full-page theatrical advertisements which appeared in the regular editions of the New York "Journal" between October, 1908, and October, 1909, each set beside the reward thereof

The American Newspaper

(Continued from page 18)

knew that the "Journal" offered a page advertisement and a Brisbane editorial for a thousand dollars. It was remarked that Brisbane would not "boost," under this arrangement, any play which he did not like—but his tastes are catholic. Just as well was it understood that for five hundred dollars the "Journal" would give a half-page advertisement, and a "special," with illustration by Nell Brinkley, together with liberal "news notices."

The "Journal" generally signed no contract for these transactions; it was just a gentleman's agreement between the solicitor and the manager. Of course, what the managers really wanted for their thousand dollars was not the advertisement, but the editorial.

The "Snapper"

MR. BRISBANE himself furnished the true climactic touch—what writers of fiction call the "snapper"—to this story. Liebler & Company, who produced "The Battle" and "The Dawn of a To-morrow," mentioned above, produced also Joseph Medill Patterson's newspaper play, "The Fourth Estate." Mr. Patterson hinged his drama on the control of newspaper policies by advertisers. To stimulate interest the Liebler press agent wrote to editors all over the country asking whether they believed that advertisers ever slanted or tainted the news columns. Afterward he made public some of the replies. And Arthur Brisbane wrote:

"I have never found that advertisers tried to control the policy of any newspaper with which I was connected. Therefore, I have never given such a possible situation the earnest thought which it doubtless merits."

Brisbane is an employee; whatever blame there is for this policy must rest on Hearst. And Hearst used others among his star special people. Owing to his eminence as an exponent of the "new journalism," however, Brisbane's part has attracted more attention than that of Nell Brinkley, for example. The activities forced on that clever young woman by her employers have been far more productive of revenue, to judge by a study of the half-page theatrical advertisements in the "Journal," than the activities assumed by Mr. Brisbane. She has a great vogue in New York; and her bizarre drawing, if not her writing, deserves it. Her following is largest in that very class which patronizes the lighter Broadway attractions. For example, "The Follies of 1909" had a chorus of Nell Brinkley girls. Before the policy of constructive criticism came into the "Journal" she was doing a theatrical illustration and story at least once a week. The first suspicion that she was used in an advertising campaign appeared on April 18, 1908, three months after Zittel began his racing chart, in a five-column illustration and story entitled "Eva Tanguay the Human Firefly." Now Eva Tanguay had taken more advertising space on "Zit's" page than any two other performers; and she was always placed first in the racing chart. During the next year and a half she had "write-up" after "write-up" in the "feature" pages of the "Journal," sometimes by Nell Brinkley, sometimes by other stars. In fact, no United States Senator, no member of the Cabinet, drew so much space in the "Journal" during that period as Eva Tanguay. She made a graceful acknowledgment in the 1909 Christmas Vaudeville Number of the "Journal"—she bought a half-page advertisement which read:

"I take this opportunity to tell the public I owe what success I have achieved and the position I hold in the theatrical field to C. F. Zittel. A Merry Christmas to you, Mr. Zit!"

Nell Brinkley's Job

BY the beginning of 1909 Miss Brinkley's employers apparently held her as close to the half-page advertisements as they held Brisbane to the full-page. Let us follow the coincidence a little way.

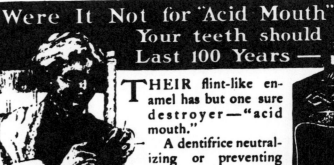

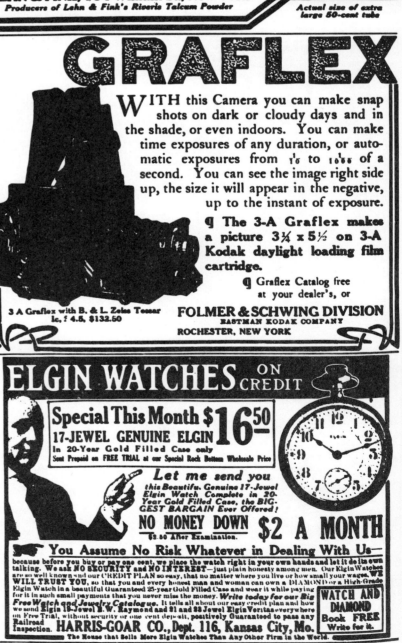

In the issue of January 7, 1909, Annette Kellerman had a half-page advertisement, the first of many. In the issue of January 16 Nell Brinkley had a five-column illustration and story, headed: "Annette Kellerman is a Sweet and Very Pretty Girl." Then, on February 2, came a story with illustration by Nell Brinkley about Vesta Victoria, who had taken no half-page, but had advertised liberally in small doses. On February 15 appeared a Nell Brinkley drawing of Eleanor Robson as "Glad" in "The Dawn of a To-morrow." That play had already received a one-page advertisement and a Brisbane editorial. On February 13, Edna Aug in a half-page advertisement. On February 23, three columns of Nell Brinkley on Edna Aug. February 27, a half-page advertisement for Stella Mayhew. March 3, three columns of Nell Brinkley—"Stella Mayhew a Jolly Bunch of Fun." March 13, a half-page advertisement for Montgomery and Moore. March 19, "Montgomery and Moore so clever they make each other laugh," a two-column drawing and story—this time by "Tad." March 20, a half-page advertisement for McKenzie and Shannon. March 26, "McKenzie and Shannon are 'It' in 'At the Waldorf'"—five columns—by Nell Brinkley. April 3, a half-page advertisement for "The Exposition Four." June 1, Nell Brinkley with illustration and story, on "The Exposition Four." April 10, and again April 24, half-page advertisements for Pauline, the Hypnotist. April 26, "'Pauline is Making a Hit with the Betty Girl,' says Nell Brinkley"—illustration and story. April 17 and May 4, half-page advertisements for J. E. Dodson in "The House Next Door." April 24, "The Art of Making Up Defined by J. E. Dodson, Its Master," an anonymous article—two columns with photographs. May 3, "J. E. Dodson in 'The House Next Door' is a Wonder," by Nell Brinkley. May 22, a half-page advertisement for "Lind," a female impersonator. May 28, a six-column illustration, with story, by Nell Brinkley on "Lind." Perhaps these are instances enough.

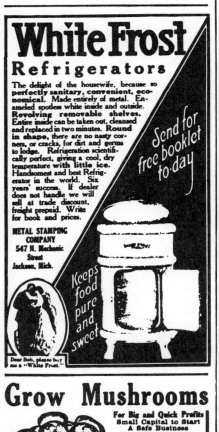

How Zittel "Made" Morris

TO summarize: in 1909 Miss Brinkley used pen and pencil on theatrical or vaudeville attractions about forty times. Not more than six or seven of these stories and illustrations went unaccompanied by a half-page advertisement. On the side of the advertiser, not one half-page advertisement went unrewarded by a "special." Now and then the "Journal" varied Nell Brinkley by Merle Johnson, Beatrice Fairfax, or "Tad"—all-star "special" people. After Brisbane stopped writing editorials to accompany full-page advertisements, Nell Brinkley was assigned to that part of the work. This remarkable correspondence between advertising revenue and artistic inspiration continued until the autumn of 1910, when the "Journal" temporarily dropped the whole policy. However, two of the coincidences call for special mention. On July 3, 1909, appeared a half-page advertisement for "The Mammoth Steel Palace Steamer *City of Worcester*." In the issue of July 10 Nell Brinkley had a five-column illustration and story, headed: "On the *City of Worcester* Down the Sound—a Worth While Trip." In the autumn of 1909 William Morris started the Plaza Music Hall at Fifty-ninth Street and Madison Avenue, a long way from the regular theatrical district. He took a half-page advertisement on November 1, 1909. Also, he kept a large standing notice at the head of the dramatic advertising columns. He was recognized on November 20 in a five-column illustration by Nell Brinkley entitled "The Plaza Music Hall, the Showhouse Delightful." By this time the "Journal," lest any reader make a mistake, was putting the name of the theater at which the attraction appeared in the headlines over Miss Brinkley's articles. And the name of the "Plaza" came out in these lines again and again that winter. Finally, the "feature page" capped the dramatic season of 1909-10 by a "write-up" of Zittel and his racing chart. It told of the Headliners from Eva Tanguay down (all advertisers, by the way) whom Zittel had made. And it touched on the Plaza Music Hall. When that theater opened, said the eulogy, the crowds would not come. But "Zit" saw that it was a good theatrical project, and began to praise it. Now the audiences overflowed the theater. As a matter of cold fact, Mr. Morris gave up the Plaza Music Hall as a bad venture at the close of that season.

A Frost for the Circus

THIS incident may illustrate the system:

A great circus came to Madison Square Garden. A circus, advertising or no advertising, is always good, legitimate news matter in New York as in Pumpkin Center; people like to read about it. The press agent of this one took his sheaf of complimentary tickets and visited the newspaper offices to see what they were going to do. At the "Journal" they informed him that the dramatic department in the business office would attend to the matter.

The representative of the dramatic department proceeded to business at once.

"For a page advertisement at a thousand dollars you'll get a Brisbane editorial and liberal feature stuff. For five hundred, Nell Brinkley and news mention."

"And if I take no special advertising?"

"Nothing!"

The press agent refused emphatically to order more than the regular condensed notice. The circus remained in New York a month, drawing column on column from the other newspapers. The "Journal" gave

(*Continued on page 31*)

The American Newspaper

(Continued from page 29)

it just one story. This was a small item noting that the circus had opened, and that a trapeze performer had broken his wrist.

All this represents the third and lowest degree of newspaper business ethics. To the publisher of this degree, the news and editorial pages are his to use for getting business whenever they may help: the only brake upon his activities in this direction is the fear that he will lose public confidence and so reduce that circulation which he is selling to advertisers. One degree higher are those publishers who believe in drawing the line between the advertising and editorial departments. "Our advertising columns," they say, "are a bulletin-board whereon any one, for a stated price, may post any notice he wishes. We pay no attention to the bulletin-board when we are making our own part of the newspaper. Hold us to the strictest accountability for what we publish as news and editorial; but we can not answer for the advertisements." So the poison of patent medicine, the obscenity of quack doctors, the lures of loan sharks, the swindling promises of mining advertisers, are all fair publication matter for a newspaper which assumes lofty attitudes on its editorial page. During the early period of the advertising craze, newspapers edited their advertising by this rule alone. Some of the best went so far as to publish freely the "personals" whose intention was so plain and so obscene that it can not be mentioned here.

The Question of a Child

PUBLIC sense of decency forced many from this absurd attitude. "The question of a child," says one newspaper philosopher, "has killed many and many a bad advertisement." For the announcements of patent medicines and of quack physicians included words which no editor would dare use in his own department. When people began stopping their newspapers because they would not have such matter on their center-tables, some publishers saw the light. The more reputable advertisers helped. They refused to appear on the same page with these indecencies; there are instances of refusal to appear at all in a newspaper so conducted. The better and more honorable publications put the knife to this class of matter. The "personals," rather a small revenue-getter at best, went first. I believe that no newspaper of any pretension to standing admits them now, although the San Francisco "Chronicle" and the Cincinnati "Enquirer" have given in only of late. More grudgingly, publishers cut out the steady and paying quack advertisements; more than half of the metropolitan newspapers have finished with these. Still, as late as last autumn, John R. McLean published in his Cincinnati "Enquirer" a column of these advertisements which verged on violation of the law against mailing obscene matter. Pehaps McLean relied for his immunity upon the fact that he owns also the Washington "Post," the unofficial Government organ. Still more grudgingly publishers pruned their patent medicine advertising. Few, however, reject this matter wholly.

Forced by the public to a new policy, commercial publishers modified the rules governing the "bulletin-board." "Let the public post anything," they said, "so long as the matter does not injure public morals." So they began to refuse quackeries, obscenities, and assignations, but they continued to admit loan sharks, whom they knew to be swindlers, crooked mining stocks, "racing tips," and clairvoyants. These, you see, do not injure public morals. The editorial page, the news column, might be attacking the faker, while the adjoining advertising section promoted his little game. In New York, the "Journal" was denouncing the race-tracks, while taking money from touts and bookmakers, to advertise tips on the races.

The Magazine Standard

OF course, this rule of the commercial publisher is disingenuous. He can not fairly assume to conduct a censor of abuses while accepting revenue from these very abuses. It is true that the distinction between fair and false advertising is sometimes very fine. But certain advertisers, certain whole classes of advertising, are known to be fraudulent; and unless it reject them, the newspaper can not be consistent. As a matter of fact, only a few are. The New York "Evening Post" has always been highly virtuous in this regard, as in all others. Some of the excellent small city journals like the Springfield "Republican" draw the line honestly. Of late, the Kansas City "Star," the Philadelphia "North American," and the New York "Times" approach what advertising men call the "magazine standard."

(Concluded on page 34)

The history of that magazine standard should be a lesson to the commercial publisher. Our first periodicals took advertisements of low class; even in the early nineties, certain get-rich-quick real-estate agents hooked their dupes through the magazines. Who saw the better way is a matter of dispute, but the late Albert E. Brady of "McClure's," a genius in the business of publication, or Thomas Balmer of the "Ladies' Home Journal," first put the new standard into effect. They refused all crooked, obscene, harmful advertising. They investigated all commodities which came near the line. They made their part of their magazines so clean, so desirable for respectable company, that the great, valuable national contracts poured into them. The best of the other magazines followed this policy. To-day, not all the periodicals are free from fraud and obscenities, but the most successful are. And with that clean-up began the great expansion in magazine advertising.

National Advertisers

"WHERE you pull up a weed, a rose will grow," says a national advertising expert. "For every doubtful contract you throw out, you'll get in the long run a bigger clean contract." Perhaps he exaggerates; but there is reason to believe that the business manager, in maintaining his false "bulletin-board" policy is as short-sighted as when he stultifies and gags his writers because he will not face down advertisers. Among the national manufacturers of commodities for the people only two per cent use the newspapers as a means of salesmanship. What of the other ninety-eight per cent? If they advertise at all, they generally use the magazines, where they travel in respectable company. Were the newspapers clean media, these advertisers would use them. Whether they would advertise enough to replace the receipts from quacks, poisoners, thieves, and swindlers, none can say. Perhaps the experiment is worth trying. And that ninety-eight per cent will not enter the newspapers in bulk so long as they must associate with poisoners and thieves.

Capital is timid; and the business office represents capital. Journalism should be brave. Let it be intellectual if you will, but first of all the tribune of the people must have courage. This advertising quandary is another expression of the anomaly in modern American journalism—the imperfect mixture of two antagonistic elements, and the frequent prevalence of the less admirable. Upstairs, journalists, willing to risk life itself that they may "get the story," to hazard friendship and personal esteem that they may attack special privilege and vested injustice—for such is the spirit and custom of the craft. Downstairs—usually—a publisher frightened at the loss of a hundred dollars in advertising.

Cowed by Phantoms

AT what phantoms, what sheets on sticks, does he cower! When the public first demanded suppression of "massage parlors" and assignation advertisements, the business managers responded that newspapers could not exist without them. But the public and the editorial staffs prevailed. The personals went; and no newspaper failed. The business office could not spare patent medicine advertisements. No; but after the exposé of 1906, public feeling and new laws forced these salesmen of poisons out of newspapers by thousands of columns. And no one failed. On the contrary, general experience squared with the opinion of the national advertising expert. Where one weed came up, two roses grew. Finally, and most pertinent of all to the public, I have seldom known a case where newspaper resistance to advertising control—if the advertiser was not backed by larger interests—did not eventually profit the newspaper. Again and again, publishers, irritated by unconscionable demands on the part of some advertiser, have answered with a flat refusal. Always, the advertiser withdrew; and almost always, after his blood cooled and his business judgment asserted itself, he came back—because he "needed the newspaper in his business"—with renewed faith in that particular journal as an advertising medium. When the department stores of Denver boycotted the newspapers, they simply emptied their own aisles and filled the shops of little competitors.

These publishers walked up to the phantom, and it vanished. They dared risk revenue, and their courage paid in cold cash. Nevertheless, the advertiser does not always, does not usually, stand alone. And when he represents not only himself but all the vested power there is in our modern world, he is not a phantom. He is a creature of flesh and blood, weapons and mail; he will not vanish before a brave front. That combination and its effects we shall consider in the next article.

XI

"Our Kind of People"

In this, by far the briefest article of his series, Irwin sketches the outlines of what since has become a commonplace charge among critics of the press. Irwin calls it recognition by the publishers that the proprietors of big business are "our kind of people." Today it's called "country club journalism" or some other name that implies the publisher's values are the same as those held by the big businessmen of the community. Irwin observes that those business interests are a "complicated web of mutual interests, mutual concessions." In his day the influence of such interests on newspapers frequently was wielded with subtlety that would do credit to the highest paid public relations men today. The Mica Axle Grease incident illustrates this and presages development of the more unhealthy aspects of the corporate public relations arm. Presently, however, some critics suggest that the influence of big business has so permeated the mass media as a result of the media themselves becoming big business that it's sometimes doubtful whether influence need be consciously exercised.

The American Newspaper

A Study of Journalism in Its Relation to the Public

By WILL IRWIN

XI.—"Our Kind of People"

The line where advertising influence becomes undeniably dangerous to the public interest — when advertisers slant or choke editorial policies. The process, still more dangerous, where the advertiser is the club of "big business" over the newspaper. Examples from the history of the Standard Oil Company, the Sugar Trust, the Coca-Cola Company, and other "interests," point the moral of this article

THE business manager of a lively little metropolitan newspaper sat one morning receiving reports from his staff. The publication was new; it had worked up a limited circulation by exposing a few ugly corners of the city, to which its older and more conservative rivals remained blind. Though sales and subscriptions had arrived, advertising lagged.

A solicitor entered.

"Nothing doing with the Sound Coal Company's ad," he said. "You remember you told me to ask why they advertised with the 'News' and the 'Globe' at their rate, and not with us at ours?"

"Yes."

"Well, they said the ad in the 'Globe' was a mistake, anyhow. They didn't intend to keep it up. They're going to do all their advertising in the 'News' hereafter. I asked for a reason; of course I knew, but I wanted them to put themselves on record. And they were fools enough to do it."

"What did they say?"

"'We give our business to our kind of people.'"

And "our kind of people"—the newspaper which I have called the "News"—was weaving a curious web of history. A fine, established property, it had been offered for sale two years before; the price was probably about $1,500,000. A financial reporter, able but penniless, had bought it and become its visible head. Reformers and rivals suspected where the money came from, even found the bank upon which the reporter drew; they could never trace the real purchaser. From that time forth the "News" went on, an excellent journal technically, free and wise on national issues, sharp in reporting unimportant local news, but blind to certain political and corporate abuses in its own city and State. So was it "our kind of people"; and so it prospered in the department of advertising.

Here was an example of that stage in advertising control when the process grows dangerous to a free press and a free commonwealth. It would seem on the surface that the ordinary suppression of news, as when a department store keeps its own accidents and scandals from the public, matters very little in the aggregate. That is not true, as every honest newspaper man knows; such things work with marvelous certitude to take the spirit and independence out of a newspaper staff—but let that pass. When, however, the advertiser presumes to dabble in editorial policies, the harm is patent and beyond argument. Still less is there room for argument when he slants or silences newspaper policies on behalf of what we call "big business."

For to a degree varying with the locality, "big business" is a complicated web of mutual interests, mutual concessions. The coal company, like this one which favors "our kind of people," has borrowed from a bank, and hypothecated its stock with a trust company. Its directors have intimate relations with directors of public utility corporations and trusts. And "big business," though often torn by internal dissensions, divided into hostile factions, presents a fairly undivided front to the outsider. So, from high finance to the small advertiser, comes an influence which affects the greater policies of newspapers. This is not yet a system, although certain pirates have tried to make it one. Nevertheless, it is a potent influence.

As an example of the first stage of this process—the advertiser looking out for his own—take a late social phenomenon in Chicago. The newspapers of that city, detractors to the contrary notwithstanding, are fairly free from advertising control over the news. Some of them even give the name of the store in reporting a shoplifting case—a little thing, but significant. Nevertheless, there are ugly spots in Chicago, fair game for newspaper investigation, which have never seen the light because an advertiser has protected them. In 1909, after the investigation of the "White Slave Traffic" in New York, the Chicago newspapers got up some excitement by exposing a like condition in their slum district. One-half of the story they never told. A feeder of the dive and brothel is the cheap department store, which pays wages at a scale below the lowest cost of living, and all but forces its girl employees to supplement their wages by other means. In this respect Chicago is perhaps a little worse than the average. And, although the reporters who investigated the white slave traffic itched to shout it out to the public, no Chicago newspaper whispered the fact that this business policy makes "white slaves." The publishers have their defense; but it will not stand in court. They say that the white slave prosecutions came out in regular course of the news, that they would have to "go out after" the department store feeder. But the Chicago newspapers were all "going out after" things which did not touch their interests; just then the "Tribune," free again after a period of half-control, was departing from its news-routine to attack Senator Lorimer's election. Even such an enlightened and independent newspaper, upstairs and down, as the New York "World" showed its fear of department store advertising when it rejected the late O. Henry's "Unfinished Story." The author was then under contract to deliver a story a week. He had scourged or ridiculed all Manhattan—"society," and slums, clergy and police alike. This story, however, treated of a store-girl who was weighing her meager seven dollars a week against her virtue. Out it went, although, after a magazine published it, "The Unfinished Story" became O. Henry's most popular tale. I give the "World" absolution, however. When, last year, Gimbel Brothers entered New York with a new department store and tried to change the name of Greeley Square to Gimbel Square, the "World" risked its advertising to resist them.

Now let us carry the matter one stage further back. If "big business" be well enough organized, the advertiser may ask extension of the favor, claim the privilege for other companies and corporations in which he holds shares, or with which he is allied by interest and sympathy. Philadelphia has poor transportation facilities. Not only do the Philadelphia department stores press hard on newspaper policies which touch their immediate interests—as when they tried to suppress news of the late general strike—but they stand guard between the newspaper and the transportation companies. Though better transit would halve the time between suburb and shopping district, thereby bringing more customers to the stores, the alliance between street railways and banks, banks and department stores, holds advertisers to a policy against their own ultimate interests.

Denver saw the system come clean to the surface. Colorado was engaged in the desperate war between the Mine Owners' Association and the Western Federation of Miners—vested injustice against mob violence. The factions cleft the State; business sided with the mine owners, labor with the Federation. T. M. Patterson's "News" and "Times," alone among Denver newspapers, supported the miners. If Patterson was pleading partly for his private interests, so were the others; if he had only half the right on his side, so had the others. When the fight reached its climax, the advertisers in formal meeting withdrew their support from these important newspapers. The department stores left in a body. But for an accident, Patterson must have thrown his whole fortune into the doubtful balance, or failed. He found that $40,000 worth of stock in one department store was on the market. He purchased this share for spot cash; as a member of the company he forced the advertising back into the "News"; and the other department stores, by the law of competition, had to abandon "principle" and follow.

Standard Oil tested this peculiarity of journalism in the nineties, and found it good for the purposes of Standard Oil. The company was in the desperate pipe-line war. It had bought a string of newspapers from Oil City to Cleveland, but it could get no other support. All Ohio journalism was snapping at its heels. Dan O'Day, the clever old Standard Oil "fixer," visited Toledo to see what could be done.

"I've got it—Mica Axle Grease!" he said one day.

Mica Axle Grease was a new by-product of Standard Oil. One small factory was manufacturing it as an experiment.

With every Ohio newspaper worth considering, O'Day placed an advertisement for Mica Axle Grease. He drew the contracts to run eighteen months, cash payment monthly. Nearly all accepted. Some, seeing the purport of this advertisement, asked four or five times the regular rate. O'Day held them to their cards. He said not one word about policy. He merely sent out the contracts and the monthly checks, and waited.

By two months the tone of the Ohio press had changed. By six months, some of the stiffer-necked, relying on the certainty of Standard Oil payment, had begun to discount the monthly check at the bank in advance of its arrival, whereupon they, too, "shut up." By a year the "knocking" of Standard Oil ceased in Ohio.

"It Pays to Advertise"

THIS campaign had one unexpected result. Before the eighteen months expired, Mica Axle Grease had put up six new factory buildings to meet the demand. From an unconsidered by-product it became a most valuable profit-maker This story, therefore, illustrates in two ways the value of advertising.

Respect for the advertiser and his backer held part of the Southern press in line for the old régime during the prohibition wave The Anti-Saloon League, the power behind the movement, nominated no candidate of its own. Instead, it threw its power always to that candidate of the old parties least committed to the liquor interests, and most friendly to prohibition. So, when once it got over the ridge, it rolled down hill like a snowball, gathering in politicians. Men who drank their pint of straight whisky a day took the stump successively for local option, for county option, for State-wide prohibition. Had they looked more to subscribers than to advertisers, nearly all the newspapers would have made the same bid for popularity But brewers and manufacturers of "bottle goods" advertise heavily, and especially in prohibition districts, where the consumer must order by mail. The brewers and distillers issued a few warnings by ceasing to advertise in newspapers which "went dry." The lesson stuck. Certain struggling journals, just above the margin of profits, looked affectionately on their three or four columns of liquor advertisement. Without one word of warning from politicians or liquor firms, they opposed prohibition, or, in districts where the sentiment was too strong, held their peace. The brewers bribed newspapers, it is true: in Missouri they subsidized—and may still be subsidizing—many country editors. The country newspaper is either the angel or the devil of journalism. But this fear for revenue was, after all, their best card.

The "Tacit Offer of Friendship"

THE American Tobacco Company has availed itself of this weakness in the press; and, more recently, the Sugar Trust. The late sugar exposé, in which Secretary of War Stimson won his spurs, came in two episodes—a little tempest, prematurely lulled, and then the storm During the lull the Trust inserted in the newspaper trade journals advertisements and "reading notices," proclaiming a $100,000 advertising campaign in the newspapers, and communicated with publishers to the same effect They never asked any favors—doubtless, like O'Day, they were too wise to take that risk. They must have known that the sight of such a large, profitable advertisement in his pages would influence a weak brother here and there, make him tone down his editorial attacks or withhold his hand altogether A national advertising expert who has done such work sums it up as follows: "Advertising is practical psychology I know that the advertisement is a kind of tacit offer of friendship. It won't silence all the press, nor even most of it, but I calculate that it will take at least twenty-five per cent of the force out of a general newspaper attack."

We have just witnessed, however, a case where the work must have been done not with a rapier but with a bludgeon The Coca-Cola Company of Atlanta, maker of a popular soda-fountain beverage, has been through another phase of its litigation with the Government's pure-food experts. Dr. Harvey W. Wiley charged that the addition of free caffein to the mixture was in violation of law. The case was tried in Chattanooga, and the company won. Now Coca-Cola is one of the greatest of national advertisers, and it uses the newspapers liberally in the "dry" South, where its wares are widely consumed as a non-alcoholic substitute for liquor. Many Southern newspapers demanded that the Associated Press carry news of the trial, the Associated Press, being servant to the whole body of its newspapers, very properly acquiesced. So the decision was freely reported—even as far north as New York, where a Hearst paper carried the story Not only that; hard upon the decision some Southern newspaper or other printed a leading editorial deploring "the attack on a great Southern industry" This editorial was clipped in full all through the Southern press, even in districts far too remote from Atlanta to be affected in the least by the success or failure of the Coca-Cola Company. A clipping of the editorial used to arrive in the newspaper offices in the same mail with the advance advertising copy of Coca-Cola. A word to the wise which was usually sufficient.

In the panic of 1907 and the curiously brief hard times which followed, the press of the United States generally published its idea of the exact truth about the situation in Wall Street, far, far away, and kept still about the home situation, or lied. Certain managing editors present a vehement defense for this course "The end justifies the means." They say that the depression was brief and harmless, as compared to the hard times of 1873 and 1893, just because the newspapers howled prosperity and hid the real conditions. This might stand as a defense, except for one fact. Newspapers which lied most brazenly were assuming to be tribunes of the "common people", and on the common people this policy often weighed most cruelly. Pittsburg was hard hit. Two banks had failed, mills were closing every day. The Pittsburg newspapers suddenly began printing "news" of a great industrial revival. So, thought the financial powers, people would spend their money instead of hoarding it, and business would go on. Well, it did go on, and Pittsburg recovered But four thousand discharged mill-hands from outside cities read these false reports and crowded into Pittsburg, to find further poverty and misery.

Or again: the Chicago banks weathered the crisis well, yet many of them refused cash to depositors, issuing instead cashier's checks to pay running expenses. Why? They were getting from New York call loan rates on their money. This was oppression—taking advantage of distress to fill their pockets. The financial reporters all knew about this process. It was news—good news. Perhaps they turned the story into their offices; more likely they saved themselves the trouble At any rate, none printed it.

In 1901, when bubonic plague first appeared in San Francisco, "big business" and the advertisers decided that the newspapers should be not only silent but false, lest tourists, settlers, and customers shun the city. The publishers met in the famous "midnight conference" All save the Hearst man pledged themselves to lie about the plague situation; and the Hearst man joined the majority before long. The Government experts found that the plague had arrived. The newspapers reviled them, hampered their work, rendered their quarantines ineffective. The plague lingered. San Francisco is only just finished with fighting it. Had the newspapers told the truth in 1901, they would have saved the city some lives, and millions of dollars. In this case no one directly threatened withdrawal of advertising; the fact that the financial powers, including the great department stores, were strongly on one side was enough for publishers and managing editors trained in the modern commercial school.

Writing in Fetters

NOW this process, going on in every corner of the country, has subtly but importantly changed the whole character of the editorial executive. For, generally speaking, by his financial success alone is the managing editor or editor-in-chief known to the owner or the syndicate of owners. He who has slashed recklessly, regardless of business office receipts, has characteristically been identified with failing or languishing newspapers. Though he have ability, integrity, news sense, and energy, he is not transferred up from Oshkosh to Peoria and from Peoria to Chicago. When the executive vacancy occurs in Chicago, the owners, of course, study the records of candidates. Brown is able—yes. But see how much money his rival made last year, how little his own newspaper! There is Green. His Peoria newspaper has made money. And Green gets the job, not because he is a great editor, but because he has known how to placate advertisers and "big business." Green may have all kinds of messages for the people. He will attack, defend, or expose as freely as any one else when the pocket of his newspaper is untouched; but on such local issues as affect the backers of his advertisers, he will make compromises. He goes to the top, and Brown stands still.

Still, that most managing editors are cravens before big business interests is not quite true. Unlike the publishers, they characteristically struggle against the system, try to evade and to elude it. They reach through the bars which imprison them, striking a blow here, whacking a head there; often they yield sullenly, and by their sullenness make ineffective a policy which owners or advertisers have imposed upon them. I know one great newspaper in the Middle West whose directors forced the editorial staff to support a highly corrupt politician. The underlings who did the work wrote half-heartedly; and by tiny insinuations in the news columns they hurt the cause as much as they helped.

Local Inconsistencies

BOND-SLAVES to convenience, and to a system which was none of their making, directing editors pick and choose, now avoiding a dark place because a watch-dog of advertising sits on guard before it, now using all persuasiveness to convince the publisher that publication of this or that derogatory story will not harm his business in the long run, now confessing absolute defeat and renewing the battle on another line. Heney was struggling in San Francisco to convict Patrick Calhoun of the United Railways, and, going further, to curb the Southern Pacific machine. But two San Francisco newspapers, and, in the end, only one, fought with him. Joseph W. Folk came lecturing; and all the San Francisco newspapers praised Folk. In St. Louis, the organs which ridiculed Folk when he was trying to convict Butler, praised Heney in news and editorial. The Philadelphia press supported Quay or held its peace; but it denounced Tammany. Now some of this arises from the bandages which prejudice and acquaintance draw over all eyes when it is a question of local issues, but more from forced reverence for the sources of income. The managing editor is become a diplomat, standing between his newspaper's integrity, its inherent mission of truth-telling, and a hundred influences at work on the proprietor to "get the story in" or "keep the story out." Daily he compromises; and compromises not only with the advertiser and the powers behind him, but with certain influences from within which hamper free presentation of the news and of his opinion thereon.

The daily press as "Our Kind of People" would like it

XII

The Foe From Within

HERE IRWIN does more than point out the obvious fact that as newspapers become big business their owners take on the coloration of socially prominent big businessmen. He foreshadows developments which increasingly perplex today's society. As big business, the press (in the broadest sense in which the term is today used, including magazines, radio, and television, as well as newspapers) is frequently involved directly or indirectly with other big businesses. Great is the dilemma which results when the role of the press as tribune of the people conflicts with its role as corporate embodiment of the stockholders' profit motive.

The American Newspaper

A Study of Journalism in Its Relation to the Public

By WILL IRWIN

XII.—The Foe from Within

How the social and financial struggles of the proprietor affect the freedom and truth of metropolitan newspapers. The "Social Lobby" at Washington and its effect on the press. The whole illustrated by a romantic episode in the history of the Omaha "World-Herald," a melodramatic crisis in the history of the Pittsburg "Leader," and a series of inner diplomacies in the history of the Chicago "Tribune." The final perplexity of American journalism

"BIG BUSINESS" is a complex web, binding this near department store to that remote trust company, this near insurance corporation to that far bank. Since the metropolitan newspaper also is a large commercial venture, involving millions in capital, hundreds of thousands in annual profit or loss, it follows the rule. Its capital is a thread in the same fabric. If the visible owner bought it full-fledged, he made the purchase with money acquired or inherited from big business. He serves on boards of directors with railroad presidents and trust company managers. His fortune, outside of the newspaper investment, may lie in interests connected with the public-service corporations which serve his city. If, on the other hand, he be a self-made publisher, if he came up from the reporter's beat, the editorial chair, or the business office, he has been obliged to borrow money somewhere along the upward march; and he knows that he may have to borrow again. His loan office is a bank, master-thread in "big business." As wealth accumulates, he makes outside investments. So he comes to sit at the same directors' table with those powers which are the perplexity of American finance and politics.

More pertinently: he sits often at the same dinner-table. The financial brake on free journalism is twisted and intertwisted with the social brake; scarcely can we consider them apart. As polite society goes in this democracy, money is the *sine qua non;* except in the more conservative Southern cities one can scarcely succeed without it. And that very publisher who battered up from the ranks is just as amenable to social influence as he who entered journalism with ten million dollars—often more so, for this parvenu is a social struggler. In journalism, as in Washington statecraft, many a man unpurchasable with money has sold his birthright for an invitation.

The Meeting Point

FOR if you have a few millions of newly-made dollars, a million in a newspaper, the rest in railroads, public-service corporations, and local industries; if you have climbed into the approved clubs, brought out your daughter under patronage of the local Chesterfield; if you take your week-end ease at the country club—then, unless you have an uncommon character, you are not, you can not be, a free journalist. You must protect your "crowd," see that your business associate of to-day, your host of to-morrow, be not attacked in pocket or pride. Else he may refuse you this or that loan, else he may cut you at his club. More, his wife may strike the name of yours from her visiting list. Further, you are an exceptional human being if you keep long your unclouded vision. You tend toward the views of "our crowd." Your managing editor, if he be a sycophant, respects all your corporation affiliations, your social connections—and behold, imperceptibly yours has become a fettered newspaper.

I asked an able editor-in-chief how his "boss" had managed to hold the newspaper to its function of public service. For though that boss is a very wealthy man, he practises free journalism.

"Well," said the editor, "he keeps his outside funds in Government bonds and railroad stocks. The Government doesn't put the screws on bondholders; and when it comes to railroad news or editorial, he leaves it absolutely to the staff—we've definite orders never to talk railroad with him."

I asked almost the same question of a Western publisher. He began as a penniless reporter; he has succeeded through entering cities where the light of the press was screened, and illuminating the ugly places. He is rich now, and powerful.

"I begin in my own home," he said. "My wife, thank heavens, has no social ambitions!"

The home line drawn by Henry Watterson binds me also; it prevents me from citing large, obvious examples of the social influence, since wives and daughters enter into the account. I may speak, however, in general terms. The editors of one American newspaper receive from the publisher, upon taking their positions, "List A" and "List B." "List A" is long; it includes all who have assisted the owner and publisher in his social struggle. The people on that list are to be treated kindly, mentioned pleasantly; in the absence of the owner, any and all news must be suppressed at their demand. It is different with "List B," which is shorter. These people have offended the "boss." Their names must not be mentioned at all unless they do something disgraceful. Then—as the editors express it—"Soak 'em." And List A and List B, formulated or unformulated, written or unwritten, rest in the bottom drawer of many and many an editorial desk, symbol of an exploited profession.

William G. Beale — The "Third Trustee" in the Chicago "Tribune"

One instance of social influence is fair for publication, because it does not involve "the women folks." That J. Pierpont Morgan had some hand in the New York "Sun" during the Roosevelt corporation war, the world believes. With the clever, adroit bitterness which is the dross in its inheritance from Dana, the "Sun" ridiculed, flouted, hammered Roosevelt so excessively as to defeat its own purpose. The opposition charged that Morgan owned "Sun" stock, or had lent to the late William M. Laffan, its publisher, the money by which he bought his controlling interest.

To the best of my belief, this is not true. Here—again to the best of my belief—are the facts about Laffan's control:

When Charles Anderson Dana died, he left his stock mainly to his son Paul. The compositors of the "Sun" struck over a matter of monotype machines versus hand labor. This fight extended to a great general boycott of "Sun" advertising by labor unions. Sick of this interminable brawl, Paul Dana decided to sell. Laffan, then the business manager, secured an option; but he had not the ready money to complete the purchase. At the last moment, a financier, hardly more than an acquaintance, advanced the loan. This backer was not J. Pierpont Morgan, nor yet one of his close associates.

A Case of Rabies

BUT Mr. Laffan and Mr. Morgan were friends. Each was a collector; in certain lines, such as porcelains, these two were the supreme court of taste in America. Laffan in his smaller way, and Morgan in his larger, bought from the same agents, interchanged specimens, visited back and forth between their collections. Doubtless, Laffan's outside investments were in the Morgan interests. So he became one of the "Morgan crowd"—its journalistic member. And so, when Roosevelt hit at the foundation of the Morgan power, Laffan saw only as his crowd saw; here was a madman, a demagogue, an offender against social order. Nothing else—except Laffan's own fighting nature—is necessary to explain the "Sun's" attack of rabies concerning Roosevelt.

This social influence affects not only the heads of our newspapers but also the rank and file. If for a paragraph I leave the publisher to discuss the reporter, the digression is only to illustrate how snobbery and desire for social esteem may influence all journalists, great and small. The social lobby at Washington is a great theme unwritten. More by society than by money do the powers influence our legislation in this period of the Republic. The Representative from Oshkosh enters Washington burning for glory. In his first session he acquires an appetite for distinction in the capital; he looks no longer so much for the esteem of his home folk as for that of Washington. He is an atom among four hundred Representatives. The process of advancement through the mere business of legislation is slow; unless he be a very genius of personality and ability, he can scarcely show above the crowd in his first term, nor yet in his second. There is, however, another ladder—society. By his dinner cards and his invitations is he known to his fellows. And the dispensers of valued cards and invitations represent "big business"—"our kind of people." To those who favor them "our kind of people" are warm; to the others, cold.

Now reporting goes largely by acquaintance; and valuable acquaintance in Washington involves surrender to the Washington point of view. The most useful correspondent is he who has the best news sources. Such a man must respect "our kind of people" and the Washington idea, even though he tell only half truths. So Washington correspondence, viewed in bulk, tends always toward the side of the powerful. Says an Insurgent Representative: "I've seen a correspondent sail into Washington shooting guns to port and starboard and turning all his searchlights on the shame of the Solons. I've seen him six months later eating out of every official hand between the White House and the Capitol." Hearst himself could never keep his Washington correspondents militant. The Washington reporter surrenders to the very influence which may be binding his employer at home.

The financial drag on newspapers is fair game for illustrative example. Here, the law of libel hampers me, as it hampers the free contemporaries of certain slavish newspapers. It is not enough to tell the truth; one must be able to prove it. That one newspaper exists to fight the battles of a railroad; that a second stopped attacking a great and corrupt corporation at the price of a loan from a bank; that a third fell into the same silence concerning the same corporation because its publisher made a profitable investment in the corporation's lands; that a fourth keeps hands off the local political gang because it borrows from the trust company which finances the public service corporation which uses the gang—all these things I know with the private certainty which is just short of public proof. The names and cities are in my mind as I write.

But the process comes now and then to the surface —sometimes years after the fact. We know now, as we suspected then, that Senator Clark secretly owned a string of newspapers, and that Marcus Daly subsidized another string, during the copper feud in Montana. The world has long believed that James J. Hill exerted an undue influence over certain newspapers of the Northwest. We know now that the Great Northern Railroad owns $170,000 worth of bonds in that excellent newspaper, the Seattle "Post Intelligencer."[1]

An interesting illustration of the way of a bank with a newspaper came out of Omaha in 1892. That is a long time ago; moreover, the controlling influence sought not to affect policies, but to suppress an important piece of news. Still further, the publisher thus gagged has been an exemplar of militant journalism and honest politics; this example shows only how one must sometimes jettison cargo to save the ship. But the story is worth telling for its own sake.

On one side of the street was Edward Rosewater's established evening "Bee," a newspaper not disposed to do anything to hurt any one who had a great deal of money; on the other, Gilbert M. Hitchcock's lively but struggling morning and evening "World-Herald." One spring morning a country correspondent telegraphed that ex-Judge Joseph Clarkson had been drowned in Honey Creek Lake. Scarcely any sudden death would have made more sensation in Omaha. Every one knew him, and most liked him. He was a figure.

The "World-Herald" sent out all its available forces to Honey Creek Lake. They found half the lawyers in Omaha wading across its shallow bottom.

Medill McCormick, "a good publisher upstairs and down"

James Keeley, "the world's greatest news impresario"

Joseph Medill, founder of the Chicago "Tribune"

The case seemed perfectly plain. Clarkson had gone alone to the lake, fishing. At nightfall he told the lodge-keeper that he wanted a swim. He launched a boat and rowed away. He did not return; and next morning the keeper found the boat, empty except for Clarkson's clothes, at the mouth of a far creek. But persistent dredging failed to discover the body. A fact which, as the event proved, had nothing to do with the case, stirred up suspicion in the "World-Herald" office. Clarkson had $25,000 insurance. The "World-Herald" mentioned this fact, and Clarkson's partners protested at the insinuation. The managing editor let his intuition play on the case; and he assigned E. A. Grimm and Thomas Hunt, reporters, to confirm his suspicions.

Tommy Hunt, now a Chicago newspaper man, then a cub reporter just promoted from office boy, walked on to the first clue. On the bank by the abandoned boat he saw the tracks of a brand-new shoe. Inch by inch he went over the ground. The tracks led straight away from the boat. In the bushes he found some bits of cloth. They were tags such as makers sew into ready-made clothes—and new. He interviewed the keeper again. Yes, Clarkson had brought a bundle to the lake. In fact, it "seemed like" he had taken it with him in the boat. Ready-made clothing tags bear the chest, waist, and leg measure. Hunt noted these figures on the tags, compared them with the measurements of Clarkson's abandoned clothes. They corresponded.

Proceeding on the theory that Clarkson had taken a full set of ready-made clothing into the boat, had changed before landing, and had disappeared deliberately, Hunt and Grimm worked in secret for two months. They discovered the clerk who sold the clothing. His memory of his customer matched their description of Clarkson. They followed all the roads which their suspect might have taken. In the shed of a schoolhouse they found some torn bits of paper. Pieced together, these formed a notice of insurance assessment which Clarkson had received the day before he disappeared. Through infinite trouble, they got a photograph of their man. A barber who kept his shop a mile or so beyond the schoolhouse remembered having shaved that face on the day after Clarkson disappeared. Finally came a little psychological touch. A few days before he disappeared, Clarkson had held a conversation with a tramp concerning the life of the road.

Everything was ready; stage by stage, Grimm and Hunt had worked out a perfect piece of circumstantial evidence. The managing editor assigned three star writers to prepare seven columns of sensation. Hitchcock, the publisher, saw and approved; he even wrote the headlines. Next morning the "World-Herald" roused in Omaha that "gee whiz!" emotion which Arthur McEwen said should be in the front page of every newspaper.

The "Bee" came out that afternoon with a story which pleased the "World-Herald" staff a great deal. It showed that they had stirred things up. The "World-Herald" was a ghoul, said the "Bee"; it was making sensation out of grief. But while the "World-Herald" staff chuckled at their desks, Hitchcock received a telephone call. The bank wanted to see him—the bank from which he had borrowed some of his working capital. And in the directorate of that bank sat a relative of Clarkson.

Hitchcock came back pale. He wrote and signed two columns of apology, which he published next morning on the front page. The "World-Herald" was a liar. The editors, the star special writers, and the reporters were liars. On behalf of the newspaper he apologized to Omaha. As for Judge Clarkson, his honored bones rested at the bottom of Honey Creek Lake.

One reporter wanted to thrash the "boss"; and the other cried. The managing editor consoled them with philosophy. The "Bee" could rave and the "World-Herald" apologize, he said; but every man, woman, child, and banker who read their story knew that Judge Clarkson was not in Honey Creek Lake. "Just wait, boys," he added.

"And the boss used to slip a cog once in a while," says an incumbent of the "World-Herald." "He'd be sitting with the managing editor nights, and he'd shift feet and say: 'I wonder where Clarkson is?' And the managing editor would say, dead serious: 'Why, at the bottom of Honey Creek Lake!' And then they'd both smoke a while and think their own thoughts."

Spring and summer passed; and with the first frosty day of autumn the staff reported at the office to find the publisher getting out an extra. Clarkson had come back. He visited the office that afternoon to congratulate the staff on their acumen—"even the agricultural editor, who didn't know he'd left town," says my informant. In the last analysis Clarkson had no reason for his performance except a mania for disappearing. Since that time, in fact, he has done it again.

There is the "Leader" of Pittsburg. Journalism in the steel city is not exactly militant; and I can not give the "Leader" a wholly clean bill of health. It has been a voice in a great silence, but a husky and blatant voice; and it has had its own silences. Nevertheless, it has sometimes been the one true reporter of bad conditions in Pittsburg. And the "Leader" had been advocating social reforms inimical to the banks, from one of which Mr. Moore, the owner, had borrowed money. This was a straight loan; he was paying interest, and paying it on the notch.

Nevertheless, the bank sent for Moore. He found himself in a meeting of twenty-five bankers. The chairman went straight to the point.

"Stop it!" he said. "If you don't, none of us will take care of you." That is, the bank would foreclose; and no other bank would issue Moore a loan. He had the alternative of failure or of silence.

"You may break me," answered Moore. "It is in your power. You can't keep me from writing. Gen-

(Concluded on page 30)

[1] This would have been the proper place for narration of that incident in the history of the Boston "Traveler" where John H. Fahey declared that William A. Gaston and Robert Winsor tried to force him out as publisher because he would not accept political dictation from them. Allegations have been brought forward from the other side which vastly complicate this case; and since the witnesses are now scattered all over the world, it has been impossible to get at the truth in time for publication in this issue. We will return to this subject after the close of the present series.—THE EDITORS.

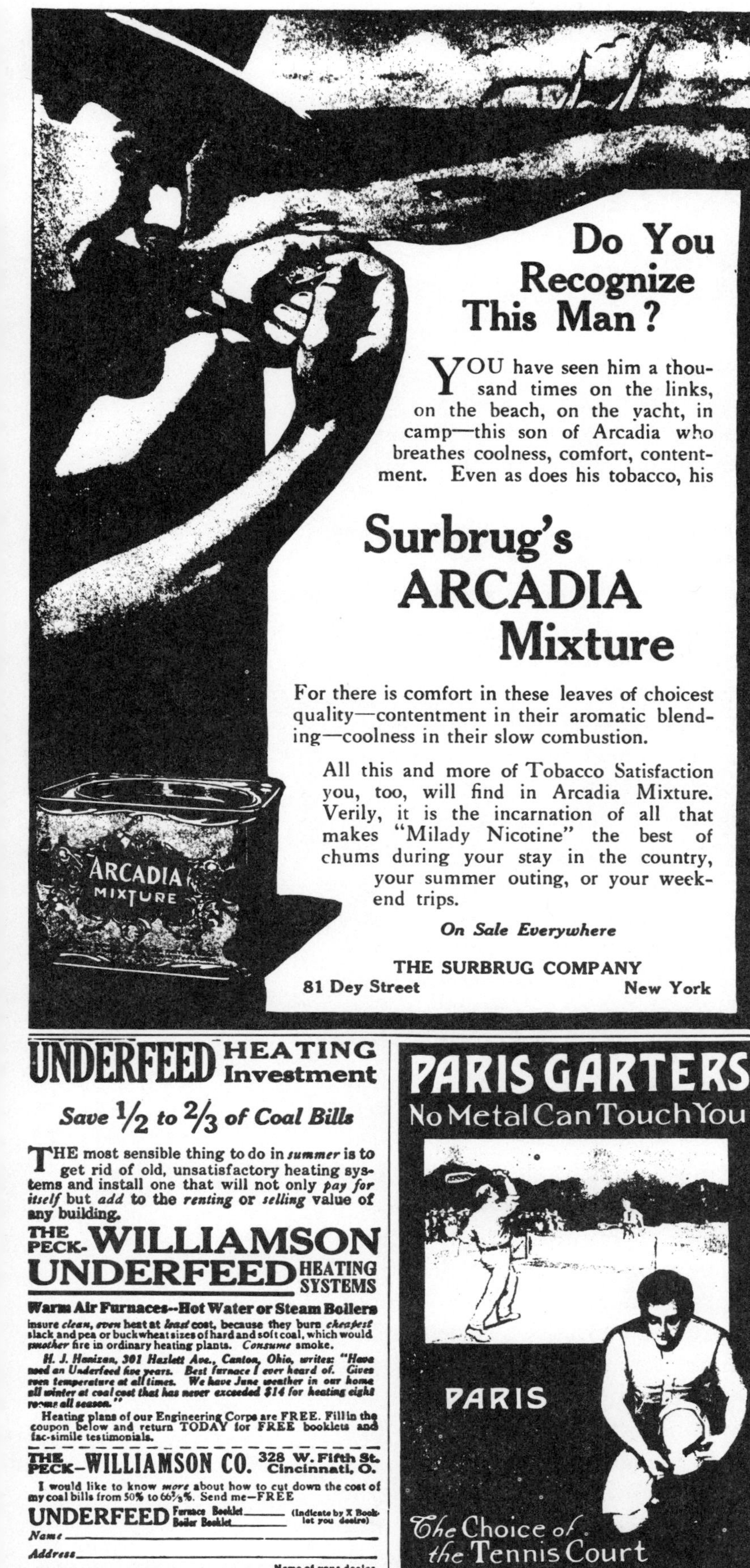

The American Newspaper

(*Concluded from page 18*)

tlemen, my signature to an article is worth some attention. And if you force me out, I shall have just enough money left to print and distribute a handbill. I'll drop it in every doorway, I'll paste it on every fence; and it will be the most interesting reading ever offered the city of Pittsburg." He left the meeting, he continued his policy, and he heard nothing further from the bankers.

How many a newspaper must have lived through such a drama—only with a different climax! For when the publisher lies down, swallows his dose, and keeps the friendship of the powers, we do not hear about it. Alone, the experienced journalist, compendium not only of publishable news but of unpublishable information, sees the change in policy, remembers where the newspaper got its money, and, by putting two and two together, knows what he can not prove.

The Syndicate Influence

WHEN one man heads a newspaper, he at least is responsible for its shortcomings and compromises. Though he be rich, he may remain more journalist than business man, as are Pulitzer in New York and Nelson in Kansas City. But when the newspaper is owned by a stock company, when its directors meet but to shave this year's expenses and increase next year's dividends, commercialism usually binds it. The height of its policy is then enlightened selfishness. If it approximate free journalism, it usually does so only because freedom may pay in the long run.

The remarkable history of the Chicago "Tribune"—not a "stock proposition" but a paper of several joint owners, nevertheless—illustrates this point: it illustrates also how the social poison mixes by chemical affinity with the financial poison.

Joseph Medill founded the "Tribune." He was of the Greeley school—a fighting, war-time editor with a blasting pen. He made it the great journal of the Middle West. Before he died, in the late nineties, journalism had become transformed. He saw the new era, as Greeley might not have done, and he made news efficiency march with editorial efficiency. In this his son-in-law, the late Robert W. Patterson, was a most able assistant. He was a remarkable news editor.

Medill owned most of the "Tribune" stock. His will left his holding in a twenty-five-year trust with three trustees of equal power. One was his son-in-law, Robert W. Patterson; a second his other son-in-law, Robert S. McCormick, later Ambassador to Hungary, to Russia, and to France; and the third, his old associate and personal attorney, William G. Beale. Under this management the publication went ahead wonderfully. Probably no American newspaper has ever employed so many men of ability verging on genius as the "Tribune" in the last decade. James Keeley is supreme in the United States as a news editor. No one else perceives so clearly and subtly what news value is; no one else can make such drama out of the day's events. William Hard, Joseph Medill Patterson, Tiffany Blake, nearly revived the lost arts of the essay in their editorials. Medill McCormick was a good publisher not only upstairs but downstairs, not only in furthering the intellectual ends of a newspaper but its business needs. Clifford Raymond was one of the great American reporters. John T. McCutcheon originated a new form of cartoon—and these are only a few out of many. On make-up, or purely mechanical appearance, on taste in news-writing, on criticism, it came to lead the country.

The Dictator of the "Tribune"

WITH all this modern cast, it continued to hold most of Joseph Medill's old power as an editorial advocate. Its circulation is moderate, as compared to the myriad Hearst readers, but it reaches the brains of Chicago and the Middle West. It remains one of the few American newspapers of which one can say with certainty that it will help any cause that it advocates on the editorial page.

But Beale served on the board of trustees, and voted one-third of the Medill stock. And Beale is not a journalist. He is a corporation attorney. He has the corporation point of view. He believes, probably, that the people prosper only as superior beings take care of them. Doubtless he believes that there are two kinds of morality—home and business. We can not quarrel with his opinions and motives. He is what nature and environment made him, and nature gave him great diplomatic ability, as environment this point of view.

Had the Patterson and McCormick interests voted their two-thirds of the trusteeship as a unit, Beale, with his one-third, were an unconsidered factor. But social and personal ambitions divided them. McCormick's ambition made him ambassador. And Beale, carefully widening the division, voted now with the McCormicks against the Pattersons and now with the Pattersons against the McCormicks. So, again and again, was he able to impose on editors, reporters, and editorial writers a policy which made them grind their teeth. For five or six years thereafter the course of the "Tribune" became spotted—a streak of white, followed by a small streak of dirty gray.

Freeing a Newspaper

BY all its old policies, the "Tribune" should have opposed Senator Lorimer's original election. Keeley, who finally exposed Lorimer, must have suspected then, as well as he knows now, what forces backed him. One imagines Blake with his keen, proportionate wisdom, McCutcheon with his incisive pencil, and Raymond with his gentle but effective sarcasm, panting for a chance at this representative of corruption. But Beale prevailed; the "Tribune" held its peace on Lorimer. The so-called Drainage Canal plan involved using that stream to make electricity for the municipal supply. But that would have hurt the Edison Company. Beale got the reins again, and again the "Tribune" favored the corporation side. Finally, but for Beale we might have needed no Insurgent fight on Joseph Cannon. The "Tribune" has real power, even in Danville; had it started one of its strong, intelligent campaigns against Cannon's re-election in 1908, it might have turned the balance. But Beale tightened the reins; and Cannon was elected.

In the course of these office disturbances, Medill McCormick virtually resigned as publisher. Then, when the "Tribune" seemed sentenced to silence and blackness, the situation shifted again. The McCormicks and Pattersons were brought together. Beale was squelched. McCormick returned to his desk. Keeley became general manager with full power. The paper emerged into a spot of white. Immediately the "Tribune" expiated an old sin. Keeley accepted an opening to let in the light on Lorimer, found just what influences elected him, and published an exposé which, for technical efficiency, was a journalistic masterpiece.

The "Leader" episode, the "World-Herald" episode, the history of the Chicago "Tribune"—these are glimpses beneath the surface. And only glimpses. They express a whole situation, in the last analysis the perplexity of free journalism. The direct control of the advertiser may pass with more enlightened business methods, but so long as our American capitalism retains its insolence and its ruthlessness of method, commercial publishers of million-dollar newspapers must recognize this influence whether they like it or no. And many of them do like it.

The Opposing Pulls

LET us, in closing, look one thing squarely in the face. Though we view society as radicals, not as Tories, we must concede to the other side the right to an organ. That a man takes the side of property is no crime. Society proceeds by checks and balances. There must be radicals, or we shall have rule by barons; there must be conservatives, or the fagots will blaze behind street barricades. A newspaper which stood openly for class and corporation rule, wrote its editorials and colored its news to that end, would be a worthy, dignified, and honest institution. By no such method do our barons proceed; and our quarrel is with the method. Publicly, the controlled newspaper assumes to exercise its ancient office of tribune of the people. Privately, it serves wealth. Publicly, that it may keep subscribers, it pretends to favor progress; privately, that it may guard its owner's sources of revenue and social position, it suppresses and denatures news which would assist that progress. The system is dishonest to its marrow.

Let us clear our eyes again, and face another fact. Circulation and advertising, the people and the interests, exercise opposing pulls on newspapers. Advocate popular causes cleverly enough, and you gain circulation. If you do not believe in these causes, and howl them out only to increase subscription lists, then are you a dishonest publisher. Newspapers have built on this policy, and built only to betray when they got themselves established. But the ratio of this kind of dishonesty to the other and deeper kind is the ratio between circulation receipts and advertising receipts—or about one to four.

XIII

The New Era

In 1911, wrote Irwin, the newspaper's commodity was truth. Today the news media, a good deal less ambitiously, declare that their basic commodity is information. What has caused the change in emphasis?

Many related factors appear responsible. As newspaper competition diminished, survivors, in order to serve larger, more disparate constituencies, seem to have committed themselves more to the objective pursuit, rather than the subjective presentation, of "truth." This of course helped create similarity among competitors, which facilitated still further reduction in competition. Moreover, wire services and news syndicates presented largely middle-of-the road products in order to reach customers to the right and left of center on current issues. But these are pragmatic, down-to-earth reasons. Perhaps more significant in the long run has been the effect of the fledgling sciences of human behavior, psychiatry, psychology, and sociology. While they may not have taught us much about ourselves, they have established the intangible nature of essential truth, and thousands of graduates have taken that lesson from the campus to the newsroom. One result of all this has been better reporting of what has increasingly been seen to be a very complex world.

One thing has changed remarkably little since Irwin's time: why newspapers fail economically. Modern publishers are fond of ascribing failure to high production costs, intransigent labor unions, competition from other media for advertising, and other causes. Without question, such factors are influential. Yet the main reason for newspaper failure today is probably as it was in Irwin's day: loss of public support. "What, in the end, alienates public support? A reputation for lies, either of expression or of silence." Today we are less direct. We say "lack of relevance." But we mean the same thing. The strictly honest newspaper was a valuable property then as now. Irwin cites Victor Lawson's Chicago *Daily News*. "Even should it change hands, should a get-rich-quick policy destroy its character, the 'News' would go on paying for a generation by power of its old honesty," he prophesied. Following Lawson's death in 1925, the paper was sold for thirteen and a half million dollars, a record price for a newspaper.

The American Newspaper

A Study of Journalism in Its Relation to the Public

By WILL IRWIN

XIII.—The New Era

Truth as a commodity of journalism. The controlled game is the short game. "Good-will" as the chief asset in the newspaper business. The cause of failure in most established newspapers which go to the wall, and the reason why such properties as the Chicago "News" and the Kansas City "Star" are considered the best investments. Passing of the "wildcat" era in publication

OF ALL the pretty theories by which mankind sugars unpleasant fact, none so poorly stands the proof of experience as the belief that it always pays to be good, that truth and honesty, in the end, get the champagne and truffles, lying and dishonesty the lees and crusts. For when the journalist, with his learning in the written and unwritten gossip of his times, reviews our world of fact, he discovers that the material rewards go very largely to the wisely and discreetly dishonest. Too often Crœsus owns his country estate, cruises in his steam yacht, because he has taken rebates or kept rotten, germ-eaten tenements. Too often Solon sits in the Senate because he has compounded, secretly and cleverly, with the weasels and rats of the city tenderloin, the vultures and wolves of the State lobby. If their sin finds them out, it discovers them in their closets, not their counting-rooms; the temporal punishment strikes their characters, not their pockets.

Yet journalism, among all human institutions, seems most to vindicate popular belief regarding the reward of virtue and of vice. Reviewing the whole field of publication, following from beginning to end the history of newspaper after newspaper, one finds that those which have gone on to great and stable profits are those which have most clearly expressed on the surface what exists beneath. In the business of journalism it seems that virtue does get its final material reward.

To understand this peculiarity of journalism, it is necessary to dismiss morals and view it as a business proposition. The advertiser pays most of the revenue. But he is paying for circulation. The greater the circulation, the greater the advertising rate, and the more eagerly advertisers will buy. This is a kind of double product, a double sale. You must have circulation first, last, and all the time, though circulation pay you no profit, except as you turn it into advertising—as a stock-feeder gets his profit not from his hay and corn, but from his fattened steers.

Truth as a Commodity

WHAT, in the last analysis, is the editor selling to his subscribers? Truth. For that they take his newspaper—to get at the truth about their times, as the imperfect human editor sees truth. The great, the damning indictment against a corrupt newspaper is the accusation of lying. Ask any stranger in smoking compartment or hotel lobby what he thinks of his home newspapers, what adverse criticism he has to bring against them? Typically, bromidically, he answers: "You can't believe half you see in them." Intuition lies deeper than reason, and mankind perceives before it formulates. Your chance acquaintance has perceived that the commodity of a newspaper is truth.

Now the gentlemen of the Crœsus type, who prosper by lies and legalized theft, have usually been moral in one thing. Their ultimate, economic product has been good, or the public would not long have bought it. John D. Rockefeller stands as type of this evil-born prosperity; but Standard Oil was good oil. The picking, stealing, and chicanery came in somewhere along the line of distribution; it did not consist in poor refining nor adulteration—if adulteration of petroleum be possible. The railroad Crœsus strangles competition by bribing legislators, or he grows fat with rebates. But his railroads run on schedule; they handle the business. If he grows too careless about safety devices, too economical about passenger accommodations, he invites boycott and competition. He, also, dare not adulterate the product.

Now when an editor habitually states what he knows to be untruth or half-truth, when, to favor his crowd, his advertisers or his financial source of supplies, he taints or suppresses good news, he is watering the milk. He is manufacturing an adulterated product, and violating a law of commercial success.

The merely commercial and conscienceless newspaper proprietor sees, or thinks he sees, a way to beat this law. Whiten your sepulchers, rouge your sores. Cleverly and adroitly color the news at demand of your advertisers, and the powers behind them; sell your policy for money; do the work of the unclean element of your political faction; and conceal it all by cleverness. Like a conjurer, attract attention to one hand, while working the trick with the other. Advocate with sincerity a good cause which touches no interest, that you may remain silent about a good cause which touches all the interests. If a reformer raise the cry of rotten tenements, speak him fair, give him perhaps perfunctory space, and start next day a public fresh air fund subscription with the richest tenement-holder at the top of the list. So you may fool your reader into giving you circulation to sell to the real profit-maker—the advertiser.

A fine plan, apparently. Yet men who have staked their fortunes on it are borrowing quarters on Newspaper Row and wondering what happened. For it had just one concealed flaw, which they might have discovered by consulting any advanced treatise on English composition. The hidden intention, the back thought, has a way of shining through the written word. Sincerity is a foundation of all sound work in letters, and insincerity in print can not be made convincing. Because he was false, Oscar Wilde stands merely a study in a phase of style, instead of a supreme figure; because, after life had beaten his cynic humor all to pieces, he became momentarily sincere, he left "The Ballad of Reading Gaol" for his monument. By one of those subtle, hidden powers of mind which the science of psychology can not weigh, the world in general perceives sincerity; and none who ever wrote was great enough to defy his own perception of truth.

William R. Nelson

Dean of active American newspaper publishers. His Kansas City "Star" is not only a great force for good, but one of the most valuable newspaper properties in the country

The conscienceless publisher who sells his influence sees his plot fall because the public finds him out in the end and gradually withdraws its support. Usually, by only one method may his game be made profitable. That is to play it wholly like an adventurer and a pirate. Enjoy your first flush of hectic prosperity; when you feel the end coming, sell the sucked lemon to some dupe, and move away to new fields. This is like the Japanese treatment of leased orchards, at which the Western farmer girds and riots. Pick, don't prune. Wring all you can out of the trees in three or four seasons; then get out, and devil take the orchard.

As for the gentleman of high finance who buys a newspaper outright to boom his private enterprises, his finish comes with greater expedition and certainty. Eventually, he finds that the newspaper in itself does not pay. If it is worth his while to retain it for assistance in his larger commercial and social plans, that is another matter. His profit must come in some coin other than business office receipts.

Letting Down the Bars

IT IS like the hotel business. Suppose you are an innkeeper, with a fine, respectable establishment. To stimulate profits, you take down a few bars, begin to admit disreputable and unpleasant people. Your hotel enjoys great prosperity for two or three seasons, then suddenly falls toward bankruptcy. The hotel bore a reputation for respectability; the soiled characters wanted to enter it in order to conceal their real nature and intentions. The newspaper bore a reputation for sincerity; prostitute causes wanted to enter it in order to get by association the color of truth. As time passed, more and more disreputable people came to the hotel, so that it lost utterly its old reputation. As time passed, the newspaper had to lie more and more boldly, suppress more and more brutally, and the public began to perceive. Finally, even the disreputable abandoned the hotel because it no longer covered their intentions. Finally, the corrupt powers which fed the newspaper discovered that its word carried no more force, that it was unable to further their causes, and they abandoned it to failure.

This is not exactly a rule of newspaper publication, but it is a strong tendency. Here and there—especially in cities which have no free journalism in opposition—exist newspapers which have grown rich, continue rich, settle into an appearance of stable respectability, on the insincere process of tricking their circulation. But the main current runs in the other direction. The properties which have remained longest in the field, that have risen to the greatest and most stable profits, are those which have kept furthest from control.

Ask any well-informed publisher what "one edition" American newspaper he would prefer to own. He would take into account, of course, not only this year's profits, but past records and future prospects; and on that calculation he would name, doubtless, the Chicago "News," the New York morning "World," or the New York "Herald." Bar New York, Philadelphia, and Chicago, and he would be likely to choose the Kansas City "Star" or the Los Angeles "Times." Now each of these newspapers has its faults and virtues in different degree; but they have this common characteristic: they have been sincere. They have expressed the view of the personality behind them. Least admirable of all, perhaps, is the New York "Herald." It has seldom stood for a good cause; usually, it has stood for no cause at all. It has been sensational under a veneer of bourgeois respectability, it has published advertisements atrociously immoral. But it has been so because Bennett the younger wanted it so. He has not sold his birthright to trust nor magnate; he has not compounded with the other interests whose securities lie in his strong-box. The "Herald" has expressed Bennett. So it has kept a certain level of sincerity, shown truth, though through an off-color lens.

The New York "World," final expression of Joseph Pulitzer's extraordinary talent, compounds a little —but very little—with its advertisers. Nothing else binds Pulitzer. If he own outside properties, they probably influence him not one whit. He speaks as he sees, and so does the staff under him. It matters not that he often sees ugliness before beauty, evil before good. The thing expresses Pulitzer; it is sincere. So he rolls up his profits by the hundreds of thousands, invests them by millions.

General Harrison Gray Otis
The fighting publisher of the Los Angeles "Times"

Victor Lawson
Publisher of the honest and independent Chicago "News"

James Gordon Bennett the Younger
Absentee publisher of the capricious New York "Herald"

An Honest Newspaper

BEYOND a few small reciprocal favors to advertisers, the Chicago "News" is an honest newspaper, first, last, and all the time. It is perhaps a tint and not a color; it would satisfy our ideal of journalism better if it fought harder. But therein it expresses only the opinions and character of its head. The "News" is not borrowing money from banks, and it does not need support from trust or corporation. It presents Chicago and the world as Victor Lawson, its publisher, and an editorial force which he chooses, see the world. In some respects it goes far beyond any contemporary in allegiance to truth. When the "News" calls a despatch foreign correspondence, it is just that; it is not matter rewritten in the office from foreign newspapers. Its specials on last night's news are its own; they are not rewritten from this morning's newspapers. And the "News," according to general report among publishers—who have their own means of knowing—makes $800,000 to $900,000 a year. Even should it change hands, should a get-rich-quick policy destroy its character, the "News" would go on paying for a generation by power of its old honesty.

The Unapproachable "Star"

JUST so with the Kansas City "Star"; but here is a color, not a tint. Not only has Colonel William R. Nelson held his organ to truth, but he has gone forth from his battlements and fought to make his city a better place for honest men and women. He has investments outside of his newspaper; I believe that he has never let these investments color his policies. In the periodical campaigns which the "Star" directs against the gang and the unfair public utility corporations, his opponents have charged underhand connection with the "interests." These charges, at worst, are not proved; probably they are the invention of desperation. And Nelson has succeeded to the height of any publisher's imagination. His business is so fortified, so stable, that it almost defies competition. He need make no concessions to advertisers; they come to him. If they would reach the people of Kansas City they must have the "Star" and "Times." Where others appeal, he dictates. He has even been able to maintain a competition-strangling policy of circulation—morning, evening, and Sunday paper at ten cents a week —which has generally failed elsewhere just because nowhere else is there so strong and healthy a business. General Harrison Gray Otis, with the Los Angeles "Times," illustrates both sides; in his career we see sincerity making dividends and insincerity shaving them. He is a forceful, knobby character; and for a long time he was himself. He represented the spirit of his community. It is a business spirit; the hustler, transplanted from the Middle West, made and maintained Los Angeles. Fairly, freely, he told the truth as he saw it. He fought for Los Angeles. He defeated the Southern Pacific, the great master of corporations in California, on the harbor project. When, in his unfair campaign against labor unions, he daily colored the fact, he expressed after all only his own knobby temper—as he did in his war on the Los Angeles school bond issue, begun because the superintendent of schools offended him.[1] But the corporation attitude crept into Otis's policy. Perhaps it was his mutual investment with the Southern Pacific in lands; perhaps it was only the weight of his millions. And now, though the "Times" is still a great money-maker, the Hearst "Examiner" on one side, the measurably free "Express" on the other, are cutting into circulation and advertising. Once almost as much a dictator in Los Angeles as Nelson in Kansas City, Otis dictates no more. His intention has pierced the written word.

The Case of Milwaukee

TAKE Milwaukee. There journalism is at rather low ebb financially. In no other American city, probably, are newspaper profits so small in proportion to the population. The "Free Press" is the boughten press of Senator Isaac Stephenson. He uses it to keep himself in the Senate, to protect the fortunes which send him there; and when there is a deficit he pays it patiently. The "Sentinel" is picket of Milwaukee's Black Horse Cavalry, whose commander is Colonel Pfister. The "Wisconsin" is weakly conservative. The most profitable newspaper in Milwaukee, by all odds the best property, is the "Journal." And the "Journal" is precisely that English newspaper which has the least traffic with corporations. Nearest of all, it approaches truth. Most of all, it dares speak out to its public.

Precisely so it goes with those publishers who have built up newspapers not by units but by groups. First among these in circulation is Hearst; in number of newspapers, the Scripps-McRae League. Except for difference of method, Scripps might appear as large to the public eye as Hearst. But the latter enters a city preceded by a calliope and a brass band, while the former steals in on gumshoes. "We want every man, woman, and child to know that Hearst is here," says a Hearst executive. "We want each of our subscribers to think he is the only subscriber," says the Scripps executive.

Now, year in and year out, through all his queer, tacking course in journalism, Hearst has steered for one beacon. He has never forgotten the subscriber and his interests. Neither—or at least not until recently—has he permitted any outside interest to get a hold on his policies. It is true that in the nineties Collis P. Huntington of the Southern Pacific bought the silence of the San Francisco "Examiner," then Hearst's only newspaper, with an advertisement. The contract called for $1,000 a month, to run thirty months. The Hearst men say that a resident manager made this deal during the proprietor's absence --Hearst was in Europe on his first long vacation. Before the thirty months was out, the great railroad strike came. The Southern Pacific was at war with the very class to which Hearst looked for circulation support. Hearst repudiated the contract—and Huntington made the transaction public. Ever since, Hearst's rivals have thrown in his teeth that dishonest contract. But in his own curious way, Hearst did stand by the subscriber and against the corporation. Perhaps that was the crossroads in his career. Perhaps had he turned the other way, respected not only his written word but also feared the blackmail which Huntington held over him, he would have descended, not risen. And he must have learned the lesson. For ten years, during which he faced the batteries of abuse, none charged control against him. He was looking always toward the subscriber.

It is "profit-taking time" with Hearst; for the last two or three years he has shown a disposition to trick the subscriber on behalf of his own larger interests; in Boston he is very quiet now, and in the city of his beginnings he is silent about the Southern Pacific—nay, during the Heney prosecution of Calhoun he fought its battles. Last year he took up the cudgels for Diaz of Mexico against magazine attack. His only visible reason for going without our borders to make a campaign against liberalism is his holding in Chihuahua lands, a bounty from Diaz to him and his father.

Commercialized Sincerity

AS FOR Scripps-McRae, who conduct twenty-two metropolitan and small-city newspapers under one central organization, the subscriber and the subscriber's interests are the foundation-stone of their policy. Scripps finances his own newspapers; his individual publisher, set down in a city with a small share in the property, does not have to borrow from a bank. The Scripps men are trained to keep an eye always on the subscriber, to serve his interests first. And the typical Scripps subscriber is a working man. If, here and there, a Scripps executive, in his haste to make returns, lies down before the advertiser, it is only here and there. The wholly commercial ideal of these newspapers is the presentation of all the truth from a popular point of view, in order to keep pure and plentiful the blood of their business. Dollar for dollar of investment, unit for unit of subscription, they make even Hearst journalism seem profitless. Further, the older ones are fine, established properties worth dollars where certain wildcat newspapers of equal circulation are worth dimes. E. W. Scripps, after all kinds of experience with all kinds of newspapers, has learned that nothing profits a newspaper like truth; he has commercialized sincerity.

"Purposely Independent"

THE negotiations for the sale of a newspaper came recently under my notice. An editor, just then out of a position and in possession of some funds, wanted an organ of his own. He consulted a newspaper broker, who led him to the chief owner of a small-city journal in New England. This vender had decided to try other fields, he told the buyer; but the "graft was great."

"Just look," he said, "we've a gubernatorial campaign coming in the fall. Smith and Jones [I disguise the names] are sure to be the nominees. There's a fine chance to collect off either—*I've purposely kept the paper independent.* You'd better go for Jones, I guess. We've already got a lot out of Smith, and Jones will have a bigger sack."

Then the vender went into details of stock and ownership. "I wish," said the proposed buyer afterward, "that I could have kept the list—it was so

(Concluded on page 25)

[1] Let no one deduce from this that we are defending by inference those—whether union men or not—who blew up the "Times" building. Truth compels the statement that the Otis war on the unions has been grievously, almost absurdly, unfair.

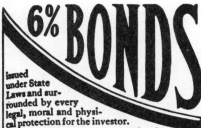

The American Newspaper

(Concluded from page 16)

typical of a certain kind of newspaper. The gas company, so many shares; the banks, so many shares; the railroad, so many shares. But the remark which closed the negotiations was most typical of all. He said: 'I'll tell you what I'd do if I were you. I'd just wipe all these shares off my books and make them come through again. They've already had their money's worth out of me!'"

Now the point and moral of this story is in the beginning. The newspaper was for sale. There was no more juice in it for banks or for gas company or for the nominal owner. The owner had sucked the lemon, and he was handing over the skin.

Why Newspapers Fail

A YOUNG newspaper may fail through any of the causes which wreck new business houses. When an old, established one fails, the type-reason is bartered influence or corporation control. The "Alta California" was the pioneer newspaper of San Francisco. During the seventies it stood supreme in its field. But the get-rich-quick policy drew its blood. It trafficked with corporations, it fought and suppressed for the Southern Pacific and its allied interests. The "Alta California" languished. Finally, circulation fell away until it became useless even to the corporations; and one day it simply stopped. Trace the history of any established newspaper which has died like this; the corporation germ is usually the cause of the disease. Within two years after John R. Walsh bought the Chicago "Chronicle" and began to use it in support of his tangled, crooked financial transactions, it had ceased to pay. When the great downfall came, when Walsh went to prison, its estimated valuation was only that of its Associated Press franchise and its down-at-the-heel printing plant.

Indeed, this instance gives another angle on the newspaper as a business proposition and freedom as an asset. As every business man knows, good-will is a tangible if somewhat mercurial asset of all commercial institutions, a thing to be bought, sold, traded with. Good-will is by far the greatest property of a publication, whether magazine or newspaper. The Chicago "Tribune," exclusive of its building, is worth, I believe, about $8,000,000. Its visible assets, as plant and circulation apparatus, can hardly be worth more than two and a half millions. What is the other five and a half millions? Good-will. Business prestige, reputation as an advertising medium, long contracts, enter into the account; but the main item, after all, is its hold with the public. What does the public buy, or expect to buy, from the "Tribune," or from any other popular newspaper? Mainly truth. What, in the end, alienates public support? A reputation for lies, either of expression or of silence. And, since the intention eventually shines through the written word, concealing, slanting, denying truth is by way of cutting into capital, breaking into cargo.

New Times, New Methods

I HAVE divided the history of American journalism into three eras. In the first, the editorial advocate, the tribune of the people, was lord and mentor. The second was the riotous era of news. The third brought yellow journalism and commercial journalism, which allied themselves for curious results. It may be that we are entering a new era. Perhaps even those publishers who recognize neither conscience nor ethics are learning that free publication pays best, that the controlled game is the short game. After the period of wildcat banks, bankers settled down to stable finance, not so much because they disapproved of wildcat methods as because the times would no longer tolerate them and wildcat banking no longer paid. So, after a period of wildcat publication, we may enter an era of greater stability and honesty. The times runs in that direction; it is a hopeful sign for a free press.

The publisher alone, however, will never wholly reform the greater abuses of journalism. The impetus must come from the actual journalist, writing upstairs while the proprietor sells his wares downstairs, and from us, the public; not from the middleman, but from the producer and consumer.

XIV

The Press of Two Cities

Of the whole series, this article most nearly conforms to the muckraking archetype. It was apparently written as something of an afterthought. It was not announced in the schedule of the series run with the first article on January 21, 1911. And it was substituted on July 22 for what would have been the last of the fourteen announced articles. Thus the series ran to fifteen, one more than announced on the cover of the January 21 *Collier's*.

In presenting the two case studies Irwin shows very clearly the importance of the news media to a community. A good newspaper may not be able to prevent corruption from taking hold, but a corrupt newspaper will assure that it does.

The American Newspaper

A Study of Journalism in Its Relation to the Public

By WILL IRWIN

XIV.—The Press of Two Cities

The danger of a controlled press as illustrated by present conditions in Cincinnati and Pittsburg. How Boss Cox and his gang have strangled criticism of machine methods in Cincinnati. The "Post's" reformation, and its influence in breaking the Cox power. The real cause of the graft indictments in Pittsburg. The long newspaper opposition to the "Pittsburg Plan" of municipal government; its causes and its methods. The curious case of the "Leader".

COPYRIGHT 1908 BY HARRIS & EWING

John R. McLean
Owner of the Cincinnati "Enquirer"

THE last five articles of this series have been running on the tack of the adverse, stating the darker side of American journalism. It would be called "muckraking," I suppose. But keep in mind that the daily newspaper, for all its power and value, is still absurdly young. Remember that journalism of any kind has yet to celebrate its three hundredth anniversary, and that journalism as we know it now is hardly a century old. Remember, also, that men yet alive took wet from the press the first copy of Bennett's "Herald," parent to every modern American newspaper. Except Darwin's scientific method, no plant of thought ever grew so great in so short a period. By human necessity it has grown in size and strength at the expense of perfection, developed flaws which it must correct by process of years and wisdom and excesses which society at large must curb and regulate. Also, it has served well in bulk. We have expected more of our journalism than any other modern people, and it has given more. The marvel is not so much that it has developed tyrannies and dishonesties, as that it has rendered this service.

Yet before I am finished with muckraking—let me accept the term—I must clinch my points by some general examples. Reverence for the sources of advertising income, reverence for the sources of social and political approval, reverence for the sources of necessary capital—to what end may they lead journalism? The answer is the present condition of press and politics in Cincinnati and Pittsburg, cities now struggling to free themselves from the tyrants of democracy.

The Rule of Boss Cox

CINCINNATI, as the world knows, has been ruled by George B. Cox, a graduate saloon owner, a survival in the newer age of that dynasty which thimble-rigged American municipal politics in the blind and lawless era of our democracy. He has held his power by all the familiar tricks, from persuading outcasts at election time to favoring bankers with city funds. He has maintained the old alliance between the rat and the wolf—the dissolute little people of the vice district and the respectable big people of the public-service corporations. On behalf of his small group of insiders, he has formed an organization so strong that every road to public preferment in Cincinnati has run through the office of George B. Cox. His favorites have gone up through certain definite stages of promotion to the bench, to the City Council, to Congress; and the speed of their promotion has depended upon their usefulness to the machine. To do this gang justice, it was not distinguished by pickings and stealings along the line. The "honest graft" went to the heads of the organization. The rewards of the faithful were promotion and personal advancement.

The Federal census has just demonstrated mathematically the effect of this hard-and-fast control by a select body of "insiders." During the last decade the average American city of Cincinnati's class increased in population 39 per cent, and the average Ohio city of more than 25,000 population 36.2 per cent. Cincinnati grew in the same period only 11.5 per cent. Analyzed to the last factor, gang control is the answer to this problem in social arithmetic. A modern city grows largely by suburban trolley lines; and the gang, working with the transportation companies, made free development of suburban trolleys an impossibility. A city of Cincinnati's character grows largely by new manufactures. What encouragement had a manufacturer to enter a city where the insiders would hold him up for every privilege, from side-tracks to sites? When the automobile came, Cincinnati had perhaps the best carriage works in the United States. Nothing easier than to turn the expert carriage makers of this city into automobile workers. But there stood the gang, asking its bit of all industry—and the automobile business went to the near-by cities of Detroit, Toledo, Dayton, and Cleveland. So much for the background.

Senator George T. Oliver
Owner of two Pittsburg papers

Now the Cox machine is nominally Republican; and Cincinnati has four English newspapers—two Republican, one Democratic, and one independent with a labor bias. Until recently not one of these newspapers has lifted a voice of protest against Cox and his gang.

COPYRIGHT BY CINCINNATI "POST"

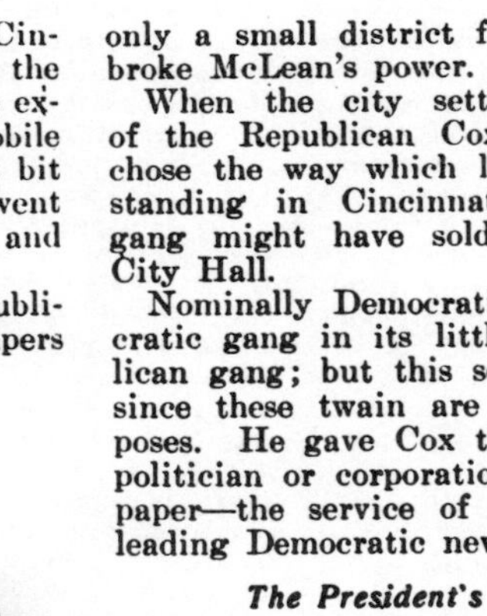

George B. Cox
The Cincinnati Boss

John R. McLean, publisher also of the Washington "Post," owns the Cincinnati "Enquirer," a morning "independent Democratic" newspaper which stands alone in its class. Year in and year out, it has been one of the cleverest of our journals, one of the sharpest in newspaper technique. Also, it has been one of the most salacious. Wherever the news offered an excuse, it has skirted the law against sending obscene matter through the mails. Not even the London "Pink 'Un" or the Boulevard sheets of Paris publish a feature more openly and subtly salacious than "Durandel's New York Letter," which appears weekly in the "Enquirer." It clung until the last hope to the outworn "massage" form of assignation advertisement. There is much cleverness and little decency in the "Enquirer."

From such a newspaper one could hardly expect the fulfilment of public duty. It has lived up to expectation.

In the stormy old period which culminated in the Cincinnati riots of 1884, McLean himself was a kind of boss; for at that date Cox ruled only a small district from his saloon. The riots broke McLean's power.

When the city settled down under the rule of the Republican Cox, the Democratic McLean chose the way which led to safe profits and easy standing in Cincinnati. For all of him, the gang might have sold the windows out of the City Hall.

Nominally Democratic, he supported the Democratic gang in its little flurries with the Republican gang; but this service was merely negative, since these twain are one for all practical purposes. He gave Cox the best service that corrupt politician or corporation fixer can ask of a newspaper—the service of silence. So much for the leading Democratic newspaper.

The President's Brother's Newspaper

CHARLES P. TAFT, brother of the President, owns the "Times-Star," "independent Republican," a good newspaper technically. President Taft is a mild radical sprung from the midst of fattened conservatives. Charles P. Taft, in so far as we can judge him from his public acts, represents that extreme American Tory who makes the English Tory appear like a Socialist.

To such a man, capital appears sacred, business a god, reform of the outworn institutions which served us in our period of ground-breaking a blasphemous irritation or a bitter joke. He was not so in the beginning. He started as a free newspaper publisher of moderate means; and in the early nineties he was fighting Cox. Then, through marriage and inheritance, money came his way—much money, until to-day he is the richest man in Cincinnati. He owns the largest and best hotel; his hand is in all the public utilities. One can not visit Cincinnati for a day without paying tribute in some form or other to Charles P. Taft.

As his millions grew, he began to let gang politics alone. He accepted a Congressional nomination from the machine. He himself became Cox's man, his newspaper Cox's organ. Not but that the yoke

(Concluded on page 25)

The American Newspaper

(Concluded from page 13)

chafed now and then. There is none too much of strong heart in Cox. Twice, after minor reform victories, he has "announced his retirement," only to slip back into the saddle. Upon each of these retirements the "Times-Star" has advised in guarded language the "need for new leaders." Not the destruction of the machine, notice, nor yet the reform of machine methods, but new leaders—perhaps Mike Mullen of the Eighth Ward, whose poetically named Silver Moon lodging-house harbors the riff-raff of the rivers on the night before election. Mike Mullen it is who gave a picnic to the poor of Cincinnati on one day, and on the next whipped through council a bill to hand over the city water-front to a railroad. President Taft's Akron speech denouncing Cox and his rule in southern Ohio is a high spot in his record. His brother's newspaper, the "Times-Star," denatured that speech by cutting out every reference to Cox and the gang. So the "Times-Star," also, pays tribute of silence to the boss.

Commission to the Sheriff

THE "Commercial Tribune," "independent Republican," has been gathered from the wreck of several older journals, conspicuously the "Tribune," which was founded as a reform newspaper and died for lack of capital before this century was born. As the "Times-Star" plays its Republican game, so does the "Commercial Tribune"; only perhaps it prospers less. One of its office secrets came out in 1906. The reformers, by a partial victory, had sent a legislative delegation to Columbus. They forced an investigation of Cincinnati affairs, which was going merrily until the gang stopped it by a technicality of law. And the business manager of the "Commercial Tribune" testified before this body that both his newspaper and the "Times-Star" were paying 33 1-3 per cent "commission" to the sheriff's office for county advertising. He had talked this matter over with Mr. Taft once, he said; and Mr. Taft had declared that 33 1-3 per cent was entirely too much—it should be 20 per cent. For this and correlated reasons—and for the main reason that it serves the complaisant individual to placate the gang—the "Commercial Tribune," "independent Republican," pays its own tribute of silence to Boss Cox.

There is one more newspaper in Cincinnati—the independent "Post," owned by the Scripps-McRae league. This, like the other units in that organization, is an economically conducted newspaper, published avowedly for working people. Through a decade of Cox's control, the "Post" also played the game of convenience and held its peace. Cincinnati owns a railroad, the Cincinnati Southern, built after the Civil War to bring the resources of the South to that gateway of the North. In the darkest days of Cox rule, the gang conceived the idea of selling that road for a ridiculous price. And through the agitation and the subsequent election the "Post" took no stand. It "threw open its columns" to both sides—in short, it printed their arguments as advertising matter at advertising rates. An unconsidered factor in Cincinnati politics averted this calamity—that is another story and a good one. But no newspaper now existing in Cincinnati had anything to do with this victory for the people.

The "Post" Takes a Hand

THE "Tribune" died, and deposited its bones with the "Commercial Tribune." For five or six years the people, as against the gang, had no voice in Cincinnati. During that period Cox, with his allies among the rich and his lieutenants among the poor, "sewed up" nearly everything in Cincinnati not already double-stitched. They all but succeeded in rendering useless the improvement of the Ohio River by handing over a water-front elevated franchise to the Louisville and Nashville Railroad. Then, in 1904, the reformers reached Scripps, who was just in the stage of his development as a publisher when he was beginning to support reform issues everywhere. The "Post" declared itself against the gang, and it never faltered. Its process of opposition was simple. It published the news. By virtue of this support, the reformers began to win partial victories. First, they got a legislative delegation in 1906. From that proceeded the legislative committees of 1906 and 1908, mentioned before. These bodies, before the machine stopped them by injunction, gathered enough information to accuse Cox of perjury. The reformers were in no position to get an indictment until 1908, when, led by the "Post," they elected District Attorney Henry Hunt and Judge Frank M. Gorman. They could not bring affairs to a head until 1910, after the reelection of Hunt and Gorman. Then came the indictment and a series of legal moves. The prosecution, as all expected, was beaten from court. I say no more of this lest I be libelous. However, the very fact of the indictment was a hard political blow to Boss Cox. Even this meager result would have been impossible without the assistance of a free newspaper.

Alas, Poor Pittsburg!

THE social and political condition of Pittsburg is so complex, such a veritable Pittsburg smelting-pot of large human forces, that I have no room to relate it even in summary. It is necessary to remember that a body of reformers, including some of the most powerful men in Pittsburg, have been fighting toward a new social consciousness, and that they have encountered not only a municipal machine and a loosely allied State machine, but remnants of several older machines. The Voters' League, expressing all that is best in Pittsburg, has secured in the last two years 149 graft indictments, involving 111 individuals, against councilmen, politicians, and bankers. On these indictments they sent several men to the penitentiary. This scandal brought the state of affairs vividly to the attention of the country. Not even Pittsburg realizes, however, that these small politicians, these bank officials, only half guilty since they but plied the old trade as their craftmasters taught it, were sacrificed to a silent press.

The reformers were not fighting men so much as systems and conditions. They recognized that the best tool of the bosses and grafters was the councilmanic system. There were two houses, elected from small districts—in one period Pittsburg had one hundred and fifty-five councilmen! Such a government tends inevitably toward graft. To replace this antiquated municipal legislature with a small councilmanic body elected at large—the system which crystallized in the Pittsburg plan—was their main object. First of all, they, the large enlightened people who understood conditions, must inform the little, bewildered people of shop and mill—the voters. For this they needed a newspaper which would find the news and tell it. When they began this open fight against the system two years ago, they looked over the seven daily English newspapers in Pittsburg, and beheld this state of affairs:

The "Gazette-Times" (morning) and the "Chronicle-Telegraph" (evening) are the property and personal organs of United States Senator George T. Oliver. He is a machine politician of the old, trading Pennsylvania school. His son, George S. Oliver, an excellent newspaper man, conducts these journals for him. Report has it that the younger Oliver is considerably more advanced in social outlook than his father; that he might, if left alone, make these newspapers champions of popular right. However, he must consider always his father's political interests, which lie, generally, parallel with the interests of the dominant machine in Pennsylvania. Further, the Frick-Mellon banks are, or have been, their creditor; and in Pittsburg, as elsewhere, the weaving and interweaving of interests allies banks and political gangs. These are, take them all in all, the best written, most modern newspapers in Pittsburg; but there was no certain hope for the reformers in them.

The Barr newspapers? No more hope there. Barr owned the "Post" (morning) and the "Sun" (evening). They are now in the hands of a receiver, who has changed their policies. I speak of them here as they were during the graft fight. What Barr might have done of his own volition, no man but he knows. He was already in financial difficulties. The "Post" had paid. Then he started the "Sun" and found no room for another evening newspaper in Pittsburg. He borrowed heavily from the Farmers' National Bank, a city depository involved in the graft cases. This, if nothing else, insured silence on the part of the "Post" and "Sun."

Five of a Kind

THE "Press" was the old working-class organ of Pittsburg, resembling in cast, though not in character, the Scripps-McRae newspapers of more modern days. Its founders established its circulation and advertising by intelligent response to the news needs of humble readers. Then a company controlled by Oliver P. Hershman bought it. Hershman's friends were Chris Magee and William Flinn, the old bosses of Pittsburg politics. Although new bosses rule, the remnant of the old

gang is still powerful. Paradoxically, Hershman, who came into his business through the machine, leans more toward freedom than the average Pittsburg publisher. But by policy the "Press" takes no strong political stand. After they "break," it reports with measurable fairness and freedom such matters as the late graft indictments; but it never "starts anything." Gang-established, gang-favored, unwilling in any event to take the first step—the "Press" was of no use to the enlightened purposes of reform.

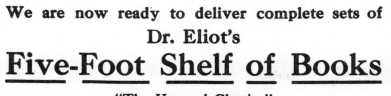

These five newspapers, in so far as they concerned the general good, presented one type. All were "tied up," in some manner or other, to the financial and political powers. All took their positions on local affairs with a view to the immediate financial, social, and political interest of the owners. There remain two newspapers of different type.

The "Dispatch" and the "Leader"

THE "Dispatch" is one of those settled, conservative journals which grow fixed in the affections and habits of settled and conservative people. These are perhaps the "soundest properties," as a class, in the newspaper business. The "Dispatch" is in a position to be independent, for C. A. Rook, who manages it, boasts that he has never passed a dividend. But Rook, apparently, looks at the newspaper business as a means of profit and personal aggrandizement, and nothing more. He plays the gang-game of silence when it best serves the kind of advancement which he covets for himself and the other owners. From the "Dispatch" most was to be expected, owing to its position, and least to be hoped, owing to its policy and traditions.

The other exception is a newspaper hard to classify, a very sulphite of journalism—the "Leader." Once Colonel John I. Nevin owned it; and in his day it served well its public. Nevin belonged in mental attitude to the elder school of Greeley, Godkin, and Raymond. His was the truculence, the likable eccentricity, the zeal for the common good, the joy in journalism for its own sake, which marked that breed. Pause by the way to hear this story: Nevin always read every word in the "Leader" with the critical eye of the expert editor. He discovered once the name of a "prominent citizen" in capital letters. The next morning he called the staff together for one of his office orations. "In future," he said, "the 'Leader' will print only two names in capitals—God Almighty and John I. Nevin." This may not be true. Like Lincoln, he was the kind of man who gathers stories unto his fame. But it represents him.

All his life Nevin fought for a better Pittsburg. His work bore spring fruit in his times and autumn fruit in these. The reformers of the Voters' League and kindred bodies, who are slowly changing and redeeming Pittsburg, build every day on the foundations which he laid. He died in the maturity of his powers, leaving his traditions and his stock in the "Leader" to his descendants and relatives. They carried on the "Colonel's" policies. But the time came when cash from the sale of the "Leader" seemed best to serve the interests of the Nevin family. William Flinn, the old joint-boss with Chris Magee, a contractor grown rich on city jobs, backed Alexander P. Moore in its purchase. Flinn, it is said, has complained at times that he "can't control the darn thing."

The Pittsburg Millionaire

MOORE rose from the "Press"; he had always been affiliated with the gang. He proceeded at once to make the "Leader" a yellow newspaper, and, as a Pittsburg attorney puts it, he "adopted the proposition that the best news is the dirtiest news." Politically, he followed roughly the old "Leader" tradition of righteous independence. However, not only the Flinn loan but his indefensible news policy made him a poor prop for reform. I give him credit for more true militant spirit than do some in Pittsburg, who may have confused honest differences of opinion with bad intention; but I agree that this yellow newspaper, owing backstairs allegiance to a time-expired boss, measuring the worth of a story by the scandal which it involved, could serve a reform cause but imperfectly.

This rapid summary of the circumstances and motives which govern individual Pittsburg newspapers ignores some characteristics common to most of them. They grant the franchise of suppression to the advertisers and the banks as frankly and freely as the worst. Kaufman's department store, for example, has killed story after story. Indeed, so many powerful Pittsburgers have this privilege that two or three free-lance correspondents flourish by selling to other cities the personal news matter suppressed in Pittsburg. From this state of affairs has come one curious effect. The term "Pittsburg millionaire" has become an American joke, a synonym for wild, crude expenditure and gaudy scandal. These irresponsible correspondents have put this tag to Pittsburg by labeling any news-beset business man with a living income "millionaire" or "society leader."

A Little on the Side

THE Oliver newspapers—most modern in their cast and methods—pay measurably good salaries to their editorial employees. The others literally pay less on the average to the men who write their news reports and editorials than to the linotype operators. Twenty-five dollars a week is a "star" salary to a writer. Frankly, the publishers do not expect that this shall be the whole pay of their men. They wink at the collection of half-tainted money "on the outside" because it enables them to get efficient men at a starvation wage. In short, they barter the independence of their writers for the small coin of politicians, theatrical managers, commercial adventurers. The press-agent of Pittsburg works more commonly from inside the newspaper offices than from the outside. The political reporter of the "Dispatch" is head of the Civil Service Commission, a bounty of the city machine, at a salary of $2,400 a year. The political reporter of the "Press" is a member of that same commission at a salary of $2,000 a year. The political editor of the "Gazette-Times" serves on the Registration Commission, a gift of the State machine, at $2,400 a year. Why pay big salaries when the going is so good?

Direct venality is not common among newspapers and newspaper men. Least of all is it common among reporters. He of that adventurous temperament which makes a good news-getter and news-writer is not inclined to look toward money as a main reward. He prefers "the story." Nevertheless, a suppressed chapter of confessions in the Pittsburg graft cases shows that when the gang "cut the melon on a big job," they often gave a share to the reporters. The "tips," on one list, ran from $450 down to $50. Perhaps these men were discharged afterward. I do not know. And I am not greatly blaming them. I blame whoever invented and promoted this system of paying journalists.

Forcing News Into Print

SUCH was the condition of the press when the new civic spirit ran through Pittsburg. Some one must get the state of affairs in city government to the "common people"—in short, some one must tell the news. Since the daily newspapers could not be depended upon to do this voluntarily, the reformers adopted an intensely modern method. They found out themselves the exact extent of graft in the city departments; they employed Wilson, the "praying detective," to trap councilmen; they persuaded the Federal Government to trap bankers; they sprung their arrests and indictments suddenly and dramatically; and so they forced the newspapers to take notice. Suppression has its limits. Here was news so big and astonishing that the newspaper which ignored it would have stamped itself a fool or a knave.

Yes, the seven newspapers of Pittsburg published the news, but they withheld still their editorial support. Bar the "Leader," and one could print in two pages of COLLIER'S all their editorials on the graft indictments, arrests, and convictions—a process which lasted nearly two years.

Further, most of these editorials took the mild tone—"if it is true it is really a pity." When, in the later stages of the fight, the details grew less glaringly sensational, they held back in their news columns. In that period, indeed, the information of most vital interest to corporate Pittsburg often came to light solely in the bulletins of the Voters' League. The newspapers held back while the Charter Committee carried the Pittsburg plan up to the Legislature, held back until A. Leo Weil charged before the State Legislature that a vice machine had been constructed under the city administration. Only when commercial body after commercial body, leading citizen after leading citizen, had endorsed the new charter movement, only when the very local improvement clubs met but to discuss plans for reform, did the newspapers give even half-hearted assent to the Pittsburg plan. Indeed, only three of them wholly endorsed it. Tribunes of the People? Heralds of the Powers!

These leading cases of Cincinnati and Pittsburg are extreme examples. Form no picture of our American press as a whole from such models as these. They illustrate only the dangers of a controlled press, and by contrast, the uses of a free press in bolstering the weaknesses of democracy.

XV

The Voice of a Generation

In this final article Irwin voices his general evaluation of the American press of 1911. It is, he says, wonderfully able, wonderfully efficient, and wonderfully powerful: with real faults.

As we look back to 1911 we can see that the ability of the daily press was clearly on the upsurge, a probable result of what Irwin recognized as "less genius but more trained and specialized talent." The era of news was underway, with its need for straight, factual reporting, and with its power to stimulate change by imparting information.

And the efficiency of the press was increasing too. Not only were reporters sent out to corners of the city which would have been ignored fifty years before, the mechanical means of decreasing the time gap from event to reader were receiving constant attention. The great printing presses developed by R. Hoe and Company a few years earlier, the "decuple," "double sextuple," and "double octuple," had sent newspaper sizes to 80, 96, and 128 pages with outputs of up to 72 thousand 32-page papers an hour. Soon would come Teletypesetter, Wirephoto, and run-of-paper color, so that within 25 years the state of newspaper technology would approximate that of today.

Irwin correctly realized that the power of the press lay in the news columns, but he also recognized that news was only one aspect of the power aggregate. Economic power, at least in the long run, was important too. In 1910 there were 13 multiple ownerships, or chains, among daily newspapers. Within a quarter of a century the number of chains would increase to 59, and the number of chain-owned papers would grow from 62 to 329. The great consolidation, or weeding out, had begun.

What Irwin failed to suggest, however, was the general development of the mass media as we know them today. That development, we now see, was already well underway. But there is little suggestion in his series of the scope the mass media were to have in the near future, and of the impact other competitors would have on the press. Within 15 years of the time he wrote, the radio networks would be establishing themselves as permanent and important parts of the mass media picture. So would the movies, and so would the ancillaries of today: public relations, advertising agencies, and even schools of journalism.

Irwin's major criticism of his day's press was that

taken by and large, "it does not speak to its generation." Tempting though it may be—in view of evidence of how the press has thrived, and with it the nation, during the ensuing half century—to dismiss Irwin's criticism as sheer idealism, the sensitive reader will not. Irwin saw his generation as one concerned with the taming of powerful social forces released by the preceding generation, which had lost sight of morality in the "dust and scuffle of their war with unharnessed nature." To the younger generation, Irwin asserts, "Our press is speaking . . . with a dead voice, because the supreme power resides in men of that older generation." Perhaps it is useless to speak of "might have beens," yet one must wonder whether the country's lot might have been better had those powerful proprietors of the 1911 press heeded Irwin's advice to be more relevant to their times.

The American Newspaper

A Study of Journalism in Its Relation to the Public

By WILL IRWIN

XV.—The Voice of a Generation

Being the final article in this series. The remedies proposed for the abuses of our press, and their general futility. The danger in stricter legislation. The limitations of an endowed press; the impracticability of the "adless newspaper." The older generation, and the means by which it keeps young talent from the control of newspapers. The "right of protest" in the Associated Press as a bar to newcomers in the publishing field. "In the profession itself lies our hope"

LOGICALLY, I should close this series with a view of the present state of American journalism. It is impossible, however, to do that with fairness and certitude. No one can state his own period in terms of time and eternity. His eyes are too near the object. Then, too, there is a special difficulty. This is a transition period. In American journalism, as in American statecraft, we are sloughing off dead skin; and the new is not yet hardened to use. Spite of the evils and excesses in our journalism, the curve of progress appears to run upward. In all matters of technique—even in the writing of editorials—we have improved vastly. We may have no Julian Ralph or Murat Halstead reporting news, no Horce Greeley or Arthur McEwen writing editorials; but we have a vast body of university-trained reporters, skilled to perceive truth closely and record it accurately, a great body of university-trained editorial writers, informed in the sound principles of economics and sociology. The art of "editing" has advanced; it shows greater discrimination, a broader point of view. Twenty years ago certain stock stories were always "good," and certain other classes of news which the public likes—and should like—were ignored. At that time any murder was news, and any hanging, no matter how remote or uninteresting, called for space on the front page.

Our Broadening Horizon

FOREIGN news was scanty, and, except in the greatest newspapers, generally trivial to a ridiculous degree. The yellows, it is true, brought in the "personal note," which is three-fourths low curiosity; and from the time that the yellow flood overflowed, great public measures have generally occupied scantier space. Yet the handling of such news is more intelligent. To print the debates on reciprocity in full, as the old-age newspaper would have done, avails less with a busy people than to print the general drift of the speeches, the general sentiment of Congress, together with the high points in the debate, as when one Congressman makes a telling point or drops a felicitous phrase. All technique has advanced. Our newspapers are sharper, quicker, more moderate, nearer to the truth and to sound principles of sociology, than the newspaper of twenty or thirty years ago. We may have less genius, but we have more trained and specialized talent. If you doubt this, ask not the veteran newspaper man, who must look at his sturdy years, as all men do, through rose-mists. Just consult the files.

In the "invasion of private right," which means the publication of stories and details in stories which wound sensitive individual feelings, there has been, it would seem, little change in bulk. The yellow influence, on the one hand, lowered standards in this respect, while on the other the advent of writers and editors better educated, better trained, improved it. If our newspapers, following the yellow custom, are more likely to dig up and print the intimate details of such events as divorces, separations, bank failures, and crimes, they are less abusive to their antagonists. No politician, whatever the cause of irritation, would draw nowadays such volleys of billingsgate as the Republican newspapers fired at Grover Cleveland. The swollen size of our newspapers is a problem which concerns the craft, after all, more than the public. The reduction of the spruce and hemlock forests, from which we get our wood-pulp, must in the end reduce the number of pages. At present the editor, especially in his Sunday edition, may shoot wide at broad targets; he may print a great deal of matter which interests only a class of people here and there. In the day of the inevitable reduction, he must try to make every story tell—to select nothing which will not interest nearly every one. Indeed, the era of reduction is already at hand; and it would have arrived long ago but for the advertisements. Even that consideration will not halt the shrinkage long. The advertiser buys "display"; and display is relative, not absolute. It does not matter whether the chief advertiser buys half a page or a full page, so long as he gets twice as much space as his largest competitor. The ninth article of this series carried a facsimile of Ehrich's three-quarter-column advertisement in the seventies and Gimbel's page advertisement in 1911. Each was the largest single "ad" of the issue. Now it is probable that Ehrich got about as much advertising value, to the unit of circulation, as Gimbel. We shall probably see smaller newspapers and, correspondingly, more tersely written ones.

DRAWN BY F. G. COOPER

The New Journalism

Youth: "I'll take the pen — they want to hear from ME now"

Concerning the ultimate honesty of journalism and its higher function—to guard popular rights—one may speak with little certainty. Undoubtedly, the direct sale of columns is now somewhat uncommon where once it was flagrant. Undoubtedly the custom of taking subsidies from politicians has been cast off by most great city dailies, although it is still a curse of the country press; undoubtedly the yellow influence made our newspapers better disposed—whether sincerely or no—to expose the evils of the body politic, to let in that light which Emerson called "the best policeman." On the other hand, the dishonesty, conscious or unconscious, arising from necessarily close relations with capital and the owners of capital, has grown. I have written five articles in vain if I have not made clear how its own finances are a menace to the freedom of the press. That is the point of perplexity; that is the disease which the public must help the free journalist to cure.

By what means, then, may we direct this new force into its proper relation toward progressive civilization? How shall we curb its audacities, check its unfair violation of private right, while leaving it free to fight the common enemy and to tell necessary truth?

No Gag Laws

THE first and most obvious proposal, of course, is stricter legislation. Those who urge that the law should take the newspaper in hand are usually those who see nothing wrong about our newspapers except the "violation of privacy." Let us amend our laws of libel and contempt of court, they say—broaden their scope, increase their penalties, stretch them somehow so as to make intimate and personal details exempt from newspaper publication. We have even reactionaries who would return to British common law, and make it illegal to publish certain news harmful to the individual until the police or the courts have officially approved its truth.

Any particular law may be meat for the English and poison for the Americans. Law is the last resort of society, the ultimate social corrective when all others have failed. For many evils which beset us, the English have their unofficial correctives of custom and habit. For example, most laws need be less strictly and minutely drawn with them than with us, since the orderly Englishman by habit obeys the letter and spirit of the law, while the American, with his tradition of Yankee independence and smartness, tries to take advantage of the letter to violate the spirit. Again, he of the stiff, steel-hearted mother-race has, in his unyielding code concerning his tiny personal rights, a method of correction which is lacking in American society.

The corresponding function, with us, has been generally assumed by our unhampered press. England has never been "muckraked" in the American sense; how much of what we call "graft" exists there, we do not exactly know. Certainly, they have a good deal of anointed and consecrated graft, accepted as the prerogative of the exalted hundredth by the flunky-hearted lower and middle classes. With equal certainty I may say that such wrongs as the railroad "cinch" in New England and California, the Standard Oil "cinch" the country over, could not have grown up in England, because the English would never have permitted the evasions of law by which they obtained their hold. But given that such evils should find root in England, there is little power in the English press to uproot them—for their villains and schemers are people in private life, and the smallest printed offense against an individual in private life may be a wrong under English law. By our deplorable attitude toward law have these evils grown up among us; by the freedom granted our press are they in process of correction. Ida M. Tarbell's "History of Standard Oil" started the fight on that monopoly. Never was a contemporaneous history so temperately and accurately written. Yet her mildest chapter contained a dozen statements which would have constituted a wrong under English law; under that law Miss Tarbell could have been sent to prison on successive convictions for the term of her natural life. Had we such laws as the British enforce and glorify, John D. Rockefeller might have brought action against nearly every newspaper in this country.

What Would Happen to Us

COLLIER'S has, we flatter ourselves, performed some service to the commonwealth by throwing light on certain rubbish heaps of the body social. Under English law, Mr. Adams's patent medicine exposés which stopped the poisoning of a great part of our people, would have brought convictions enough to go around among the editors and leave a few over for the printers and pressmen. And never did we need this journalistic freedom so much as now; never before would the brake on journalism which English law enforces have worked so much harm. For we are in such a curious stage of our social evolution that the enemies of the people, the generals and chiefs of privilege, are not our elected and appointed representatives, but men in "private" life, so situated that they could entrench themselves behind any law drawn on the English plan. This is no time to prate to us of gag laws for our press.

A few features of foreign libel laws we might copy without fettering any honest editor. Germany, for example, has a good statute concerning retractions. The individual who, either through the carelessness or bad design of the editor, is the victim of a published untruth, may obtain an apology of equal space and prominence with the original statement. In this country the rule, all but universal, is to "play down" the retraction. A newspaper will publish a false and damaging statement in three columns on the front page. Being forced to eat its words either to avoid a libel suit or to mitigate damages, it will print the retraction in six lines at the bottom of a remote column. Every newspaper man knows that certain people with no reputation to lose rejoice over a newspaper libel against them as over a prize in a lottery—it is a chance for easy money. Every newspaper man knows also how reluctant are those of real pride and respectability to sue for libel. A retraction of prominence equal to the original story is what they want; and there is no reason in all justice why they should not have it.

The "endowed press" was, ten years ago, a favorite remedy with theorists. Let us have, they said, some national newspapers, supported by private philanthropy, which can afford to publish not what the public wants, but what it should have. A few newspapers endowed on this system would probably do a certain amount of good. But one major difficulty, and two minor ones, present themselves. Who, in the first place, would give the endowment? Some Carnegie or Rockefeller, doubtless. The unavoidable sycophancy of mankind would connect the editors of such a publication to the donor's point of view. From no newspaper endowed by Andrew Carnegie could we expect fair treatment of another Homestead strike; and no newspaper endowed by Rockefeller would fail in respect to 26 Broadway and its allied interests. Our endowed universities are cowards in the presence of capital. Could we expect more of the endowed newspaper?

Again: those who propose the endowed newspaper, like those who would strengthen our press laws, have proved that they recognize, after all, only one evil in the popular press—its publication of matter which hurts people's feelings and is inimical to good taste. Their ideal is something like the older New York "Evening Post." I have already shown the flaw in that admirable kind of journalism, the danger to democracy in a review of the world which ignores the ugly. It is so easy, in any organization of society, to lift a part and to degrade the mass; so easy to create a state consisting of an aristocracy and a Helot mob! It is much more difficult to lift the whole mass; yet that is the idea of democracy. The masses will not take such a newspaper, any more than they will now take the "Evening Post" or the Boston "Transcript." It must remain a class publication. And what we need is not more class publications, but more sane and honest popular newspapers, like the Kansas City "Star," which tell the truth in the language of the people.

Finally, the theorists have assumed that the newspaper occupies the same relation to society as the theater and the opera. Since an endowed theater in Europe has elevated—if not purified—the state of the Continental drama, why should not an endowed newspaper elevate American journalism? These theorists forget that while the drama is purely a luxury, the newspaper is primarily a necessity. Although it serves to spread the taste and desire for culture through the masses, it is nevertheless concerned mainly with economic and political needs; it is not an ornament to the cornice of society, but a girder in the frame-work. It is part of the workaday world; it will serve best if it is free to fight its own way toward perfection, to maintain its own athletic relations to the other forces of society.

The "Adless Newspaper"

THE newspaper endowed by its subscribers, the stock held in blocks of one share, has been suggested, has even been tried in Europe, with doubtful results. When the public becomes sufficiently well educated concerning journalism, learns what its real failings are, such an experiment may succeed to a limited degree in this country. The newspaper without advertisements — the "adless paper" in office slang—has been proposed. Even that seems impracticable just at present. To compensate for the loss of advertising revenue, it must sell on the street at from three to five cents, and it must dispense with the high-priced "features" and "specials" which embellish the great popular newspapers and which are such a lure to the average reader. For its chief commodity would be unclouded truth, seen through the eyes of a free editor; and the public, in its present state of education concerning newspapers, is not quite ready to pay good coin for truth alone. Some genius in newspaper economies may devise a plan to make an "adless paper" pay at one or two cents. If he does, he will have a profound influence

(Continued on page 23)

The Problem of American Ships

The Second of Two Articles on the Disappearance of Americans from the High Seas

By ARTHUR RUHL

Last week's article, "The Sailor's Side," explained why American boys do not go to sea. This article discusses the restoring of our merchant marine—a problem of which Mr. Thomas Clyde of the Clyde Line, in testifying before the Mercantile Commission, said: "There are more blind alleys about this one than any I ever struck." The difficulty with most articles and speeches on this subject is that they are prepared by some one who has an ax to grind. The following article endeavors to make the question clear to the average reader by presenting fairly the arguments for each of the proposed remedies:

THE most obvious difficulty in the way of increasing our merchant marine is the fact that it costs from 30 to 50 per cent more to build a ship in America than in England and at least 25 per cent more to operate it under the American flag.

The decline of our merchant marine began with the change from wooden to iron ships. So long as ships were built of wood American builders had the advantage. They kept on building wooden ships, while England went into steel and steam. After the iron ships drove out the wooden ones, our tariff restrictions continued to give Great Britain an advantage.

Our Lost Shipping

A SECOND cause was the loss of shipping during the Civil War. In various ways more than a million tons was either destroyed or transferred to foreign ownership.

A third cause is the larger returns both for capital and labor in other lines of industry. England's colonies and exports made her need ships, and our vast territory and commercial growth made us need railroads. Manufacturing has offered more attractive opportunities for investment than foreign shipping. The same is true of labor. An American sailor shipping from an American port seldom gets more than $25 a month on a sailing vessel and $30 per month on a steamship. He gets his board, to be sure, but it is sea fare and sea quarters, and it can't be shared with a wife and children. At the same port a capable mechanic would receive from $3 to $4 a day, and be free to come and go and quit when he wants to without being dragged back and forced to work.

A fourth cause is the protective tariff, which has forced capital into other more profitable channels. In 1904 the price of American steel in England was $27 per ton, and the price in America for the same steel was from $35 to $40 per ton. Most of the builders who testified before President Roosevelt's Merchant Marine Commission stated that an English builder could buy American plates delivered in England for $8 per ton less than they could be purchased here. And what is true of steel is true of nearly everything that goes into the building—of wages and the general standard of living which have made ship-building as well as ship-operating more costly for Americans.

One of the few steamships which fly our flag—the Ward liner Saratoga

A fifth cause is our registry law, which prohibits giving American registry to vessels built abroad.

The large number of ships built in British yards has made standardization, with its consequent savings, possible. Mr. Lewis Nixon testified before the Merchant Marine Commission: "I have known one great yard in this country where they had five slips, every one capable of building a *Lucania*, and they were building there at one time a steamer, a ferry-boat, a tug, a battleship, and a yacht. The Almighty Himself could not practise economies under those conditions."

It is true that steel imported for the construction of vessels to be used in the foreign trade is not subject to duty, but two things have prevented importation: (1) Delay in getting plates and the fact that they may be injured in transit—"People do not know," testified Mr. Nixon, "the heart-breaking difficulties of the chances of the boat being belated, of delay in shipment, of ship-plates being bent, angles distorted," etc.—(2) and, far more important, the fact that no vessel built wholly or in part of this foreign non-dutiable material may be used in the coastwise trade of the United States for more than two months of any one year.

Back to the Sea

MILLIONS of words have been written and spoken about the "decline of our merchant marine." There are some 2,000 books and pamphlets in the Congressional Library, each furnishing the only proper solution.

President Roosevelt's commission held hearings in the Atlantic, Pacific, Great Lakes, and Gulf cities, and received testimony from ship-owners and builders, railroad men, and the sailors themselves. The published report of these hearings contains 1,481 pages of extremely interesting suggestions. Some of them are paraphrased here, and I must acknowledge special indebtedness to Mr. Walter T. Dunmore of the Western Reserve University, whose little book, "Ship Subsidies," is the briefest and best summing-up of the various arguments yet made.

The plans for the restoration of our merchant marine group themselves under three heads:

The American Newspaper

(*Continued from page 16*)

on his own city; for when one is telling the whole truth the others must be chary of half-truths. But that also is a mighty parlous undertaking at present.

We may assume then, with all the certainty which ever attaches to prophecy, that we must go on for a time as we are going at present, with newspapers published to make money, their investment closely allied to "big business," with the real producers of journalism arranged in groups, each under the dominance of a capitalist.

In the profession itself lies our greatest hope. In spite of all commercial tendencies, its personnel and intelligence are improving year by year. Visiting from newspaper shop to newspaper shop last year, I was struck with the general and noble dissatisfaction of the men over the present condition in their craft. It was not the whine of the half-baked old-time newspaper man—"this is a rotten business!" They are coming to realize the importance of their profession, its usefulness, its potential standing. Their dissatisfaction is only disgust for a control which forces the reporter to drop a "good story" because it leads to the iniquity of some "friend" of the paper, which forces the editorial writer to write against all his opinions because the source of income is involved. The sentiment is young, but growing; it has not yet crystallized in results. In ten years of journalism, I have not known five writers for the daily press who left their employment over a matter of opinion.

The British Idea

THEY order those things better in Britain. The best English journalists will not take dictation from the sources of revenue, and will not write against their opinions. When a London newspaper changes editorial policy, switches from Whig to Tory, for example, the editorial writers resign as a matter of course. No such code in this country! Some of the most bigoted Republican Protectionist editorials of these times proceed from the pens of Socialists and Single Taxers.

It is a great deal to expect—but there is some hope that we may get the higher code into American journalism. When that time arrives, the brains of the profession—and in no human activity is brain related so directly to profit—will refuse to suppress or color truth for greed of revenue. Then the system will cure itself. Let us take an analogy from medicine, that profession so admirable on its ethical side that it has lately, through its "preventative work," set about to reduce its own source of revenue. Suppose a business man of great wealth, cleverness, and enterprise were to arise and say: "These fellows don't get half the money out of it that they might. Look at all the cheap cases they take! I'll get them together. I'll start a medical institute in every city, offering the doctors better money than they're getting now. I'll have a corner on doctors. I'll advertise 'em, I'll exploit 'em, and I'll force the public to pay what it's worth to save life! And I'll make millions for myself." The plan is perfectly feasible, except for one thing: no physician of ability and reputation would give it a moment's countenance. That journalism will reach this height is improbable; the very haphazard nature of journalistic education makes against it. But with every notch it rises, corrupt commercialism in newspaper-making will fall a corresponding notch.

Indeed, were the abler among the younger generation of journalists free to go forth and start newspapers of their own, we might find at once a corrective for the gagged press. A single journal telling the truth to its community will cure the "suppression habit." When the lottery fight was on in New Orleans, every newspaper of that city was so deeply influenced by its capital, its advertising revenue, and its social connections that none told the truth. The reformers started the "New Delta," which they sold on the day after the lottery was buried. In it they told the people of New Orleans what was going on; and this one clear voice of truth prevailed.

The Million-Dollar Phantom

UNFORTUNATELY young brain is no more generally associated with old accumulation of wealth in journalism than in any other form of industrial activity. Also, there is a general impression that it takes a million dollars to start a city newspaper; and the stable old publishers who hold the business under their control have done nothing to remove that impression. The youth with a free message has no million dollars; if he manages to borrow it, he must go, usually, to the very institutions which pull the wires on his contemporaries.

That million-dollar valuation is a bugaboo, however. There is reason for believing that a city newspaper can begin small and grow large like any other commercial institution. E. W. Scripps, than whom no other man sees further into a newspaper "business proposition," has said: "All two young men need to start a newspaper is a basement, a second-hand press, four linotype machines, and a message!" And, indeed, his experience proves his maxim. Mr. Scripps experimented for many years with many kinds of newspapers. In his middle age he began his "string." He picks a town which needs "shaking up" and selects from his organization an editor and a business manager whom he thinks adequate to the task. He establishes them in humble quarters with the second-hand press and the linotype machines, gives them a small salary and a block of stock, and puts them to work. Now he controls twenty-two newspapers, all but two or three started on this plan. And here is the significant general fact about them: *none of his successful papers has cost more than $30,000 to start.* I have, from the Scripps organization, figures concerning the Dallas "Dispatch." It is four years old; it claims a circulation of 12,000 in a city of 92,000 population—a circulation great enough to get any truth to the people. It cost $17,000 to establish the "Dispatch." In its fourth year, the editor, who owns twenty per cent of the stock, made more from his shares than from his salary. "Any young newspaper man who is thoroughly sincere and intelligent," says Mr. Scripps, "can with $10,000 or $20,000 found a people's newspaper and outstrip in the race for popular favor any old-established journal which depends only on the wealth of its owners and the favor of the so-called capitalist class." Of this there is one serious qualification. Behind the Scripps newspapers is Scripps experience and the marvelous Scripps business method. The zealous young independent publisher must start without that.

One institution which has been a jewel of American journalism stands now in the road of the ambitious young publisher—the Associated Press. Axiomatically, you can not run a newspaper on local news alone. And in some cities which need fresh newspapers just now, the situation in the press bureaus, which supply news of the outer world, forbids new journalism.

The Trouble With the "A. P."

WHEN Victor Lawson and others gathered up the wreckage of the old press bureaus in the late nineties, and formed the new Associated Press, they needed funds. It was part of their policy to make an Associated Press franchise valuable. They issued bonds; and the newspapers which took these original bonds were given forty-one votes in convention, against one vote to the newspapers which came in later. These original purchasers nearly all represented that "commercial" brand of publisher which rose after the Civil War; and they have controlled the organization ever since. The radical publishers, first fruit of insurgency in the younger generation, have tilted at this control from time to time, but with no success. The conservative majority, strong in commercial wisdom, put into the constitution the "right of protest." This article, stripped of its complexities, means that the original members may unite to shut out any newcomer from their field. A suit at law made them modify this rule. Now, the applicant protested by his elder rivals may appeal to the annual meeting; and if he gets a five-sixths vote, his petition is granted. He never does get such a majority, of course. New York votes against the applicant from St. Louis, that St. Louis may vote against the next applicant from New York. Nothing except outright purchase of a newspaper could get to-day an Associated Press franchise in New York, Boston, Philadelphia, San Francisco, St. Louis, or any other of the greater American cities. Melville E. Stone, a genius at conciliation, took charge of the organization. He was a tremendous success. He made it without doubt the most efficient press bureau in the world. Even now, when respect for the mighty sources of news is slanting it toward the side of the powerful, it is, for freedom, as a yeoman to a slave beside most European press bureaus. For a time it had no competition worth considering. And the Associated Press franchise to a morning newspaper, from a mere piece of paper, has become a tangible asset—worth from $50,000 to $250,000 in most big cities. At these figures it can be bought, sold, or mortgaged like a piece of real estate. That consideration, if nothing else, kept the founders true to the "right of pro-

(*Concluded on page 25*)

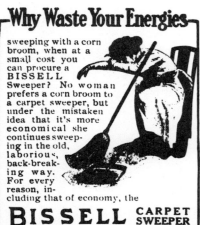

The American Newspaper

(*Concluded from page 23*)

test"; for if you make the Associated Press free to all comers, you wipe out this piece of property at one stroke.

The Scripps newspapers, as they began to dot the West, gathered up from several old ventures a service of their own—now called the United Press—which they maintained as a general press bureau. They have only an "evening wire," however. Still, within three years they have begun to disturb the Associated Press. They have already made an evening Associated Press franchise almost valueless. Most of those founders with forty-one votes in convention owned morning papers, and they had put in the constitution such rules about hours of delivery as seriously embarrassed evening Associated Press newspapers—for example, the wire "closed" for the evening service at four o'clock, and it was impossible to publish the late sporting news, such as baseball and football scores, except by purchasing it from the telegraph companies. The United, taking full advantage of this fact, kept cutting into the Western territory. The United has hardly attempted as yet to cover the territory east of Ohio. In the West, however, it is growing fast—far faster than its rival. It is a private concern, run for immediate gain, while the Associated Press is cooperative. This handicaps the United Press. Although its point of view is far less influenced by power and place than that of the Associated Press, it is as yet, owing to its youth, less efficient.

"Mouthpiece of an Older Stock"

IN the morning field—and here grow the newspapers of most general service to public intelligence—there is still no rival of equal strength. The New York "Sun" Press Bureau, called also the Laffan Bureau, is a supplementary bureau, useful to enrich the other services because it gets illuminated "Sun" writing into the news. The Hearst bureau distributes Hearst news; that does very well for the avowedly yellow newspaper, but it does not satisfy general needs. Hearst is extending this bureau; he may in time modify its policy to make it available for all kinds of newspapers; it is too early as yet to tell. But until something happens to break the "right of protest" in the Associated Press, until there arises a general morning and evening press bureau from which any newspaper may draw by paying the tolls, the way to directing journalism will be barred, in many cities and States, for the young man of brains, enterprise, and purpose who can not buy a newspaper outright.

And, indeed, this quandary stands for a general criticism of the American press. Most of the faults which I have enumerated in showing the darker side of our wonderfully able, wonderfully efficient, and wonderfully powerful daily journalism, might all be gathered under the cover of this one generic fault—take it by and large, *it does not speak to its generation.* It is the mouthpiece of an older stock; it lags behind the thought of its times.

For in the uninterrupted flow of the coming and going of men, time somehow arranges generations like the generations of a family. We had one such after the Civil War. The men of that day broke ground. They performed miraculous labors; they tamed a continent. In the dust and scuffle of their war with unharnessed nature, they took little time to analyze the nicer moral questions, or to consider the ends to which their warfare led. They worshiped success and its rewards; the stories which made their hearts glow were stories of poor boys grown rich and great—they never inquired how. John D. Rockefeller was long, to his own generation, the pattern for youth that he is to himself.

"We of the Thirties"

THEN, after that little Spanish War, so poor in action, so rich in consequences, a new earth held up its smoky hands to the same old heaven. We in our thirties and forties, who are now doing and directing the work of America, are not nearly so respectful toward immediate success. We found the continent broken and tamed; we are considering the new forces loosed by the work of the nineteenth century, and wondering how we may reduce them to the power of law before they overwhelm us. It may be a less able generation; it is surely a more moral one. And our chief concern with such a phenomenon as John D. Rockefeller is to see that no one ever repeats his kind of success.

To us of this younger generation our daily press is speaking, for the most part, with a dead voice, because the supreme power resides in men of that older generation. Could the working journalists of our own age tell us as frankly as they wished what they think and see and feel about the times, we should have only minor points to criticize in American journalism.

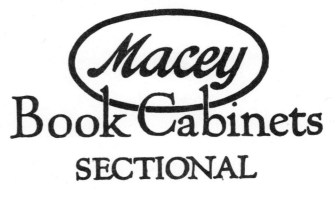

"Brickbats and Bouquets"

From the first, Irwin's articles were greeted with praise by the readers of *Collier's*. On February 25, 1911, the week after the third article had run, the magazine printed twenty-one letters, nearly all from newspapers, congratulating *Collier's*. The Chicago *Tribune* asserted the series promised to be "one of the most notable of *Collier's* many notable enterprises. . . ." Over the next eight months, some seventy letters were published in the magazine, and the ratio of praise to criticism was overwhelming.

But the letters do not tell the whole story. The editors of *Collier's* soon realized they had struck a vein of acute reader interest. They telegraphed the managing editors of 100 major newspapers across the country, asking them to answer the question "What is news?" The replies were presented from week to week as a symposium to supplement Irwin's articles. And to the general readers $50 was offered for the best letter about a newspaper in each of 56 American cities. In the first two weeks of the contest 5,000 letters arrived, and by the end of the contest period the number had risen to 10,000.

Reaction of prominent publishers to the articles varied. Hearst, through an attorney, threatened a libel suit as soon as *Collier's* announced that one of the articles would deal with yellow journalism. And as soon as the article was run, Hearst announced the filing of a $500,000 libel suit. In the end, nothing came of it. H. H. Tammen, one of the publishers of the Denver *Post*, expressed delight at Irwin's treatment of him, although it was by no means gentle. Tammen ordered 250 copies of the April 1 issue, saying he would send them to the 250 persons "in the world who don't take *Collier's*." And by telegram he offered a further characteristic anecdote. He told of leaving to close a business deal (possibly one of the unscrupulous schemes he and his partner, Bonfils, were widely assumed to be working), when Bonfils wished him on his way. "Good-by. Remember the last three words of the Jewish Bible, 'Get the Money.' " Adolph Ochs, publisher of the New York *Times*, responded through his friend and business manager, Louis Wiley. Irwin had called Ochs "the best and highest example of the commercial publisher." Ochs apparently took the well-intentioned remark as a slur. He really was more concerned with the editorial performance of the paper than with money-making, wrote Wiley in a long letter which *Collier's* ran as a separate article.

The Irwin series also stimulated further articles in *Collier's* on newspaper work. On September 23, nearly two months after the last Irwin piece, the magazine ran an article by Tiffany Blake, editorial writer of the Chicago *Tribune*, on "The Editorial: Past, Present and

Future." On October 7 Richard Harding Davis had a piece on "The War Correspondent." And on October 28 "Confessions of a Managing Editor" ran anonymously.

To this first major series of articles on the American newspaper published by a large-circulation magazine, the response of readers clearly showed widespread awareness of the importance of the press in 1911. Clearly, too, the newspaper had entered maturity as a mass medium of communication.

The following pages represent a selection of "Brickbats and Bouquets," starting with the February 25, 1911, issue, the first published reader response.

Brickbats and Bouquets

Editors and Readers on the Newspaper Series

IN A SPIRITED article in COLLIER'S of this week Mr. Will Irwin begins a series on "The American Newspaper" which, if we may judge by this sample and by the prospectus already published, will be one of the most notable of COLLIER'S many notable enterprises. . . .

The COLLIER'S series should accomplish an important public service. In addition to its own intrinsic value, it will provoke discussion in and out of newspapers throughout the country, and that is highly desirable both for the press and for the public.—Chicago (Ill.) *Tribune*.

✤

It is a great compliment to the newspapers—the fact that they are criticized more than any other institution except the Church and the Government. COLLIER'S is astute in its choice of a subject for prolonged discussion.
—Syracuse (N. Y.) *Post-Standard*.

✤

The newspaper has become a mighty important factor in modern civilization, and COLLIER'S WEEKLY has not overestimated the significance of the institution in making a series of articles on the American press the dominant feature for the coming year.—Kansas City (Mo.) *Times*.

✤

The series promises to be of unusual interest both to the maker and reader of newspapers.—Logansport (Ind.) *Journal*.

✤

Both the newspaper and the public will no doubt be greatly enlightened. This will be especially the case, if COLLIER'S adopts the same attitude toward the newspaper that it has toward other subjects and forces in American life which it has discussed.
—Aberdeen (Wash.) *World*.

✤

Will Irwin, formerly a newspaper man of this city and an alumnus of Stanford, has begun in COLLIER'S WEEKLY a remarkable, instructive, and entertaining series of articles on the American newspaper press.—San Francisco (Cal.) *Call*.

✤

It has come at last—a series of articles on the American newspaper. Will Irwin, that sunny and clever reporter, is to tell the story, and the vehicle by which he expects to reach the public is COLLIER'S WEEKLY.—Pittsfield (Mass.) *Eagle*.

✤

We trust that COLLIER'S WEEKLY, in its forthcoming series of articles on American journalism, will point out how great a breach of etiquette it is to call on a busy editor and stay all morning without leaving cards.
—Newark (N. J.) *Evening News*.

✤

COLLIER'S is doing a good service by printing what promises to be an instructive study of the virtues and faults of American newspapers, a subject needing agitation—Boston (Mass.) *Common*.

✤

The current issue of COLLIER'S WEEKLY contains the first of a series of articles by Will Irwin on the subject of the daily press, with a full-page drawing of a city editor surrounded by persons offering the good and the bad, the true and the false, as news. The city editor is in a dilemma—in the picture. And there are, perhaps, very few city editors out of pictures who are not constantly in a dilemma to know what is news, what to display prominently, and what to suppress or barely record. For in the long run news is a matter of taste. And tastes differ.
—Columbus (Ohio) *News*.

✤

COLLIER'S is attempting to prove "that the power of the press is not waning, but on the contrary is vastly greater than in any previous age." COLLIER'S has the reputation for finishing everything it starts, and, as the articles are clearly stating both or all sides of the question, the coming ones will be awaited with interest.
—Vallejo (Cal.) *Chronicle*.

✤

COLLIER'S has commenced the publication of a series of articles on newspapers. The series starts out well and indicates that there will be much information which the public will be benefited by knowing published. It is a fact that people know less about newspapers than almost any other subject.—Lawrence (Kans.) *Journal.*

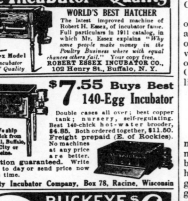

✤

Professor Hugo Münsterberg, in the current "McClure's," indicts the American reporter for incorrectness and for wilful distortion of news, while in COLLIER'S Mr. Will Irwin pays tribute to the news-gathering force of the public press as the real power of that institution. . . .

We commend Mr. Irwin's article to Professor Münsterberg and suggest that the "eminent psychologist take himself less seriously." One man's grievance against a few ribald reporters is not sufficient to convict journalism of habitual distortions of fact.—Denver (Colo.) *Republican.*

✤

The public sees that in many things the newspapers fall short. The best newspapers, like the best men, try to do their best; but, also like the best men, they are occasionally guilty of sins of commission and omission. What the public should realize is that it is an accessory before the fact in many cases, and after the fact in almost all cases, in not writing to the newspaper freely and frankly what it thinks ought to be done. While every citizen and all editors may not agree with what he says, it is probable that Mr. Irwin's articles will do a great deal of good in calling attention to the merits and demerits of American journalism, increasing the public's appreciation of the former and desire to reform the latter.

—Houston (Texas) *Chronicle.*

✤

The initial number of what promises to be the greatest magazine series of the year is printed in full herewith.

—Birmingham (Ala.) *News.*

✤

The newspaper series you have started is a very excellent enterprise. It is going to give your paper about ten million dollars' worth of advertising for a comparatively small outlay of money, and it is going to help a lot of newspaper men in finding themselves. HERBERT HUNT, Editor Tacoma (Wash.) *Daily News.*

✤

I think the series of articles you are running by Will Irwin will be the most interesting and instructive that have appeared in your publication in several years.

D. R. BARBEE,
Montgomery (Ala.) *Advertiser.*

✤

COLLIER'S is the most independent and influential journal in the United States, and therefore is better qualified to handle this subject than ordinary periodicals.

—Abbeville (La.) *Vermilion News.*

✤

COLLIER'S, New York.

My Dear Sirs—Myself and many others of the "Capital" staff have read your first article on newspapers. The article is full of interest, maintains a splendid point of view, and sets a high standard for the other articles to follow. We congratulate COLLIER'S very much on the series as outlined. Very truly yours,

LAFE YOUNG, JR.
Des Moines (Iowa) *Capital.*

✤

I suppose every *real* newspaper man—I mean the gentlemen upstairs who get the news, and groan when the business office butts in—is glad to see your yarn and hopes the newspaper business is about to get a little wholesome publicity. Since I got into the advertising business I have realized more than ever before the necessity of teaching newspaper men the power they possess. WINFIELD W. DUDLEY.

✤

It should be a great story. It is a story that has never been scratched. COLLIER'S should keep out all signs of animus and treat the topic fairly, as it generally does its topics. Sometimes even COLLIER'S is a bit vicious.

Recently COLLIER'S has been a trifle sensational in an effort to fight truly sensational frauds. It has kicked the "get-rich-quick schemer" into jail in collaboration with Postmaster Hitchcock: it has frightened the fake medicine bunco-steerer out of business and it has muckraked generally to mighty good advantage.

The history of American newspaperdom may be written without fear and with great justice and beneficent results. Though newspapers do not like to write of newspapers, there is no logical reason why they should not.

Power to the elbows of Will Irwin. If newspapers can not stand the white light of truthful publicity, heaven save the profession!—Butte (Mont.) *News.*

BRICKBATS & BOUQUETS

MANY newspapers in the country participated in the effort to get a third-rate lawyer of shifty disposition, long tied up in the affairs of a pernicious corporation, ousted from the office of Secretary of the Interior where he might do great harm to public interests, but the leader in that effort was COLLIER'S WEEKLY, which furnished a large quota of the ammunition.
—Columbia (S. C.) *State.*

✚

LOUISVILLE, KY.

Mr. Rice and I have just returned from a trip around the world, and it may interest you to know that in the most remote places we invariably found three American institutions—Standard Oil, the Singer sewing-machine, and COLLIER'S WEEKLY.
ALICE HEGAN RICE.

✚

That COLLIER'S has done a splendid public service in exposing Ballinger and Ballingerism every impartial person will readily concede.
—Johnstown (Pa.) *Democrat.*

✚

They didn't dare do it until the election was over—exonerate Ballinger. You know that COLLIER'S rendered the verdict of the American people in June in two words—*Ballinger, Shyster.*
—Little Valley (N. Y.) *Hub.*

✚

It would be far better, of course, to have another man than Mr. Ballinger in charge of the people's interests in Alaska; but it is a fine thing to have a condition in which an official who has a wrong conception of the square deal has got to administer the square deal anyhow. For which thanks be to Mr. Glavis, Mr. Pinchot, Mr. Brandeis, and COLLIER'S WEEKLY.—Kansas City (Mo.) *Star.*

✚

The great value of the fight led by COLLIER'S WEEKLY for the retention of the Alaska coal-fields as the property of the people of the United States appears in the majority report of the Ballinger Investigating Committee.—*Life.*

✚

COLLIER'S WEEKLY says that England produces more humor of the higher kind than America. The writer is, perhaps, thinking of our new schemes of taxation.
—London (England) *Opinion.*

✚

These articles will certainly be read with interest. Irwin is an entertaining writer and knows his subject.
—Modesto (Cal.) *News.*

✚

COLLIER'S earned its title of The National Weekly not alone through its widely quoted editorials, or its fight against public wrongs, or its authentic weekly record of the world's progress, or its extraordinary short stories, or its unique printing of notable art subjects, but through *all* of these things and others, collectively. This is done by presenting weekly the best in all things which go to make a great national weekly.
—Abbeville (La.) *News.*

✚

Even COLLIER'S WEEKLY admits that America is the best country in the world and we feel better now.
—Concord (N. H.) *Monitor.*

✚

COLLIER'S editorials are always interesting and deal with the vital questions of the day, and no better example of this policy can be found than in this recent utterance on the "progressive and developing South of to-day."—Charleston (S. C.) *Keystone.*

✚

We resent the suggestion that COLLIER'S WEEKLY be given a mush ladle. We owe COLLIER'S for books bought on the instalment plan.—Topeka (Kans.) *Capital.*

✚

It is probably the first time that the power of the press, the value and the equality of newspaper work, and the work of various newspapers has been studied carefully. It should be the duty as well as the pleasure of every citizen to read and consider this series of articles carefully.—Lexington (Ky.) *Herald.*

✚

The introductory indicates that there is to be much truth-telling, as the author sees the truth, and that often the truth will hurt and perhaps hurt those of us who least expect to be hurt.

But exploring an uncharted country is dangerous; sometimes the explorer wanders far without discovering much of real value. The start, however, does not justify the early conclusion that the effort will not be entirely successful, contributing to the general good and the good of the American newspaper as well.
—South Bend (Ind.) *Tribune.*

✚

COLLIER'S WEEKLY has decided that the men of the future shall be bald. Posterity, however, should be mighty thankful that COLLIER'S hasn't scalped it.
—Joplin (Mo.) *Globe.*

✚

And are we at last to have the truth about the "American Newspaper"?

Is the press in truth a molder of public opinion? Is it a force for good or for evil? Does it tend to uplift or drag down literary standards? What should be its principal function? . . .

Mr. Irwin spent eighteen months in the preparation of these articles, and made a tour of the United States for the purpose of studying the question exhaustively. His treatises will be elaborate as to detail and will prove highly interesting, no doubt, both to expert and layman.
—Birmingham (Ala.) *News.*

✚

COLLIER'S WEEKLY is now engaged upon a series of able articles telling how the newspapers should be run, but the man who comes in to impart that information to the editor personally seems to call about as frequently as usual.
—Columbus (Ohio) *Journal.*

✚

That these articles will be interesting is sufficiently probable from their author's name, and the first of the series is indicative of the value of all.
—Chicago (Ill.) *Public.*

✚

COLLIER'S for January 21 begins a series of articles by Will Irwin on the American Newspaper that is fraught with intense interest. It is probably the first time that the power of the press, the value and the quality of newspaper work, and the work of various newspapers have been studied carefully. It should be the duty as well as the pleasure of every citizen to read and consider this series of articles carefully. That the newspaper is our strong factor is certain, whether stronger for right or wrong is important to consider, though each of us probably has made up his or her mind long ago.
—Lexington (Ky.) *Herald.*

✚

Mr. Collier, publisher of the magazine of that name, has bought a biplane and is getting ready for a flyer. Did we consider ourselves our brother's keeper in this instance we should advise him to keep the feet of himself and his magazine on the solid earth. But the probabilities are that he will reach terra firma ahead of his magazine.—Tacoma (Wash.) *News.*

✚

The Senate has adopted a resolution censuring COLLIER'S WEEKLY for its opposition to the Sulloway pension bill to increase the pensions for soldiers and sailors of the Civil War.
—Wichita (Kans.) *Eagle.*

✚

COLLIER'S WEEKLY in a recent editorial twice refers to the fact that those best citizens who left the Republican Party to elect Governor Dix must enjoy the exhibition at Albany.

There is no question that Republican business men who would object to being termed independents defeated Mr. Stimson.
—Watertown (N. Y.) *Standard.*

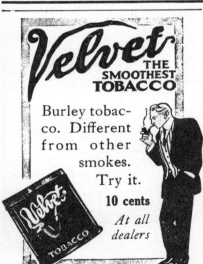

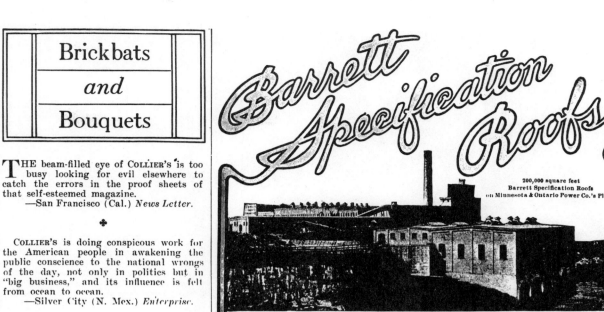

Brickbats and Bouquets

THE beam-filled eye of COLLIER'S is too busy looking for evil elsewhere to catch the errors in the proof sheets of that self-esteemed magazine.

—San Francisco (Cal.) *News Letter.*

✣

COLLIER'S is doing conspicuous work for the American people in awakening the public conscience to the national wrongs of the day, not only in politics but in "big business," and its influence is felt from ocean to ocean.

—Silver City (N. Mex.) *Enterprise.*

✣

The editor of COLLIER'S, who came to Kansas with a message, was another illustration of what a fool a man can make of himself if nobody interferes.

—Hutchison (Kans.) *News.*

✣

This week the amused COLLIER'S offers a prize to the first standpat Kansas editor who can translate into good sense one sentence in the "resolutions" adopted by the "association." Here is the sentence:

Resolved, That the association sees nothing but hope and promise in its appreciation of present conditions or of prophetic visions.

COLLIER'S is a great and far-sighted journal, and it can well afford to dismiss with a smile the gratuitous insult offered Mr. Hapgood by the standpat editors. They do not represent to any degree worth mention the sentiment of the Kansas people or of the Kansas editors.

—Kansas City (Mo.) *Star.*

✣

Mr. Hearst has given COLLIER'S a valuable bit of advertising, and whetted the public appetite for its treatment of Hearst and Hearstism. And the more the American people know about the Hearst style and method of journalism the better it will be for the American commonwealth.

—Detroit (Mich.) *Saturday Night.*

✣

Another way to swell the postal revenue is to answer COLLIER'S WEEKLY'S query as to your favorite newspaper. . . . Thank you.—New York City *Mail.*

✣

The "Comment on Congress" is wonderfully effective out here in Ohio. Speakers quote from it and the people read it.

ALLEN ALBERT,
Columbus (Ohio) *News.*

✣

SALT LAKE CITY, UTAH...

We want to congratulate you on the concise masterly reports that have come to us each week through COLLIER'S, and thank you for keeping us informed as to how our Senators voted on the various schedules. ROSCOE W. EARDLEY.

✣

Permit me to say that in my judgment your comment about Congress, appearing weekly in COLLIER'S, is doing a great work in informing the people of this country what is going on in their national lawmaking body. JOSEPH E. NORWOOD,
Editor, the *Gazette*, Magnolia, Miss.

✣

1728 CONNECTICUT AVE., N. W.,
WASHINGTON, D. C.

Much to my disgust, I find in your issue of the 18th of February an inspired article on "The Aldrich Credit and Currency Plan."

How much were you paid for the publication of this article?

And why have you not put "Adv." at the end thereof?

For I refuse to believe that your editors are so crassly ignorant of finance as to swallow, without vigorous protest, the "Suggested Plan for Monetary Legislation submitted to the National Monetary Commission by Hon. Nelson W. Aldrich," which you foolishly advise people to send for copies of. HENRY C. STUART.

Brickbats and Bouquets

I THINK the stand of COLLIER'S is a patriotic one, and that the newspapers of the country which care more for fair play, in behalf of the people they propose to serve than for the money of a millionaire fraudulent advertiser, should join it in furthering the good work so well undertaken.

T. J. MABRY,
Editor the Clovis *Journal*.

Anybody who reads COLLIER'S either does so from curiosity or as a joke, or they are inoculated and are fixed.

—The Enid (Okla.) *Events*.

✤

HAMILTON, MONT.

Mr. Irwin's first two articles portend a splendid contribution to the history of American journalism, and as one of the fraternity I wish to preserve the series.

M. L. H. ODEA,
Manager of Chamber of Commerce.

✤

LEWIS'S MAGAZINE, Liverpool, England.
COLLIER'S WEEKLY, New York.

Gentlemen—I read COLLIER'S WEEKLY, and have done for many years, because, as a progressive Briton, I must know what is going on in America; and whatever impression I may get from other papers published, I feel that from COLLIER'S I *always* get the truth. Your comments on matters relating to the United Kingdom are always correct. In fact, you forecasted the result of the last general election with the most deadly accuracy, and summed up the entire political situation in a most masterly manner in the briefest editorial I have ever read.

I simply could not do without COLLIER'S.

Faithfully yours, C. BRUNNING,
Editor-Manager.

✤

The letter, which has caused the whole country to wonder why Hearst considers it necessary to yell before he is hit, is tense with boiled-down apprehension. Here it is:

COLLIER'S WEEKLY and Mr. Norman Hapgood, editor of COLLIER'S WEEKLY, 416 West Thirteenth Street, New York.

Sirs—With reference to your proposed libelous attack upon Mr. Hearst in the Irwin article:

I am instructed to and do hereby notify you that you will be held criminally and civilly responsible for the false statements contained therein.

Yours truly, CLARENCE J. SHEARN.

Even the publisher of COLLIER'S was puzzled, as is indicated in his reply here given:

Dear Sir—While it is a fact that COLLIER'S contemplates publishing a series of articles on the American Newspaper, I do not see why the inference should necessarily follow that these articles are to be criminally libelous to Mr. W. R. Hearst.

We shall certainly be prepared to accept full responsibility for the truth of anything we print about Mr. Hearst.

Very truly yours,
ROBERT J. COLLIER.

Clarence J. Shearn, 140 Nassau Street, New York City.

Hearst was so tormented by the prospect of basking under the COLLIER searchlight that his attorney also wrote a letter to Mr. Irwin, but confined his threat merely to criminal libel without hope of pecuniary balm.

Now the question is: What so fearful wounds does Hearst anticipate that only a court prosecution will assuage them?

—San Francisco (Cal.) *Bulletin*.

✤

Speaking of the "Police Gazette," Topeka has a barber shop which subscribes to "Life" and COLLIER'S.

—Topeka (Kans.) *Capital*.

✤

The fidelity with which you have endeavored to protect the American public from the subtle and persistent power of wealth, political tricksters, and traitors will be rewarded by the loyalty of a vast number of the most intelligent readers of our country. The greater the wrongs, the more powerfully must they be combated. So, good luck to you and more power to your shoulder. Very truly yours,

R. J. BEATTIE.

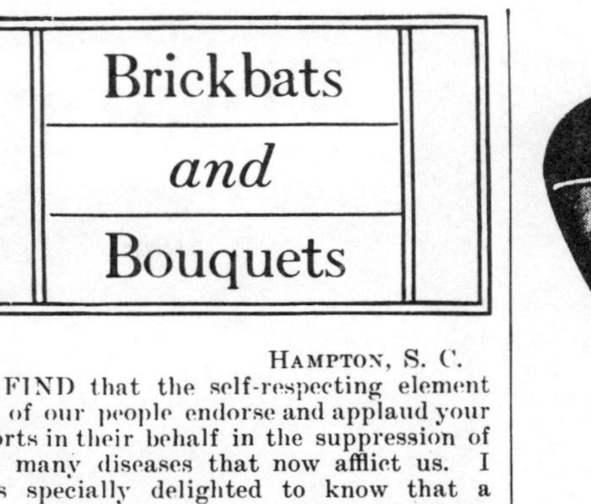

HAMPTON, S. C.

I FIND that the self-respecting element of our people endorse and applaud your efforts in their behalf in the suppression of the many diseases that now afflict us. I was specially delighted to know that a New York jury could render so righteous a verdict. It seems from this Postum verdict that some prophets are not without honor even in their own countries. The result must have been the same anywhere.

Yours truly, J. W. VINCENT.

✚

The newspapers that get full-page advertisements from C. W. Post keep mighty mum about the libel verdict for $50,000 against him secured by COLLIER'S WEEKLY.

—Abilene (Kans.) *Reflector.*

✚

It may be freely admitted that that fellow Post of Battle Creek, Michigan, has the champion grouch of the world. He thinks the country is going to the dogs on account of the labor organizations, and in every paper and magazine in which he can buy space he tells his troubles. It may be a peculiar variety of advertising, but it gets tiresome after a while. The world doesn't care anything about his troubles, and has no time for his grouch.

—Roswell (N. Mex.) *Register-Tribune.*

✚

Please accept my congratulations upon the splendid way in which you have handled the driest of all political questions. It is simple justice to say that you have made the subject live and vital for your readers.

D. M. GILBERT, Managing Editor, Harrisburg (Pa.) *Patriot.*

✚

Let me assure you that the press of the country, at least the newspapers in the Western and Central States, appreciate the stand COLLIER'S has taken and the good it is doing in the way of political searchlighting.

H. B. R. BRIGGS, Managing Editor, Kalamazoo (Mich.) *Telegraph.*

✚

May we remind COLLIER'S that there are more newspaper boys than journalists? We want to hear about them.

—Louisville (Ky.) *Times.*

✚

COLLIER'S WEEKLY turned itself into a sort of pied piper of Hamelin and old rat woman in one to make a fearful, yet bloodless, attack upon the San Francisco rodent. It was so easy for an anemic special writer to come West, secure the confessions of a few poisoned rats, and then return East to indite some several thousand words about the dangers of the plague.

—Los Angeles (Cal.) *Times.*

✚

A comprehensive and authentic study of journalism in its relation to the public has been attempted now for the first time; and, judging from the three articles already published, it will prove one of the most valuable services that COLLIER'S has yet performed.

—Toronto (Canada) *Mail and Empire.*

✚

I am very much interested in the series of articles which you are printing, and they ought to stir up a widespread discussion. Very truly yours,

F. A. WALKER, Managing Editor, Washington (D. C.) *Times.*

✚

I am sure the series on newspapers will be interesting to members of the profession, and I am led to believe that it will interest a great mass of readers.

Respectfully,

C. P. J. MOONEY, Managing Editor, Memphis (Tenn.) *Commercial Appeal.*

✚

We are all deeply interested in Irwin's series and in your effort to standardize news. That certainly was a good one you put over on Willie Hearst.

Very truly yours,

J. G. A. MONTAGUE, Richmond (Va.) *News-Leader.*

✚

COLLIER'S WEEKLY, with that acuteness and truth that has made history for America these last few years.

—Indianapolis (Ind.) *Sun.*

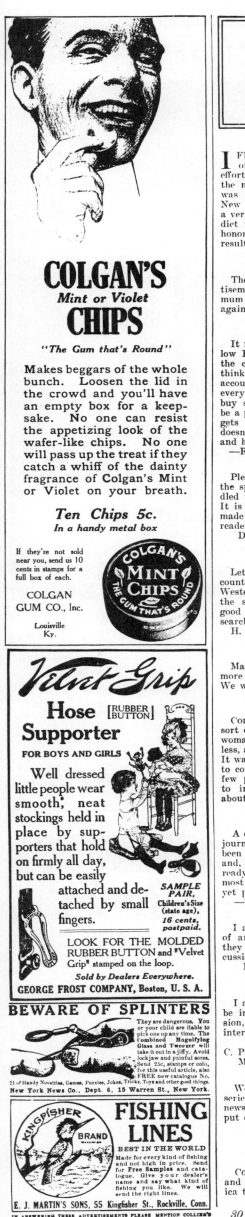

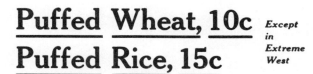

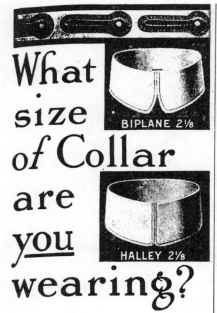

BRICKBATS AND BOUQUETS

P. O. BOX 186, HONEY GROVE, TEXAS.
P. F. COLLIER & SON,
416 West 13th Street, New York.

GENTLEMEN—I wish you to stop sending me your paper at once. Your thrust at Senator Bailey is the culmination of your straight Republican, hypocritical righteousness, disguised under the small mantle of little Willie Hearst of the Independence Party.

Very respectfully, J. F. PARRISH.

✤

It now turns out that the most serious charge lodged by his captors against the "Herald" man made a prisoner of war by Mexican Federal troops Friday was that he was reading a copy of COLLIER'S.

—El Paso (Texas) *Herald*.

✤

I don't think it is necessary to tell you with what interest I have read the articles, recently published in COLLIER'S, touching on and appertaining to the triumphant march of American journalism.

H. H. TAMMEN, Denver (Colo.) *Post*.

✤

TOPEKA, KANS.

I believe the newspapers of this country are, as a rule, truthful and give the news as they get it, and depend on that fact to make themselves popular with the reading public, in marked contrast to your paper, which is sometimes spoken of as the "book-pedlers' weekly," a sort of annex to your book-peddling business. D. O. MCCRAY.

✤

COLLIER'S WEEKLY is running a series of articles on newspaper making. They expect to continue the series throughout the year. The articles so far have been splendid and are attracting the attention of newspaper men everywhere.

—Des Moines (Iowa) *Capital*.

✤

COLLIER'S WEEKLY is asking prominent editors what is news. Well, here's our answer: If Harry Lauder gave $1,000 to a university, if St. Louis won the pennant, if Gotham streets were in good condition, and if everybody liked the "G. W. Gazette," that would be news.—New York *Mail*.

✤

PHILADELPHIA, PA.

As one who has for many years taken a deep and active interest in the purification of the press, I wish to express my appreciation of the propaganda which you have inaugurated in the series of forceful articles now appearing in your journal.

I have long wished some magazine to take up all the phases connected with the ethical side of journalism, that in this way public opinion might be so educated that a reform would follow. . . .

The Council of Jewish Women has its branches or sections in fifty-six cities throughout the land, embracing a large number of influential and prominent Jewish women.

Hoping that the agitation of the subject in your columns will bear good fruit.

Very truly yours,
CORNELIA KAHN,
The Council of Jewish Women.

✤

The articles are well written, and show a deep investigation into this always interesting subject. COLLIER'S is the most independent and influential journal in the United States.—Abbeville (La.) *News*.

✤

COLLIER'S WEEKLY is merely seeing ghosts again.—Portland (Ore.) *Oregonian*.

✤

I wish to express to you the satisfaction I felt, as a newspaper man, when you announced Mr. Irwin's great series and my gratification at the way he is fulfilling the promise. I wish every one in my community could read the series.

Very truly yours,
CHAS. M. VERNON,
Editor, Manhattan (Kans.) *Mercury*.

✤

The youthful editor of COLLIER'S is one of the several individuals who were recently made to look very silly by Mr. Taft.

—Pawtucket (R. I.) *Times*.

✤

COLLIER'S WEEKLY, which likes to be known as the National Weekly because of its inclination to dabble in everybody else's business, has just given an exhibition of crass ignorance that is attracting widespread attention.—Butte (Mont.) *Review*.